Operation
Citadel

Janusz Piekalkiewicz

Operation

Kursk and
The Greatest
of the Second

Translated from the German by Michaela Nierhaus

"Citadel"

Orel:
Tank Battle
World War

PRESIDIO

Published by Presidio Press
31 Pamaron Way, Novato CA 94947

Library of Congress Cataloging-in-Publication Data

Piekalkiewicz, Janusz.
  Operation "Citadel."

  Translation of: Unternehmen Zitadelle.
  Bibliography: p. 282
  Includes index.
  1. Kursk, Battle of, 1943. 2. Orel, Battle of, 1943. 3. World War, 1939–1945—
Tank warfare. I. Title.
D764.3.K8P5413 1985   940.54'21   86-21279
ISBN 0-89141-254-9

Printed in the United States of America

Table of Contents

Foreword

The assault in the Kursk Salient "must succeed quickly and decisively!" Thus Hitler orders his generals in the operational instructions for Operation "Citadel."

But Hitler's last attempt to consolidate his wavering authority in Europe with a great summer offensive failed. What he did not anticipate at that time was that Operation "Citadel" would be directed at Red Army forces prepared for an attack. The best German divisions, which should have been held in reserve for countering a foreseeable Soviet offensive, were used up in this operation. By the end of April 1943, the German chances of success in Operation "Citadel" already were no longer favorable and dwindled rapidly with each postponement.

In those days of July 1943, the Red Army succeeded for the first time in defeating the Germans in summer, under favorable weather conditions and on ideal tank terrain. The OKH's (Oberkommando des Heeres, or German High Command of the Army) operational plan also contributed to the failure of the German offensive at Kursk for it lacked any element of surprise, strategic or tactical.

The concept behind Hitler's offensive was to eliminate the Kursk Salient and to neutralize Soviet reserves in order to retain the vital coal area in the Donets Basin and Orel Salient. Following the debacle of Stalingrad, this plan, however, overtaxed the capacities of the Wehrmacht. And as Colonel General Guderian noted, Germany was already "no longer able to replenish the Eastern Front with fresh forces in the course of 1943." On the other hand, Soviet defensive operations at Kursk owed their success to the well-timed concentration of strategic reserves. It was the Fifth Guards

Tank Army of the strategic reserve that proved decisive on the battlefield at Prokhorovka in the greatest tank battle in history.

The Battle of Kursk became the Waterloo of the German Panzer forces. Even after the first few days, the planned German "Panzer raid" was only inching forward laboriously. In spite of three months of preparation, the thrust of the Panzer forces was contained in the depth of the Soviet tactical lines and suffered very heavy losses.

The Soviets managed to build up their forces at the Kursk Salient to the extent that the defensive battle of Kursk lasted only seven days, whereas the Red Army's defensive fighting in the forefield of Moscow had lasted more than two months, and at Stalingrad approximately four months.

This was the beginning of a new phase in the Panzer war: the tank tactics which the Germans had applied with the greatest success up to now were adopted by the Soviets and their western allies. With Kursk began the agony of the Panzer Troops and the Luftwaffe: both were no longer able to exert decisive influence on the operations of the German army. Thus Operation "Citadel" proved to be a fiasco resulting in irreplaceable personnel and material losses and ultimately forcing the Wehrmacht to forfeit the strategic initiative.

The Battle of Kursk and Orel was not only the climax of the eastern campaign but it was also *the* decisive battle of the Second World War: the failure of Operation "Citadel" signified the beginning of the last phase of the war, which ended with the Red Army marching into Berlin and paved the way for the rise of the Soviet Union to world power.

The other factor that greatly influenced the outcome of the Battle of Kursk-Orel was that for three months prior to the launching of Operation "Citadel" Stalin had received reliable running information about the German High Command's intentions. But what is astonishing is that the information did not come from the reports of a Soviet spy ring in Switzerland, as many publications maintain to this very day. It came from Winston Churchill, who thanks to his secret Ultra operation was able to listen in on top-secret, German High Command radio transmissions.

Military Theater

In the deep gorges of the gentle hills covering the countryside lie endlessly long villages. As there are few forests here, the cottages in these villages are made usually of stone or clay. The fertility of the black earth and the industry of the inhabitants brought the villages, in Soviet terms, a certain amount of prosperity.

The Kursk-Orel region is part of Central Russia but has some of the characteristics of the Ukraine: a fertile black-earth region, similar to the rolling steppe, cut by deep gorges called balkas, which afford good cover on the one hand but present difficult obstacles for attacking tanks on the other.

The Central Russian ridge with the cities of Orel in the north, Belgorod in the south, and Kursk in the middle is also a wide plain interrupted by numerous valleys, little rises, and scattered hamlets and villages, as well as a few rivers and brooks. The Olkhovatka chain of hills, covered with wild currant and gooseberry bushes forms the heart of the ridge. The Oka River springs from the picturesque eastern slopes as do many brooks and little streams. From Olkhovatka one can see the chimneys and onion-shaped turrets of Kursk on the horizon. Whoever holds the high ground also controls the lowland stretching between the Oka and the Seym.

Kursk, the district (oblast) capital of the Mordvinian Autonomous Soviet Socialist Republic, lies 600 kilometers south of Moscow. As early as the eleventh century, it was mentioned as a junction on the Kiev trade route. Kursk is situated where the Kura flows into the Tuskora. Since ancient times, the town has been famous for its numerous tanneries. It is also an important center for the production of candle wax, a by-product of beekeeping, which is widespread in this region. In the spring of 1941, Kursk had a population of 120,000. The ruins of old settlements, Gorodischtsche and the Hun burial mounds, and kurgans, encountered in the steppes of the surrounding region, are reminders of the dark ages of the barbarian invasions.

The very rich, high-quality magnetic ore deposits between Orel and Belgorod, among the largest of their kind in the world, are responsible for the "Kursk Magnetic Anomaly," which has always fascinated geologists. This layer of iron ore causes compass needles to deviate considerably above ground and thus interferes with directed artillery fire and all operations requiring a compass.

In the seventeenth century, the "Belgorod line," a series of fortresses, earthworks, and other battlements intended to protect Czarist Russia from invasion from the south, ran here. Newer, more effective fortifications replaced the old ones. In 1943, even small hamlets were turned into all-round defensive strongpoints and the chalk hills of Belgorod gave the Soviet troops natural cover. Every heavy rainstorm made the dirt roads practically impassable for motorized transport vehicles. Wide cornfields covered the countryside in summer and impeded visibility. In addition, incoming roads and many hamlets were camouflaged against aerial observation with extensive screens of sackcloth. Huge munition and fuel dumps as well as numerous signs with tactical markings edged the roads in the front of the rear area.

For Official Use Only!

Military geopolitical data on European Russia
    CENTRAL RUSSIA (not including Moscow)
Prepared on 15 May 1941, General Staff of the Army, Berlin 1941

The Terrain
The terrain of Central Russia ranges from generally flat and undulating to nearly totally flat. For the most part, it consists of broad stretches of plateaus and wide ridges; in the northern half of the country there are also wide lowlands. The region is a rolling plateau deeply cut by rivers and steppe gorges. The land drops steeply to the north, sinks gently to the west, and descends in two marked steps to the east along the Don and Voronezh rivers. The high-lying areas are in the central region around Orel.

The most important "Guidebook" for the German troops deployed between Orel and Belgorod

9

The highest elevations here rise to 300 meters (east of Orel). There are large forests only in the northern part. The central and southern parts with their black earth constitute a virtually treeless steppe region with extensive farms. Great forests are confined to the lowlands directly adjacent to large rivers. The area is densely covered with rural settlements, which usually develop into large villages. Many middle-sized towns have grown from markets and farm sites. In the Ryazan, Tula, and Kursk area there is also heavy industry.

The Nature of the Ground

The most important natural boundary in Russia, namely the northern edge of the black-earth zone, stretches in a southwestward by northeastward direction running in a line through Central Russia from Konotop (Ukraine)-Kursk-Tula-Saransk to the northeastern corner of the Mordvinian Republic. Close up this boundary is irregular and overlapping. Moreover, to the south of it, particularly in the eastern section, are frequent enclaves of different types of soil.

The black earth when moist is very dark and very fertile. It sticks to one's boots. When dry it becomes fine and very dusty. Digging into it, one sees that this black earth is grayish yellow at very little depth (loess); for this reason, trenches stand out like light lines against a black background even at a distance.

Between the forest zone and the treeless steppe lies a wide transitional zone of forest steppe: a mixture of open terrain (originally steppe, but now farming and pasture land) and many oak and aspen forests. To the south, these round groves grow increasingly farther apart until they become rare. The forest region thus turns into ordinary steppe, treeless farm- and grassland. There usually are no tree lines alongside trails or roads and in Russian villages there are hardly any trees at all. Trees and shrubbery grow only in the lowlands stretching along the big rivers.

Military Estimate

In dry periods the ground, particularly the black earth except for swamps and moors, is readily passable. Most vehicles need not keep to the roads here; frequently one can drive across country just as well as on a road. In wet periods sandy ground is often better for movement than clay or the black earth.

Climate

The climate of Central Russia is a moderate continental climate with cold winters and relatively warm summers. The essential difference between it and the Central European climate are the long periods of very low temperatures in winter. Spring is marked by drastic changes. The rapid rise in temperature in April brings the thaw and causes the rivers to swell and flood large areas. Snowfall must be counted on until far into May. After a short summer the first snowfall begins in October, sometimes as early as September, and a deep blanket of snow covers the country from November on for four to five months.

10

Clouds and Wind

The cloud cover is relatively heavy. Even in summer the sky is usually half-covered. It is cloudless only in the southern part of the region. The heaviest cloud cover occurs in Central Russia in November, covering approximately 85 percent of the sky. But in winter, there are often cloudless days and nights. These starlit nights are then accompanied by temperatures of forty degrees below zero centigrade and lower. The winds generally are stronger than in Central Europe, but are by no means constant. In summer, from June to September, the winds are usually westerly to northwesterly, whereas during the rest of the year, they are predominantly southerly. In April and May, easterly winds sometimes bring a return of cold weather.

The South Central Russia Steppe Region

In winter, conditions are about the same as in the northern region, but the cold weather is approximately one month shorter and the average snow blanket is only thirty centimeters deep. Moreover, summer is considerably longer. For at least two months the average daytime temperature is more than twenty degrees centigrade. Precipitation is primarily in the form of rainfall accompanying short thunderstorms, so that summers are quite hot and dry. Annual rainfall is usually 400–500mm.

Military Estimate

The most unfavorable time for military operations is the spring from March to May. Drastic changes in temperature are extremely taxing physically and the thaw makes most of the roads and rivers impassable. From June to October the climate is rather like that of Germany, except that temperatures are somewhat higher and are more stressful to humans and animals. Optimum months for military operations are August and September.

Agriculture

Peculiarities of the individual administrative regions of the black-earth zone are as follows. In the Orel area, as the soil tends to return to podzol, wheat growing subsides and potato growing predominates. There is particularly much hemp growing (the best hemp harvest is in the flood area of the Desna; Orel is the most important hemp-growing area in the Soviet Union). In the Kursk region the proportion of farmland is especially large. There is extensive winter wheat and sugar-beet farming (in sugar manufacturing this region takes first place in the Soviet Union). Legume (peas, beans, and lentils) growing is increasing. Near cities there are large gardens and vegetable farms, poultry farms, and hog raising (the hogs are fed with refuse from the sugar-beet factories).

Natural Resources

The Central Russian iron ore deposits lie in the areas of Tambov, Ryazan, Tula, Orel, Kursk, and Voronezh. Iron ore is mined in Tula, Lipetsk, and Korobkovo near Stary Oskol (Kursk region). Moreover, there are also magnetic iron ore deposits in the Kursk region; this so-called Kursk Mag-

March 1943, Volosnaya, a village not far from Slavyansk: Winter is over, the mud period is setting in

11

netic Anomaly encompasses from sixteen to twenty billion tons of magnetic ore spread over 300 kilometers.

Mobility

The railroad network is better developed than the road network. The efficiency of the railroad leaves something to be desired even in peacetime; it could not meet the great demands a war would make. The only efficient network of roads in Central Russia is close to Moscow, lying within a radius of about 200 kilometers of the capital. As for the other roads, they are poor and not connected. In winter the unpaved roads often follow a different course than they do in summer. Furthermore, in spring and autumn they

A May evening in 1943, on a bridge over the Balakleyka, a tributary of the Donets: Partisans disguised as farm hands at work in the German Eastern Army's rear area

14

are very difficult if not impossible to use for several weeks because of the mud.

The Flatlands East of the Central Dnieper

The southern half of the Smolensk area and the western half of the Orel area belong to this region of Central Russia. In the eastern part, the country takes on a flat, rolling character with deeply incised river valleys and a system of steppe gorges. The big rivers flow from the northeast to the southwest. Here the west side of the valley is always steep and the east side usually slopes gently.

On the east side of the rivers, wide strips of forest stretch along the valley lowlands beside low, river meadowlands which are flooded in the spring. In addition, dune areas are frequent. The terrain gradually rises eastward to the next watershed and drops again to the next stream in the east. The country is relatively densely populated. Numerous little villages are scattered over the open farmland, whereas large settlements and markets lie along the rivers.

Military Estimate

Apart from the densely wooded areas, the country is easily passable for both large motorized units and infantry. In particular, an approach from the west is facilitated by the gently rising slope of the valley.

The Lowlands Along the Don and the Oka

East of the Central Russian highlands, a low, flat country spreads to the south of the meandering west-east course of the Oka. Starting in the north with a steep drop to the Oka, the lowlands stretch south to the Don. The soil is usually sandy in the north with black-earth soil in the central and southern sections. Densely wooded areas occur only in the north in the form of mixed forests. Toward the south, the terrain is open. The north is more densely populated. The density of farm settlements alone gives a population of seventy inhabitants per square kilometer.

Military Estimate

The area is particularly passable. The receding density of the steppe gorge network is a great advantage for military movement, which can also be conducted off the roads. As the preferred valleys, even the smaller ones, run north–south, and considering the general situation of the area between the more elevated steppe plateaus in the east and west, the best direction for movement is south–north. Although the rivers do not cut very deep valleys, these valleys offer some cover.

Waterways

Most of the rivers are in a natural state, i.e., their riverbeds are wild for long stretches. Their courses take many turns and often divide into many branches. Therefore, one must remember that there is sand filling in most rivers and that many change their course. During the long spells of severe cold the rivers freeze solidly every year and all of Central Russia is covered with a blanket of ice for an extended period, causing the waterways to cease being obstacles.

The Oka freezes in early November. The melting and drifting of ice occur at the end of March in the west and in April farther to the east. From time to time the ice remains until mid-May. A short, but relatively rapid warm spell melts the snow quickly in many areas all at once. As there is a great deal of snow in Central Russia (a depth up to 40 and 50 centimeters), an enormous amount of water enters the rivers in a short time, turning what in summer may be insignificant little streams into very wide and deep watercourses and thus dangerous, major obstacles. There is nothing to compare to it in Central Europe. The rising water, several meters high, is very powerful, flows over the low banks, and floods the bigger valleys for

16

many kilometers. The floods (particularly near the Volga and the Don) last about a month. Then the water level of the rivers drops to a mean level. In the summer months, the water level is often quite low.

Donets River: Right tributary of the Don; source in the south of the Central Russian ridge, south of Kursk. Width: until Belgorod 20 meters, then 60 meters. Depth: in general very flat, up to 1 meter; before obstacles up to 5 meters. Velocity: up to 2 meters per second; grade on the average 2.21 meters per kilometer. Width of valley: up to Belgorod 1 kilometer, then wider. Valley slopes: the right side nearly always higher than the left, until the Belgorod high chalk bank; thereafter, the right side often drops 65 meters down to the river. Ice cover: from 25 December to 26 March, beginning somewhat earlier in the headwaters.

Oka River: Right tributary of the Volga, main river of Central Russia; source in the Central Russian ridge; 1520 kilometers long. In the headwaters it is occasionally a military obstacle, from the mouth of the Ugra a constant obstacle. Width: at Orel 60 meters, thereafter up to 140 meters. Depth: at Orel and behind flat. Current: at Orel significant, fluctuating between 0.6 and 0.7 meters per second; at narrow passages 1–1.5 meters per second. The riverbed has many great turns and overgrown old channels; the bottom within the Orel region is at first muddy, then sandy, finally stony. The banks are low, generally flat and dry so that military bridge building is possible everywhere. Valley width: from the mouth of the Moskva on, quite wide. Valley slopes: until Orel up to 60 and 70 meters high in some places. Ice cover: at Orel from the end of November until the end of March.

Psel River: Left tributary of the Dnieper; source near Prokhorovka; 585 kilometers long. Width: often narrow. Depth: above Oboyan up to 3 meters. Current: strong. Banks: in the headwaters sandy, clay, in some places marl; then craggy, sometimes sandy.

Line of Sight and Cover

In the southeastern part of the country, observation is good on the open steppe. The uniformity of the terrain makes orientation difficult especially as there are no decent maps. The steppe gorges (ovragi), which often cannot be seen until one stands on their very edge, diminish observation somewhat. For this reason, they afford good cover. In the transitional strips between the two sections, the forest steppe, observation is better than in the northwest.

Cover is offered by the oak and aspen woods. Cover and camouflage possibilities differ from season to season all over the country. In winter, white clothing (snowsuits, snow shirts) is required for camouflage. In spring, flooding often lessens cover along river banks, in the valleys, and in the flooded forests. In midsummer, the tall corn affords cover even in the open.

17

Men in Command

Otto Dessloch

Commanding general of Luftflotte 4 (Air Force), born the son of a head forester in Bamberg/Franken on 6 June 1889.

After passing his school final examination, he joined the Royal Bavarian 5th Light Cavalry Regiment "Archduke Friedrich of Austria" as an ensign; he was promoted to lieutenant on 23 October 1912. Soon after the outbreak of the First World War, he was seriously wounded in August 1914 while riding patrol. After recovering, he enlisted in the flying corps. Then came pilot training in the Flieger-Ersatzabteilung (pilot replacement training detachment) Schleissheim. He transferred to the Feldfliegerabteilung 8 (combat flying section) in February 1915. From 1916 on, Dessloch was a fighter pilot in Jagdstaffel 16 (fighter squadron) in the west. In 1917 he became squadron commander of Jagdstaffel 17. After that he became commander of a flying school and from 1919 on he was commander of the Freiwillige Fliegerabteilung (volunteer flying section) "Dessloch."

He entered the Reichswehr (national defense forces) and was, between 1921 and 1927, cavalry captain and squadron commander in the 17th (Bavarian) Cavalry Regiment and for a time post commander in Ansbach. In 1925 he and his team of the 17th (Bavarian) Cavalry Regiment won the Grosse Heeres-Patrouillenritt (army patrol ride) in Berlin.

In 1927 he was ordered to the Staff of the 7th (Bavarian) Division; in 1932 he was promoted to major in the Staff of the 18th Cavalry Regiment.

After transferring to the Luftwaffe, Dessloch became head of the Fliegerschule (flying school) Cottbus on 1 December 1934 and in 1935 the commander of all flying schools in Germany. On 1 March 1936 he was promoted to colonel and commodore of the Kampfgeschwader 155 (bomber squadron group). On 2 February 1939 he took over the 6th Fliegerdivision (air force division) as major general. Following the Polish campaign he became commander of the II Flakkorps (antiaircraft corps) on 3 October 1939. He was promoted to lieutenant general on 19 July 1940 and to General der Flieger (air force general) on 1 January 1942. From 12 May 1942 to 10 June 1943 he was commanding general of the I Flakkorps. He was named commander in chief of Luftflotte 4 in the sector of Army Group South (FM von Manstein) on the Eastern Front on 11 June 1943.

Hermann Hoth

Commanding general of the Fourth Panzer Army, born the son of a medical officer in Neuruppin (Mark Brandenburg) on 12 April 1885.

After high school, he joined the Prussian Cadet Corps in 1904, attended Officers' Candidate School, and served in Infantry Regiment 72 (Torgau). At the outbreak of the First World War Hoth first joined the Great General Staff as captain, then became company commander, battalion commander, and chief of an air force section.

At the end of the war he was an officer on the General Staff of an infantry division. Afterwards he joined the Reichswehr and was given various command and staff positions. From 1935 to 1938 Hoth headed the 18th Division (Legnica) and later, as lieutenant general, the XV Army Corps (Jena). In the Polish campaign Hoth, now general of infantry, commanded the XV Panzer Corps assigned to the Tenth Army (General of Artillery von Reichenau) and contributed substantially to the success of operations

(*Left*) Otto Dessloch

(*Right*) Hermann Hoth

19

(*Left*) Robert Ritter von Greim

(*Right*) Werner Kempf

by attacking at strategically decisive points. On 13 May 1940 his XV Panzer Corps were the first German forces to cross the Meuse River at Dinant and reached Brest on 16 June 1940.

Following the attack on Russia, Hoth commanded Panzer Group 3 with which he, in cooperation with Guderian's and Hoepner's Panzer groups, laid the groundwork for the successes of the great encirclement battles in the summer and autumn of 1941. On 9 July 1941 Colonel General Hoth captured Vitebsk and on 17 October 1941 Kramatorsk in the Donets region (Ukraine) as commanding general of the Seventeenth Army. In the winter of 1941/42 he and his Seventeenth Army were engaged in heavy defensive fighting in the southern Ukraine. On 17 May 1942 his Seventeenth Army and the First Panzer Army (Colonel General Kleist) attacked Marshal Timoshenko's armies from the south and the Sixth Army (General of the Pz. Tr. Paulus) from the north, in order to gain jumping-off positions at the Donets and in the Kharkov area for the summer offensive to open the way to Stalingrad. On 1 June 1942 Hoth became commanding general of the Fourth Panzer Army. His units participated in the Battle of Stalingrad, and on 12 December 1941 an assault group of the Fourth Panzer Army in the Kotelnikovo area attempted without success to relieve the Sixth Army.

Robert Ritter von Greim

Commanding general of Luftflotte 6, born the son of a Royal Bavarian Police captain on 22 June 1892 in Bayreuth.

After the Cadet Corps, he joined the Bavarian Railroad Battalion as an ensign in July 1911 and transferred to the 8th Bavarian Field Artillery Regiment in November 1912. After the outbreak of the First World War, he saw action in the Lorraine. In August 1915 he attended an air observer course and then was assigned to Feldfliegerabteilung 3b (combat air force section). He then was transferred to Jagdstaffel 34 (fighter squadron).

On 11 March 1918 von Greim, as squadron captain, was the first German pilot to destroy a British tank from the air with MG fire. In air combat he won a total of twenty-eight victories.

From 1920 to 1922 he became a lawyer in Munich and worked in a bank. From 1924 to 1925 he was assigned in China as military air advisor to the Chiang Kai-shek government. From 1928 to 1933 he was head of the civilian flying school at Würzburg. In January 1934 he joined the Reichswehr and helped in organizing the Jagdgeschwader (combat squadron group) "Richthofen." On 1 August 1935 he became major inspector of

20

Jagdflieger (combat air force) and was promoted to colonel on 20 April 1936. As commanding general of the V Fliegercorps and lieutenant general, he participated in the western campaign in 1940.

Following the attack on the Soviet Union, in November 1941 he became chief of the Luftwaffenkommando (Air Force Command) East, attached to Army Group Center (FM von Kluge). In February 1943 he was promoted to colonel general and continued to command his Luftwaffenkommando East, which was renamed Luftflotte 6 in May 1943.

Werner Kempf

Commander of the Kempf Army, born the son of an officer in Königsberg (East Prussia) on 9 March 1886.

From 1897 to 1905 he was a cadet in Karlsruhe, Oranienstein, and Gross-Lichterfelde. Then he was promoted to ensign in the 6th West Prussian Infantry Regiment No. 149 (Schneidemuehl). In 1912 he was transferred in the rank of lieutenant to the II Sea Battalion (Wilhelmshaven). From 1913 to 1914 Kempf trained cadets on the Grossen Kreuzer (fleet cruiser) SM *Vineta*.

With the outbreak of the First World War, Kempf became regimental adjutant of the 2nd Marine Corps Regiment. In November 1914 he was promoted to first lieutenant and in January 1916 to captain. Then he attended general staff training in the 21st Infantry Division and in the AOK (Armeeoberkommando, or Army High Command) Army Section B. In early 1918 Kempf was assigned as second officer in the General Staff of the 3rd Marine Brigade.

After the end of the First World War, he joined the Reichswehr in 1921 as company commander of Infantry Regiment 4. From 1922 to 1926 he was an officer on the General Staff of Infantriefuehrer (commanding officer of the infantry of a division) II (Schwerin), then in the 1st Prussian Medical Section in Königsberg and in the 2nd Company of the Motor Vehicle Section (Allenstein). In 1929 he was promoted to major.

From July 1934 on, Kempf was chief of staff of the Inspectorate of Army Motorizing and from 1 June 1936 on, the inspector of Army Motorizing in the Ministry of War of the Reich. In October 1937, he assumed command of the newly established 4th Panzer Brigade (Stuttgart).

On 18 January 1939 he was promoted to major general. In September 1939 he participated in the Polish campaign as commander of Panzer Division Kempf (Panzer forces East Prussia). On 1 October 1939 he became commander of the 6th Panzer Division and in August 1940, lieutenant general. On 6 January 1941 he was made commanding general of the XLVIII Army Corps (mot.) and on 1 April 1941, general of Panzer Troops.

In the attack on the Soviet Union, Kempf captured Dubno with his corps on 25 June 1941 and on 3 November 1941 took Kursk, where he and his corps spent the winter of 1941/42. In early August 1942 the corps (renamed the XLVIII Panzer Corps on 1 June 1942) reached the southern sector of Stalingrad. In September 1942 Kempf was transferred to the Reserve Command and spent several months at home. On 18 January 1943 he became head of the first training course for division commanders and on 15 February 1943, commander of the Kempf Army. As of March 1943 this army section was assigned to Army Group South (FM von Manstein).

(*Left*) Günther von Kluge

(*Right*) Erich von Manstein and Gen. Speidel (left)

Günther von Kluge

Commanding general of Army Group Center, born the son of a lieutenant general in Posen (Poznan) on 30 October 1882.

He joined the Prussian Cadet Corps and graduated from the Army Staff College. In 1914 Kluge took the field as a captain in the XXI Army Corps, saw action in Flanders, and was seriously wounded at Verdun.

In 1919 he joined the Reichswehr and was promoted to lieutenant colonel on 1 July 1927. One year later he became chief of staff of the 1st Cavalry Division (Frankfurt/Oder); on 1 February 1933, major general and inspector of the Signal Corps; on 1 April 1934, lieutenant general. On 1 April 1935 he became commanding general of the VI Army Corps as well as commander of Military District VI (Muenster) (Wehrkreis) and was promoted to general of Artillery on 1 August 1936.

In the Polish campaign, Kluge commanded the Fourth Army which thrust forward from East Pomerania. His troops participated in the Battle on the Bruza. On 1 October 1939 he was promoted to colonel general.

In the western campaign, his Fourth Army was part of the northern flank of Army Group A (FM von Rundstedt), which moved via Dinant and Arras toward Dunkirk. After fighting the British Expeditionary Force, the Fourth Army pursued the remnants of the French Army in a rapid thrust on both sides of Paris across the Loire and farther toward the south. On 19 July 1940 Kluge was made field marshal.

In the attack on the Soviet Union, he continued to command the Fourth Army. Following the battles of Vyazma and Bryansk, his army advanced on Moscow. On 19 December 1941 Kluge assumed command of Army Group Center. Applying well-planned defensive measures he held the front against Soviet attacks for the next two years.

Erich von Manstein

The commanding general of Army Group South, born on 24 November 1887 in Berlin, a scion of military stock descending from the old aristocratic West Prussian von Lewinski family. Following the death of his parents he was adopted as a child by his uncle, Lieutenant General von Manstein.

Having spent the last six years of his schooling in the military academies of Plön and Lichterfelde, Manstein joined the 3rd Foot Guards Regiment in the spring of 1906 as an ensign. From the fall of 1913 on, he attended the Army Staff College, leaving in the summer of 1914 at the start of the First World War. Except for short assignments to the front, after having been seriously wounded, von Manstein spent most of the war in high staff positions.

From early 1919 on, von Manstein was a General Staff officer on the General Staff of the High Command of the Grenzschutz (Frontier Defense) South (Breslau). In the Reichswehr, he alternated between the General Staff and troops. He was assigned to the Truppenamt (Service Department) of the Reichswehr Ministry in the fall of 1929. Cooperation between the Reichswehr and the Red Army permitted von Manstein to spend several weeks in the Soviet Union on study trips in 1931 and 1932. This kept him—unlike the other German commanders—from underestimating the Red Army.

In February 1934 Colonel von Manstein became chief of staff of Military District (Wehrkreis) III (Berlin) under General von Witzleben, then on 1 July 1935, chief of the Operations Section in the General Staff of the Army. Promoted to major general a year later, he became chief of the General Staff. In early 1938, now lieutenant general, he was commander of the 18th Division (Legnica). Shortly before the outbreak of the Second World War, he was made chief of the General Staff of Army Group South (Colonel General von Rundstedt), which played a decisive role in the Polish campaign. From October 1939 on, he was chief of the General Staff of Army Group A (Colonel General von Rundstedt) at the Western Front. Here he distinguished himself by creating the brilliant operational plans which brought defeat to France, the concept of a tank spearhead through the Ardennes. Following the capitulation of France, he participated in the preparations for the invasion of Great Britain.

As commanding general, he assumed command of the newly established LVI Panzer Corps in the attack on the Soviet Union. He advanced so rapidly that he occupied the crucial bridges over the Dvina, nearly 300 kilometers away, within four days and shortly afterwards reached Lake Ilmen.

On 14 July 1941 he became general of Infantry. By the end of September 1941, his Eleventh Army, fighting in the Crimea, captured the "Tartar Trench" on the Perekop Isthmus.

Before the conclusion of Operation "Trappenjagd" (Bustard Hunt) (8–18 May 1942), in which the Kerch Peninsula was taken, he was promoted to colonel general. A month later, the assault began on Sevastopol, one of the strongest fortifications in the world. On 1 July 1942 this Black Sea bastion fell and von Manstein was appointed field marshal.

On 22 November 1942 he assumed command of the newly formed Army Group Don (later renamed Army Group South), with the mission of saving the hopeless situation at Stalingrad.

Walter Model

Walter Model

Commanding general of the Ninth Army, born the son of a court musical director on 24 January 1891 in Genthin (Anhalt). He joined the Army in 1909, and was at the Western Front during the First World War, temporarily in the General Field Headquarters. Then he saw action at Verdun and was wounded and decorated for valor several times. After the war Model joined the Reichswehr as captain and became commander of Infantry Regiment 2 (Allenstein). On 1 October 1934 he was appointed colonel; in 1935 he became chief of the Engineering Section of the General Staff of the

23

Ivan S. Konev

Army and was promoted to major general on 1 March 1938. A year later he was promoted to chief of the General Staff of the IV Army Corps in Dresden. In this position, Model participated in the operations of the Polish campaign. On 25 October 1939 he was chief of the General Staff of the Sixteenth Army which crossed the Mosel River at Trier, broke through the Maginot line, and captured Verdun. On 13 November 1940 Model, now lieutenant general, assumed command of the 3rd Panzer Division.

In the attack on the Soviet Union, his division formed the spearhead in the race to the Dnieper. On 1 October 1941 Hitler made him general of Panzer Troops and commanding general of the XLI Panzer Corps deployed north of Moscow.

From 16 January 1942 on, Model commanded the Ninth Army before Moscow. After succeeding in eliminating the threat of encirclement at Rzhev during the Soviet winter offensive, he became known as "immune to crisis" and "the master of defense."

From 2 to 12 July 1942 his Ninth Army led successful assaults against the salient in the front west of Sychevka.

Ivan S. Konev

Commanding general of the Steppe Front, born the son of peasants in Lodeynoye (North Russia) on 16 December 1897.

Following the outbreak of the First World War, Konev was an NCO in a Czarist artillery regiment fighting at the front in Polish Galicia, joined the Communist party following the October Revolution in 1917, and became commissar of the Nikolsk District. During the Civil War from 1918 to 1920, he was commissar of an armored train and later commissar of a rifle brigade. In the Far East Army, Konev saw action fighting the troops of White Russian General Kolchak as well as in the suppression of the Kronstadt Mutiny.

From 1922 to 1928 he was commissar of the 17th Rifle Division, attended Officers' Candidate School, and graduated from the M. V. Frunze Army Staff College. From 1931 to 1938 he was commander of a rifle division in the Far East Army. From 1938 to 1941 he was commander of the Second Independent Far East Army, then commander of Military District Baikal. In the summer of 1941 he was commander of the Nineteenth Army and on 14 August 1941 he became commanding general of the Western Front and was promoted to colonel general in September 1941. On 17 October 1941 he became commanding general of the Kalinin Front active in the decisive operations in the Battle for Moscow.

In September 1942 Konev once again became the commanding general of the Western Front and in March 1943 of the Northwestern Front. From 23 June 1943 on, he assumed command of the Steppe Military District (renamed Steppe Front on 10 July 1943).

Markian M. Popov

Commanding general of the Bryansk Front, born in Medvyedickaya in the Tsaritzyn District (Stalingrad) on 2 November 1902. During the Civil War from 1918 to 1922, Popov fought at the Western Front. In 1920 he joined the Red Army and became a member of the Communist party in 1921. He was made platoon leader in 1921, then later an adjutant. In 1922 he finished a training course in infantry operations and in 1925 another

24

in fire operations. Then he became adjutant of the chief of the regiment school, which he himself later headed; subsequently he was promoted to battalion commander. Following this, he was inspector of the Military School System in the Moscow Military District.

In 1936 Popov attended the Frunze Army Staff College. In May 1936 he became chief of staff of a mechanized brigade and later head of the V Mechanized Corps. In June 1938 he became deputy chief of staff of the First Independent Red Banner Army in the Far East and in September 1938, chief of staff. In July 1939 he was appointed commander of this same army. In January 1941 he became commander of the Leningrad Military District.

After the outbreak of the Soviet-German War he was appointed commanding general of the Northern and Leningrad Fronts (June to September 1941), then commanding general of the Sixty-First and Fortieth Armies from November 1941 to October 1942. Following this, he was deputy commander of the Stalingrad and Southwestern Fronts, commander of the Fifth Assault Army from October 1942 to April 1943, and then commanding general of the Bryansk Front.

Konstantin K. Rokossovsky

Konstantin K. Rokossovsky

Commanding general of the Central Front, born the son of a railroad worker in Warsaw on 21 December 1896. Forced to earn money as a fifteen year old, he worked as a stonemason's assistant on the construction of the Warsaw Pontiatowski Bridge.

Following the outbreak of the First World War, Rokossovsky fought against the Germans with the Russian 5th Kargopol Dragoons Regiment at Lodz and Warsaw. As an NCO, he left his home country with the retreating Czarist Army. Following the October Revolution, he was fighting as second in command of his old regiment, the 5th Dragoons, now part of the Red Army. As commander of the 30th Cavalry Regiment, he fought the White Guards in the Urals and the legendary Baron Ungern of Courland in Mongolia.

This cavalry officer of large stature remained in the army after the Civil War. In 1924 he, Zhukov, and Yeremenko were sent to a special training course in Leningrad. After graduation from the Advanced Cavalry Training Center in November 1926, he went to Mongolia as an instructor of the 1st Cavalry Division.

In 1928 he assumed command of a cavalry brigade and fought the Chinese. After attending the Frunze Army Staff School, he commanded a brigade and subsequently the 7th Cavalry Division (Samara); the commander of one of his four regiments was Georgi K. Zhukov. In September 1937, one day after assuming command of the V Cavalry Corps (Pleskau), Rokossovsky was arrested for being an "agent of the Japanese and Polish Secret Service."

Thanks to his good luck and most probably his good physical condition, he, unlike thousands of other officers, survived Stalin's purge, though with the loss of some teeth.

After three years in a NKVD prison, he was released in March 1940. Timoshenko offered him the command of his old V Cavalry Corps. At the end of 1940 he was assigned the task of activating the IX Mechanized Corps.

Following the outbreak of the Soviet-German war, Major General Rokossovsky and his newly formed IX Mechanized Corps attacked General Kempf's Panzer Corps from the Klevany Forest on 26 June 1941. Promoted to lieutenant general, he commanded the Sixteenth Army, fighting with it in the Battle for Moscow, and participated as part of the "Western Front" (General of the Army Zhukov) in the 6 December 1941 counteroffensive, which saved the Soviet capital. On 10 January 1942 he led the assault on Panzer Army 3 (Colonel General Reinhardt) at Volokolamsk.

In March 1942 Rokossovsky was badly wounded at the front before Moscow and did not return to duty until July 1942, when he became commanding general of the Bryansk Front. As of September 1942 he commanded the Don Front with which he helped in smashing the German Sixth Army (Colonel General Paulus) at Stalingrad. On 15 February 1942 the front was renamed Central Front.

Pavel A. Rotmistrov

Commanding general of the Fifth Guards Tank Army, born on 23 June 1901 in the village of Skovorovo in the Kalinin District.

He served in the Red Army and was a member of the Soviet Communist party since 1919. During the Civil War, Rotmistrov was active in the Kulak Revolt and the liquidation of Melekeskovo (1919). As an ordinary soldier, he fought in the Russo-Polish War from 1920 to 1921 and in the suppression of the Kronstadt Mutiny in 1921. In 1924 he graduated from the military unification school "VCIK," and led a company and became second in command of a battalion.

He attended the Frunze Army Staff College in 1931. From 1931 to 1937 Rotmistrov was on various division and army staffs and commanded an infantry regiment. In January 1938 he became instructor in war tactics at the Academy for Mechanization and Motorization of the Red Army. During the Russo-Finnish War from 1939 to 1940 he was commander of a tank battalion and chief of staff of the 35th Armored Brigade. In August 1940 he was appointed second in command of the 5th Armored Division; he was promoted to chief of staff of the III Mechanized Corps in May 1941.

Following the outbreak of the Russo-German War, Rotmistrov saw action at the Western Front as chief of staff of the III Mechanized Corps. In January 1942 as commander of the 3rd Guard Armored Brigade, he participated in the counteroffensive before Moscow. In April 1942 he became commander of the VII Armored Corps operating in the Yelets area and later at Stalingrad. In February 1943 Rotmistrov became the commanding general of the Fifth Guards Tank Army.

Vasili D. Sokolovsky

Commanding general of the Western Front, born the scion of an aristocratic Polish family on 9 July 1897 in Kozliki near Bialystok (Poland).

He joined the Red Army in 1918 and saw action at the Eastern, Southern, and Caucasus Fronts during the Civil War from 1918 to 1922. He became deputy chief of staff of the 39th Rifle Division, then a brigade commander, and chief of staff of the 32nd Rifle Division. In 1921 he graduated from the Military Academy of the Red Army and became deputy chief of operational administration at the Turkestan Front, the chief of staff, division commander, and commander of the battle groups in the Fergansk and Samarkand regions. For exemplary service, he was decorated with the

Pavel A. Rotmistrov

26

Order of the Red Banner. From 1922 to 1930 Sokolovsky was first chief of staff of a rifle division in northern Asia, then of the Moscow Military District, and later chief of staff of an infantry corps in the northern Caucasus. In 1928 he attended courses at advanced training academies.

From 1930 to 1935 he was commander of a rifle division; later deputy chief of staff of the Volga Military District. He joined the Soviet Communist party in 1931. In May 1935 he became chief of staff of the Ural Military District, and in April 1938 again chief of staff of the Moscow Military District. In the spring of 1941, Sokolovsky was named deputy chief of the General Staff.

Following the outbreak of the Soviet-German War, he was at the Western Front from July 1941 to January 1942 and from May 1942 to February 1943. From July to September 1942 he was chief of staff of the Western Front. In February 1943 he became commanding general of the Western Front.

Nikolai F. Vatutin

Commanding general of the Voronezh Front, born on 3 December 1901 in the village of Chepukhino, Belgorod District.

During the Civil War from 1918 to 1922, he fought against the White Russian Mahno partisans in the Lugansk and Starobelsk region. He was in the Red Army in 1920 and joined the Soviet Communist party in 1921. He graduated from the Infantry School in Poltava in 1922. In 1923 he led a platoon and was subsequently on the staff of the 7th Rifle Division.

In 1924 Vatutin attended the Advanced Officers' School in Kiev and in 1929 the Frunze Army Staff College (majoring in operational tactics). In 1934 he finished his studies at the General Staff Academy. From 1931 to 1941 he was chief of the Division Staff, then section leader of the I. Siberian Military District, then deputy chief of staff, and subsequently chief of staff of the Kiev Military District. Then Vatutin was promoted to section chief of the Operational General Staff and to deputy chief of the General Staff.

Following the outbreak of the Soviet-German War, Vatutin was chief of staff of the Northwestern Front and participated in the defense of Novgorod. From May to July 1942 he was deputy chief of the General Staff and representative of the Supreme Staff of the Staff Command (STAVKA: the Soviet High Command) at the Bryansk Front. On 14 July 1942 he was made commanding general of the Voronezh Front. In the Battle of Stalingrad from 1942 to 1943, Vatutin commanded the Southwestern Front. In March 1943 he once again became commanding general of the Voronezh Front.

Prologue

The setting sun was sinking slowly behind the horizon, its last rays illuminating the smoke clouds hanging over the city, the roofs and ruins covered with snow. Along the walls of buildings, Soviet tanks were proceeding down main roads leading into the city, firing at the invisible enemy. The streets were strewn with burning wrecks and abandoned equipment. The incessant rattling of machine guns was drowned out by the booming of the artillery and the screaming Katyushas. Long lines of crouched Red Army soldiers in white camouflage suits jumped past the fronts of buildings, shooting wildly on their way toward the center of town. A couple of heavy detonations shook the ground. Yet with the oncoming darkness, stillness fell over the city. Only single shots could be heard here and there. In the glow of burning adjacent buildings, soldiers hung a red flag from the top floor of the "House of the Pioneers." This building had artillery shells piled at its entrance, indicating that it was meant to be blown up.

It was Monday, 8 February 1943. The Soviet Sixtieth Army (Lieutenant General Chernykhovsky) had captured Kursk following an entire day of street fighting.

WHAT WOULD THE FUEHRER SAY TO IT? This slogan hanging like a Damocles' sword over the desk in FM von Manstein's rolling HQ seems to even make him pensive

Twenty-four hours later, on 9 February 1943, the Soviet Fortieth Army (Lieutenant General Moskalenko) took Belgorod. Just a week earlier the last German troops had capitulated in the northern encirclement of Stalingrad. The first half of February 1943 was marked by a series of rapid Soviet victories. Although German troops were defending the Mius line north of the Sea of Asov and were still holding the southern part of the Donets Basin, the Red Army was advancing unflaggingly on a wide front in the

Voronezh area, pushing from the east and northeast into the northern Ukraine, liberating the province of Kursk and recapturing several towns, both large and small.

On Tuesday, 16 February 1943, the II SS-Panzer Corps (Obergruppenfuehrer and general of the Waffen-SS Hausser) had to evacuate Kharkov, the fourth largest city in the Soviet Union; this against Hitler's express orders. While the troops of the Southern Front (General of the Army Malinovsky) were taking Novo-Cherkask and Rostov, General of the Army Vatutin's forces recaptured the big industrial center of Voroshilovgrad. It looked as if the liberation of the strategically and economically vital steel and mining centers in the Donets Basin was imminent. Following the recapture of Kharkov, the Red Army continued its advance to the west and was almost in sight of the Dnieper on 17 February 1943.

Six days later, on Monday, 22 February 1943, however, the Germans counterattacked between the Dnieper and the Donets under the command of one of their best officers, the commanding general of Army Group South, Field Marshal von Manstein. The counterattack was directed against the Voronezh Front (General of the Army Malinovsky). Soon the wave was rolled back. The Red Army now quickly lost all the ground in this sector that it had recaptured during the winter offensive.

On Sunday, 6 March 1943, the German Fourth Panzer Army (Colonel General Hoth) and the Kempf Army (General of the Pz. Tr. Kempf) launched an assault against the Soviet Third Tank Army (Major General Rybalko) and the Sixty-Ninth Army (Lieutenant General Kryuchenkin) of the Voronezh Front (General of the Army Vatutin) in the area west of Kharkov.

Nine days later, on Monday, 15 March 1943, after smashing the Soviet Third Tank Army, the II SS-Panzer Corps (Obergruppenf. Hausser) retook Kharkov in dogged street fighting.

On Thursday, 18 March 1943, while the remaining sections of the Soviet Third Tank Army were being decimated south of Kharkov by the XLVIII Panzer Corps (General of the Pz. Tr. von Knobelsdorff), the German Fourth Panzer Army reinforced by the bulk of the II SS-Panzer Corps and supported by squadrons of Luftflotte 4 (FM Freiherr von Richthofen) started its thrust toward Belgorod. Following hard fighting with the Soviet Sixty-Ninth Army, Colonel General Hoth captured Belgorod. As a result the entire rear area of the Soviet Central Front (General of the Army Rokossovsky) was seriously threatened.

Field Marshal von Manstein now planned a pincer assault from the south from Belgorod and from the Orel area on the north with the aim of encircling and smashing several Soviet armies in the salient of the front at Kursk. This operation, which would have made Operation "Citadel" superfluous, was foiled before it could even start by the adamant refusal of Army Group Center's commanding general, Field Marshal von Kluge, to make his units at the southern flank of Army Group Center available because they were being rehabilitated. With the approaching mud period Army Group South's counteroffensive had to be abandoned.

Although von Manstein had saved the Donets coal region, so invaluable to the German armaments industry, and had linked up again with Army Group Center without a gap, his northern flank now had a vulnerable bulge.

The Kursk Salient encompassed an area about the size of Bavaria. Situated in the center of the German defensive front extending far into the west, it offered both sides excellent geomilitary possibilities for a large-scale offensive. In 1943, it was strategically the most vital sector of the Eastern Front. On the one hand, the salient separated German Army Groups Center and South so that, in the case of a Soviet attack, its deep flanks as well as the operational rear were endangered. On the other hand, the German troops concentrated at Orel and Kharkov from the spring of 1943 on were a threat to the northern and southern flank of the Soviet forces positioned there.

In the spring of 1943, Germany found itself in a complicated strategic situation. Twenty months after its invasion of the Soviet Union, its primary objective of annihilating the Red Army was still not in sight. Its defeat at Stalingrad led to domestic and foreign policy crises at home and among its allies in Europe and Asia. Italy and Romania were intensifying efforts to extract themselves from the war, while Japan made it clear it intended to respect its nonaggression pact with the Soviet Union. Turkey finally decided not to enter the war against the Soviet Union. Therefore, a defensive strategy in the east, which would have meant abandoning large-scale assault

The end of an assembly line at the Henshel Works early 1943: PzKpfw VI Tiger at that time still the most formidable tank in the world. The armor in front of the driver and on the turret was so strong that a direct hit will not cause much damage. Its 88mm gun with 92 rounds of ammunition became one of the weapons most dreaded in WWII. This heavy tank—according to Hitler—was supposed to decide the Battle of Kursk

operations, would have been tantamount to the end of Hitler's political plans. In the first months of 1943, the Germans were being forced to defensive operations on land, air, and sea. There were signs of shortages in some vital supply areas—particularly fuel.

Hitler, who saw that his prestige was seriously endangered, said that he intended "to get back in the summer what was lost during the winter." Without question, following the loss of Stalingrad, facing a difficult situation in North Africa, a decline in the U-boat victories, a crisis in the air war, and a vacillating Italian attitude, the Nazi regime really needed a military success. The German people's faith in ultimate victory had to be restored and the disintegration of the Berlin-Rome axis stopped.

At the end of the winter offensive, there were 159 German field divisions in the shortened line of the Eastern Front (2600 kilometers), most with reduced combat effectiveness. Because of the length of the front, it was practically impossible to conduct a stationary defense against the 400 Soviet major formations, which surprisingly had quickly regained their full fighting strength. With this unfavorable combat situation, Hitler saw that the only solution was to weaken the Soviets by a powerful strategic offensive in restricted areas that would reduce decisively the impact of the imminent Soviet summer offensive.

Although the combat proportions no longer permitted any large offensive operations, the Wehrmacht was, nevertheless, still quite capable of striking rapid, effective blows, as the counteroffensive south of Kharkov showed. And elastic tactics—combined with the flexibility and tactical talent

33

Rylsk area, March 1943, in a trench: ". . . to give the Soviets a hard, exhausting fight"

of German junior officers—allowed the Wehrmacht to give the Soviets a hard and exhausting fight.

As the Germans were managing once more to ward off the impending defeat in the east, Hitler was as convinced as ever that he could still bring the war to a victorious conclusion. He stuck to his decision to launch his own assault before the mud period set in, and before the Soviets could launch their offensive. This plan was the subject of a conference between Hitler and his top generals on 17–19 February 1943, attended by chief of the Armed Forces Command Staff, General of Artillery Jodl; chief of General Staff of the Army, General of Infantry Zeitzler, as well as the commanding generals of Army Groups South and Center, FM von Manstein and FM von Kluge. They demanded that Hitler seize the initiative again

34

on the Eastern Front because, "Only offensive operations can bring about a way out of this situation."

Ideal for this seemed to be the salient extending far into the German front at Kursk. If one were to cut off this salient from both sides, not only would strong Soviet forces be trapped, but the Red Army would also lose its jumping-off point for operations against the deep flanks of Army Groups South and Center. It also seemed possible that a comprehensive assault could annihilate strong Soviet reserves standing by east of Kursk for a subsequent offensive.

To the High Command of the Army (OKH) the removal of this salient (approximately 200 kilometers wide, protruding about 100 kilometers into the German front) meant shortening the front by 240 kilometers and thereby saving reserves. For this reason OKH planned an early opening operation with a limited objective in the Kursk area as soon as the weather permitted. This would also make possible the encircling of the Soviet Central and Voronezh Fronts, thereby making a breach for later, large-scale operations south and northeast.

Hitler prophesied quick and far-reaching victories. The most important condition, however, was that any offensive in the Kursk Salient would have to be launched quickly in order to catch the Soviets off guard and in a state of relative weakness. What spoke against this plan was that this was exactly the sector where the Soviets were sure to expect a German assault and where they had especially reinforced their troops. There was the danger of exhausting one's own forces more than the enemy's. Moreover, it was quite conceivable that the Red Army might exploit the fact that strong German assault forces were tied up at Kursk and itself attack the Orel Salient.

5 March—3 July 1943

Prepa

rations

From the OKW War Diary (Oberkommando der Wehrmacht, High Command of the German Armed Forces)
Wednesday, 17 March 1943:

The Fuehrer has issued Operational Order No. 5 for the east (tactical directive for the next several months). The main effort is to prevent the enemy from seizing the initiative from us in any one sector of the front, and letting him butt against all sectors and bleed himself white. Necessary preparations are to begin immediately as the mud period has ended earlier this year than last year.

Classified SS-Secret Service Report on the Home Political Situation No. 269 (Excerpt)
Friday, 19 March 1943:

I. General: According to reports coming in from all over the Reich concerning the Fuehrer's speech on Heldengedenktag (16 March, Heroes' Day), it was met with great approval by the people.

The statement that made the biggest and undoubtedly most lasting impression was, "There is one thing that we already know today. The Bolshevik hordes that the German soldiers and their allies were not able to defeat this winter will be annihilated by us next summer!" These words have eminently strengthened the hope held by most Germans that Bolshevism will still be conquered this year.

From the OKW War Diary
Friday, 2 April 1943:

Army Group South: Road conditions have grown worse.

The Army Group has orders to prepare for Operation "Habicht" (hawk). In case the operation cannot be conducted according to schedule due to the weather, preparations should also be made for Operation "Panther." The Army Group must also be able to start Operation "Citadel" if the enemy situation should change.

A Gigantic Battle
Monday, 5 April, 1943, Moscow. A member of the Soviet General Staff reports in *Pravda*:

"There will be a gigantic battle in the summer of 1943 that certainly will free the Soviet Union from the Fascist invaders. We shall make every effort to make our tank divisions more effective and hurl them mercilessly at the enemy. We were unable to exploit completely the great successes of our winter offensive, a fact we do not deny.

"Just at the very moment that we had begun to shake the enemy's ranks in many sectors of the long front and were pursuing him, snow and mud became insurmountable obstacles for our motorized troops. It has often been said that the Red Army prefers winter as the 'season for Russian offensives' and for this reason the world has eagerly been awaiting the Russians next move, following the German victories from May to October 1942. Our troops, in fact, did seize the initiative both winters of the Soviet-Ger-

man War, but it was not as if we felt particularly comfortable in snow and frost. We unfortunately needed much time to train, assemble, and send our reserves into battle. There is every indication that our army is now able to carry out all these indispensable preparations in much shorter time than a year ago."

French Pilots on the Eastern Front
Wednesday, 7 April 1943, Moscow. United Press reports:

A representative of the French National Committee in Moscow has announced that for the first time a group of "Fighting French" have been sent into action on the Russian Front and have already shot down two German bombers. There are sixty men in the group, among them twelve well-known French bomber pilots, who had already proven themselves in the battle for France and in North Africa.

Kursk: The Objective of the German Offensive
Saturday, 10 April 1943. From the Central Front:

To the Head of the Operations Section of the General Staff of the Red Army, attention Colonel General A. I. Antonov.
Re: Your Number 11990
The objective and probable directions of an enemy attack in spring/summer 1943:

Mosalsk area, April 1943: the Free French forces' "Normandy" Squadron. Lt. Bruno de Faletans with his radio operator

39

a) Considering the present forces and resources and particularly the results of the 1941/1942 assault operations, an enemy offensive in spring/summer 1943 can only be expected in the operational direction of Kursk-Voronezh. An enemy offensive in other directions is hardly possible.

. . .

d) The enemy cannot begin to regroup and concentrate his troops in the probable assault directions and build up his supply network until after the mud period and the spring floods. Therefore, the enemy's transition to offensive can be expected approximately in the second half of May.

. . .

Chief of Staff of the Central Front

No. 4203

Lieutenant General Malinin

"Highest State of Readiness"
Monday, 12 April 1943. At the Voronezh Front:

To the Chief of the General Staff of the Red Army.
Re: Your Number 11990

At this moment there are at the Voronezh Front:
1. Nine infantry divisions in the first echelon (the 26th, 68th, 323rd, 75th, 255th, 57th, 332nd, 167th, and one unidentified one). These divisions are holding the line Krasno-Oktyabrskoye-Bolshaya-Chernechina-Krasno-polye-Kazatskoye. According to statements from prisoners, the division whose number is not known is supposed to move forward in the Soldatskoye area and relieve the 332nd Infantry Division.

This information is being checked. We have unconfirmed information that six infantry divisions are to be assembled in the second echelon. Their position has not yet been ascertained; this information is still being confirmed.

In the Kharkov area, radio reconnaissance has discovered the staff of a Hungarian division which can be put in a secondary section. . . .

The enemy's objective is to strike concentric blows from the Belgorod area to the northeast and from the Orel area to the southeast and encircle our troops positioned west of the Belgorod-Kursk line.

Moreover, an enemy thrust can be expected to the southeast into the flank and rear of the Southwestern Front. This thrust is then expected to continue north.

However, the enemy may not conduct an offensive to the southeast this year, but instead adopt another plan, namely, an offensive to the northeast following the strikes from the Belgorod and Kursk areas in order to bypass Moscow. This possibility must be considered, and adequate reserves prepared.

We therefore expect that the enemy will with his main forces push forward from the Voronezh Front out of the Borisovka-Belgorod area toward Stary Oskol and with part of the forces toward Oboyan and Kursk. Additional assaults are to be expected on Volchansk, Novy Oskol, Sudzha, Oboyan, and Kursk. The enemy is not yet capable of a general assault. The attack will probably not start before 20 April of this year, most likely in the first days of May. However, limited advances must be anticipated at any time. This requires our troops to be in a state of highest readiness.

No. 55/k

Fyodorov Nikitin Fedotov

"*. . . like a signal*"

Sevsk area, mid-April 1943: German machine gunners after night combat with Soviet reconnaissance troops

The Fuehrer   F. HQ., 15 April 1943
OKH (Oberkommando des Heeres, High Command of the Army),
GenStdH (General Staff of the Army), Op. Abt. (I) (Operational Section)
No. 430246/43

Top Secret!
Confidential!
Only for Officers!

Operation Order No. 6
I have decided to launch Operation "Citadel" as the first of this year's
offensives as soon as the weather permits.

This assault is of vital importance. It must succeed rapidly and totally.
It must give us the initiative for this spring and summer.

For this reason, all preparations must be carried out with utmost care
and energy. The best formations, the best weapons, the best commanders
must be present with great stocks of ammunition placed at key points. Every
commander, every man must be indoctrinated with the decisive significance
of this offensive. The victory of Kursk must be a signal to the world.
To this end I order:

1. The objective of this offensive is to encircle enemy forces deployed
in the Kursk area by means of an extremely concentrated thrust conducted
mercilessly and swiftly by one assault army each from the areas of Belgorod

and south of Orel, to annihilate the enemy in a concentric attack. In the course of this offensive, a shortened new front which will save strength will be gained along the line Neshega-Korocha section–Skorodnoye-Tim-east of Shchigry-Sosna section.

2. It is crucial

a) to maintain the element of surprise as much as possible, and above all to keep the enemy in the dark as to the timing of the offensive,

b) to concentrate the attacking forces into as narrow a front as possible, in order that both armies break through with locally overwhelming materiel (tanks, assault guns, artillery, rockets, mortars, etc.) in one blow until they unite and thus close the encirclement,

c) to cover the flanks of the assaulting wedges with forces from the rear as fast as possible so that the striking echelons themselves only have to drive forward,

d) to prevent the enemy from resting and hasten his destruction by pushing into the circled forces from all sides as quickly as possible,

e) to carry out the attack so swiftly that the enemy is neither able to break out of the encirclement nor bring up strong reserves from other fronts,

f) to liberate forces, particularly mobile formations for further operations, as soon as possible by quickly building up a new front.

3. Army Group South will jump off with strongly concentrated forces from the Belgorod-Tomarovka line, break through the Prilepy-Oboyan line, and link up with Army Group Center's assault army at and east of Kursk. To cover the attack from the east, the line Neshega-Korocha sector–Skorodnoye-Tim must be reached as soon as possible without jeopardizing the main effort of linking up with forces in the Prilepy-Oboyan direction. To cover the assault from the west, secondary forces are to be employed which at the same time will have the task of driving into the encirclement as it is being formed.

4. Army Group Center will jump off with its assault army from the Trosna–north of Maloarchangelsk line, concentrate its forces, and break through the Fatesh-Vereytenovo line. Its main effort will be on the western flank, and linking up with Army Group South's assault army at and east of Kursk. To cover the assault from the east, the line Tim–east of Shchigry-Sosna sector must be reached as soon as possible; this, however, must not jeopardize the concentration of forces in the main effort. Secondary forces are to be employed to cover the assault from the west. The Army Group Center forces operating west of Trosna to the boundary of Army Group South must tie down the enemy's strike forces and push into the forming encirclement quickly. Constant air and ground reconnaissance must ensure that the enemy does not break away unnoticed. If he should, a general offensive is to be mounted immediately along the entire front.

5. The forming-up of the forces of both army groups must occur far from the jump-off point using all possible means of camouflage, concealment, and deceptive measures so that the offensive may be launched on the sixth day following receipt of the orders from the OKH. Accordingly, the earliest date is 3 May. Movements to the jump-off points must be in the form of night marches using every possible means of concealment.

6. In order to deceive the enemy, preparations for "Panther" are to continue in the area of Army Group South. They must be supported by every means (conspicuous reconnaissance, show of tanks, preparation of

On the supply road
Kharkov-Belgorod,
mid-April 1943:
every inch of
ground alongside
the road is mined

crossing materials, radios, agents, spreading rumors, employment of the Luftwaffe, etc.) and kept going as long as is possible. These deceptive operations will also be supported by measures necessary to strengthen defensive forces at the Donets Front. (See paragraph 11.) In the area of Army Group Center, no large-scale deceptive measures are to be carried out. However, everything must be done to confuse the enemy's picture of the situation (false and retrograde movements as well as marches by day, spreading false information about the timing of the attack (that it would be in June) etc. In both Army Groups, new formations that are moved up to reinforce the assault armies are to maintain radio silence.

7. To ensure secrecy only those who absolutely need to know are to be briefed. Briefing is to be explained phase by phase as late as possible. There must, at all costs, be no leaks due to carelessness or negligence.

Increased counterintelligence efforts constantly will combat enemy intelligence activities.

. . .

11. For the success of the assault it is vital that the enemy does not succeed in forcing us to postpone "Citadel" or withdraw assault formations prematurely before attacking other sectors of Army Group South or Center. For this reason both Army Groups must systematically prepare for defensive battle at other threatened primary sectors with every available means by the end of the month; this in addition to the "Citadel" offensive. It is essential to speed up field fortifications, to supply the sectors vulnerable to tank attack with sufficient antitank defense, to make reserves ready locally, to discover enemy strong points through intense reconnaissance, etc.
Dated April 24th   signed Adolf Hitler

From the OKW War Diary
Sunday, 25 April 1943:

Army Group South: The Army Group has turned in a comprehensive assessment of the enemy for "Citadel" which shows that we must expect him to be completely ready defensively and capable of strong counteroffensives. But his offensive capabilities will probably not forestall the launching of "Citadel." For the execution of "Citadel," the Army Group proposes extension of forces, reinforcement of positions, deceptive measures, and coordination with the Luftwaffe.

Army Group Center: On 25 April 1943, at 0000, as a result of the new boundary with Army Group North, the 331st I.D. comes under the com-

43

mand of AOK (Armee Oberkommando, Army High Command). The transportation movements forward of the 4th and 9th Pz. Div. are in process and there is continued improvement of roads and trails.

The Army Group presents its proposals for conducting Operation "Citadel" and gives a detailed report on the enemy situation, intended assault operations, the Second Army's secondary attack plan, supply operations, defense plans on the Army Group's other fronts, and the location of the Army Group's operational headquarters during the assault.

From the OKW War Diary
Monday, 26 April 1943:

Army Groups South-Center-North: A supplemental Operation Order No. 6 is sent to Army Groups South and Center underlining once again the importance of concentration of forces; adaptation to the enemy's intentions; the significance of intelligence and reconnaissance, camouflage, and deceptive measures; and the final scheduling for the assault.

From the OKW War Diary
Thursday, 29 April 1943:

Kromy, April 25, 1943. Training in destroying tanks: the best place to attach a magnetic mine—the engine ventilator

Army Group South: Commencement of march movements for "Citadel." Transport forward and relief according to plan.

Rumors Spread by the Enemy

Thursday, 29 April 1943, Berlin. The DNB (Deutscher Nachrichten Dienst—German Press Service):

Reichsminister Dr. Goebbels explains in an article "Where Do We Stand?" the events of the war up to the present. The minister rejected rumors that the axis had sent out peace feelers to this or that side via various neutral countries. These rumors spread by the enemy obviously are wishful thinking. The exhaustion of the physical and emotional strength of a people by the long duration of the war affects both friend and foe equally, the enemy to a much greater extent. Finally Dr. Goebbels said an "overrunning" of the European continent was an impossibility.

From the OKW War Diary

Friday, 30 April 1943:

Army Group South: Transportation according to plan. March movements for "Citadel" stopped.

Army Group Center: Orders for new scheduling of "Citadel" dispatched to Army Groups South and Center.

Preparations for the Summer Offensive

30 April 1943, Moscow. The Sovinformburo reports:

The pause in fighting at the front should last for a little while yet. Just in the last twenty-four hours there has been a considerable increase in artillery fire and patrol activities. Significant German troop and materiel transportation were attacked violently in three sectors. On our side we have concentrated forces in the Kursk area which the Fascist Luftwaffe has attacked repeatedly. The present interlude does not deceive us. It is the lull before the storm. Hitler will try to turn the tide of the war in his favor this summer, and we have to be prepared for even fiercer battles and even harder tests than we have encountered before. We are now preparing blows that will upset the enemy's preparations in a decisive way. We are prepared to conduct an enormous campaign against Hitler's armies in the summer of 1943.

Korotcha area, end of April 1943. Preparations for the summer offensive: heavy Soviet KV–1C tanks after returning from target practice

45

From the OKW War Diary
Tuesday, 4 May 1943:

Army Group South: Transport movements according to plan.

Army Group Center: No significant action. During the night there was a heavy air attack on Orsha. Three hundred cars, among them three ammunition trains, burned up. Personnel losses ascertained at this time: 4 Germans killed; 130 dead and 150 seriously injured Russians.

From the OKW War Diary
Thursday, 6 May 1943:

Army Group Center: Lively enemy air force activity in the entire Army Group area focusing on the Orel area.

Radio Beromuenster (Switzerland)
Friday, 7 May 1943:

On 1 May, Stalin made public an order of the day for the Red Army which received much attention throughout the world. In this communiqué the Russian head of government forsook his reserve which he has preserved in public up to now on all questions concerning cooperation with the Anglo-Saxon allies. As is known, the Soviet Union has never made an official statement about the so-called "Casablanca Program," Churchill's and Roosevelt's war objective for the "unconditional capitulation" of the Axis powers. Stalin has now adopted this principle in the above-mentioned communiqué. Officials in Berlin interpret this as Russia's acceptance of the Casablanca resolutions. The communiqué also was received with great satisfaction in England and America. . . . What was politically most remarkable was the sharpness and bluntness with which Stalin fended off peace rumors and peace campaigns. He said a separate Anglo-American peace with Germany was just as unthinkable as a separate Russian peace with Germany.

"Total combat readiness . . ."
Saturday, 8 May 1943.

Teletype to the Commanding Generals of the Bryansk, Voronezh, and Southwestern Fronts: According to our information we can expect the enemy to attack in the Orel-Kursk or Belgorod-Oboyan direction or in both directions simultaneously between 10 and 12 May. The STAVKA Headquarters orders that as of 11 May all troops in the first defensive line and in reserve be put in total combat readiness to meet a potential enemy thrust. Special attention must be given to our air force's readiness. In case of an attack, they must not only ward off blows by the enemy air force but also gain air supremacy as soon as they go into action.

Receipt is to be confirmed. Measures taken are to be reported.

In Four Days a German Offensive?
8 May 1943:

To the Headquarters of the Supreme Command, Comrade J. V. Stalin. Re: Headquarters Directive No. 30123 of 8 May 1943.

1. Following receipt of the Headquarters directive, all armies and independent corps at the Central Front were directed to put their troops in combat readiness by the morning of 10 May.

2. During 9 and 10 May:

a) The troops were informed about possible enemy assault operations in the near future.

b) The troop sections in the first and second echelons and the reserve were put into highest combat readiness. The commanders and the staffs are inspecting troop readiness on the spot.

c) Troop reconnaissance by fire and movement against the enemy in army sectors, particularly in the Orel direction, has been increased. First echelon forces are checking the accuracy of their fire plans. Forces in the second and reserve echelons are performing additional reconnaissance in the direction of the probable action and cooperating well with the forces of the first echelon. Ammunition supplies in firing positions are being established. Blocking positions, particularly in areas vulnerable to tank attack, are being reinforced. Defensive sectors are being mined in depth. Communications equipment is being checked; it is in excellent working condition.

3. The Sixteenth Air Army has established air reconnaissance and is observing the enemy in the Glazunovka-Orel-Kromy-Komariki area. Air formations and air corps sections of the army have been put in combat readiness to fend off the enemy air force and to prevent possible enemy action.

Belgorod, May 7, 1943, Russian volunteer helpers (Hiwis) at work: fuel is one of the most crucial supply items for motorized forces

47

4. In order to thwart a possible enemy attack in the Orel-Kursk direction, preparations for counterbattery fire have been made in which all the artillery of the Thirteenth Army and the aircraft of the Sixteenth Air Army will participate.
No. 00219   Rokossovsky, Telegin, Malinin

From the OKW War Diary
Wednesday, 12 May 1943:

Army Group Center: Transport movements for the two large-scale antiguerrilla operations, "Gypsy Baron" and "Freischuetz," are running according to plan.

Heavy Air Attacks
Thursday, 13 May 1943, Moscow. STAVKA reports:

On 11 May and during the night of 12 May, strong forces of our air force conducted attacks on the railroad junctions of Dniepropetrovsk, Poltava, Bryansk, Kharkov, Orel, Krasnograd, Losovaya, Barvenkovo, Jartsevo, and others. At the same time our planes bombed enemy motorized columns. These operations destroyed or damaged many enemy railroad cars and motor vehicles containing war materiel. Moreover, our aircraft bombed several Fascist airfields.

From the OKW War Diary
Tuesday, 18 May 1943:

Army Group Center: Second Pz. Army: antiguerrilla operation "Gypsy Baron" is running without encountering significant enemy resistance. The day's objectives are being achieved. Third Pz. Army: antiguerrilla operation "May Storm" is being continued against tough enemy resistance.

Strong Concentration of German Troops at Orel-Bryansk
18 May 1943, London. Reuters Agency reports:

New reports have come in about a strong concentration of German troops in the Orel-Bryansk Salient. Hungarian, Romanian, and Italian divisions, which were deployed here up to now, have been replaced completely by German elite troops. In addition to a powerful concentration of armor, artillery, and infantry, new aircraft have arrived as reinforcements at German combat airfields. Nevertheless, in military circles the general opinion is that the Germans will not succeed in deploying as overwhelming a number of troops and materiel this year as in past offensives. In addition, German offensive preparations are being disturbed markedly by constant Soviet air attacks.

Further to the south, in the Kharkov-Belgorod area, Soviet reconnaissance planes are operating constantly over German rear areas. They have found great concentrations of German troops and armor. Although details cannot be made public, it can be stated that STAVKA is not confining itself to defensive measures to repulse a possible German large-scale offensive.

Olkhovka area, May 19, 1943. Protected against observation from the air, the crew of a camouflaged Tiger is trying to cover up its tracks in the grass

Instead, it has concentrated powerful and well-equipped armies at sensitive points that, as is being stressed in well-informed circles, "will strike shortly."

From the OKW War Diary
Wednesday, 19 May 1943:

Army Group Center: Fourth Army: According to plan, most of the troops have reached the assembly area for the antiguerrilla operation "Neighborly Help." Third Pz. Army: In Operation "May Storm," the encirclement is being drawn tighter and break-out attempts are being prevented.

An Imminent Soviet Large-Scale Offensive?
Friday, 21 May 1943, Berlin: A correspondent of the *Svenska Dagbladet* reports:

German military circles apparently expect that the lull at the Eastern Front will end. It is assumed that the Soviets are planning a large-scale offensive in the summer as soon as preparations for it have been completed. The Soviet High Command has increased its reconnaissance and recently conducted many patrol activities. In Berlin it is assumed that their first assault will be directed against the Orel Salient which protrudes far into Russian territory since the clearing of Vyazma and Kursk. This area was hotly contested in March and April, the fighting there being among the fiercest and bloodiest of the entire Winter War.

The Soviet High Command is deploying its formations south of Moscow and at Kursk. This would mean bypassing Orel with two flanking thrusts from the north and south. German intelligence reports that the enemy has already concentrated strong infantry and tank formations and particularly a lot of artillery in the sectors in question. Moreover, traffic behind the front is very active. The Luftwaffe has lately tried to disrupt the Soviet buildup by bombing communication lines and supply bases intensively.

". . . no assault before the end of May"
Saturday, 22 May 1943, 0448:

To Comrade Ivanov:
I report the situation at the Central Front: By 21 May various intelligence agencies have established that the enemy has fifteen infantry divi-

sions deployed in his first defensive line; in the second line and in reserve there are thirteen divisions, three of them armored. In addition to this we have reports that the 2nd Panzer and the 36th Motorized Divisions are being concentrated south of Orel. The information on these two divisions requires confirmation.

The enemy's 4th Panzer Division formerly located west of Sevsk has been moved elsewhere. Moreover, there are three divisions, two of them armored, in the Bryansk-Karachev area.

Thus, according to the information of 21 May, the enemy can bring thirty-three divisions, six of them armored, against the Central Front.

Technical intelligence and sightings along the Front have identified 800 guns, primarily 105 and 150mm, with the bulk of enemy artillery facing Thirteenth Army, the left flank of Forty-Eighth Army, and the right flank of Seventieth Army; i.e., in the Trosna-Pervoye-Pozdeyeva sector. Behind this main artillery group there are approximately 600 to 700 tanks deployed along the line Zmeyevka-Krasnaya-Roshcha, mainly east of the Oka.

In the Orel-Bryansk-Smolensk area, the enemy has concentrated 600 to 650 enemy aircraft. The bulk of the enemy air force is deployed in the Orel area.

Prisoners say that the German High Command knows of our troops to the south and our preparations for an offensive and that German units have been informed accordingly. Captured pilots say that the Germans are planning an assault themselves and that they are bringing in air units for this purpose.

I myself have been at the main forward position of the Thirteenth Army, examined the enemy's defense from various points, observed his activities, and have personally spoken to the division commanders of the Seventieth and Thirteenth Armies and to Commanding Generals Galinin, Pukhov, and Romanenko. I have concluded that there is no evidence in the enemy's main fighting line of an imminent enemy attack.

I may be wrong. Perhaps the enemy is very skillful at hiding his preparations; but considering the way his armored units are deployed, the insufficient concentration of infantry, the lack of heavy artillery units, and the way the reserves are spread out, I believe that the enemy cannot launch an attack before the end of May. . . .

No. 2069

Yuryev

From the OKW War Diary
Monday, 24 May 1943:

Army Group Center: Second Pz. Army: Operation "Gypsy Baron" is continuing against heavy enemy resistance while road conditions are growing worse. In Operation "Freischuetz" we are tightening the encirclement further. In the antiguerrilla operation "Neighborly Help," twenty-one partisan camps were destroyed and the encircled enemy groups pushed closer together.

A base at the East-
ern Front, May
1943. Return from
home leave

The Eastern Front
remained relatively
stable from the end
of May to July 7,
1943; in particular
at the Central Front
Sector, the Kursk
Salient

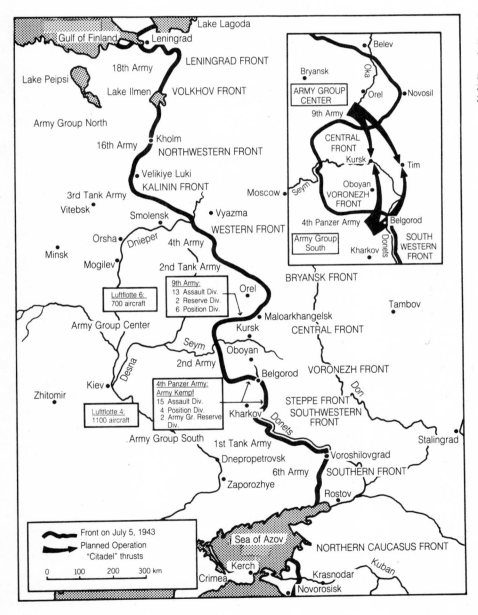

Lake Lagoda

Gulf of Finland · Leningrad

LENINGRAD FRONT

18th Army

Lake Peipsi

Lake Ilmen · VOLKHOV FRONT

Army Group North

· Kholm
16th Army · NORTHWESTERN FRONT

· Velikiye Luki
KALININ FRONT

3rd Tank Army
Vitebsk ·

· Smolensk · Vyazma
Orsha · Dnieper WESTERN FRONT
· Minsk
· Mogilev 4th Army
2nd Tank Army
9th Army: · Orel
13 Assault Div.
2 Reserve Div.
6 Position Div.
Luftflotte 6: · Maloarkhangelsk
700 aircraft · Kursk CENTRAL FRONT
Army Group Center Seym
Desna 2nd Army · Oboyan
· Belgorod VORONEZH FRONT
Kiev · 4th Panzer Army:
Army Kempf Don
Zhitomir · 15 Assault Div. STEPPE FRONT
4 Position Div. SOUTHWESTERN
Luftflotte 4: 2 Army Gr. Reserve · Kharkov FRONT
1100 aircraft Div. Donets
Army Group South 1st Tank Army Stalingrad
· Dnepropetrovsk · Voroshilovgrad
6th Army SOUTHERN FRONT
· Zaporozhye
· Rostov

Front on July 5, 1943
Planned Operation
"Citadel" thrusts
Sea of Azov NORTHERN CAUCASUS FRONT
0 100 200 300 km
· Kerch Kuban
Crimea · Krasnodar
· Novorosisk

Belev ·
· Bryansk Oka
ARMY GROUP · Orel · Novosil
CENTER
9th Army
CENTRAL
FRONT
· Kursk · Tim
Moscow · Oboyan
Seym VORONEZH
FRONT
4th Panzer Army
· Belgorod
Army Group SOUTH
South WESTERN
· Kharkov FRONT
Donets

· Tambov

BRYANSK FRONT

24 May 1943:

General: What is happening at the Eastern Front hardly concerns our fellow citizens at all. The absence of activities on our side has been noticed, whereas last year they were still "feverishly" waiting for an "offensive." The question most people are asking this year is less "When will the offensive begin?" but "Will there be an offensive at all?" Here a constantly growing number of people think that Germany is not strong enough for an eastern

offensive this year. Therefore, on the Eastern Front, the "Ostwall" (eastern rampart) should be held.

The German Buildup
Wednesday, 2 June 1943: United Press reports:

The present situation at the fronts is still considered static. There are signs, however, that this will end soon and that Germany may launch a large offensive. As far as it is known here, the German regrouping that was

Sybina, east of Belgorod, the end of May 1943. As always, bearing the burden of war: forced evacuation of the neighboring villages

53

necessary following the defeats during the winter has been essentially completed. Major shifting of divisions is no longer being accomplished.

Combat airfield near Orel, June 2, 1943; fight for air supremacy: a burning He 111 type bomber following an attack by Soviet ground attack planes

Fighting Against Guerrillas
by war correspondent E. Breitner:

As our grenadiers assembled for action on the morning of 10 May, even the weather god seemed to have allied himself with the guerrillas. It started to rain hard and long as is so typical of this region's continental climate. The swampy areas and flooded lowlands soaked up the downpour greedily, building a practically impassable protective wall around the forests where the guerrillas were hiding. Taking stock at night in this terrain and in this weather has been out of the question, so we could move only by day, while during the night every man was needed for security.

Our men had to overcome tremendous difficulties with the terrain and the weather. Every foot of ground had to be painstakingly reconnoitered and secured. Fighting guerrillas is the supreme test for any soldier.

The chase goes through the endless steppe and nearly impenetrable swamps and forests.

There is no real front and no real enemy. The vermin cunningly lie in wait in swamp holes. In this type of combat each man must fend for himself. Securing the occupied East against guerrillas is of great military importance. Bringing up supplies is vital to soldiers in the front lines and can even decide the outcome of major operations.
Völkischer Beobachter, June 1943

From the OKW War Diary
Thursday, 3 June 1943:

Army Group Center: Enemy air force attacks Orel with 115 aircraft. There were many casualties among the civilian population. The power station was heavily damaged, so it will probably be out of action for a long time. The supply line to Bolkhov, the train station, water supply, telephone lines, army commissary depot, and the army medical depot were hit.

Fighting for the Supremacy of the Air
3 June 1943, Moscow. Associated Press reports:

The fighting between the Luftwaffe and the Red Air Fleet for the supremacy of the air has taken on dimensions during the last twenty-four
hours that surpass all previous operations on the Eastern Front. The Germans tried to bomb Kursk yesterday in five waves with about 500 bombers,
but Soviet fighter squadrons were more than a match for the attacking German formations. There was a great air battle, probably the biggest one that
has occurred so far on the Soviet-German Front. Only a few of the German
planes were able to get through to Kursk.

From the OKW War Diary
Saturday, 5 June 1943:

Army Group Center: Orders for the earliest date for "Citadel" issued
to Army Groups South and Center.

German and Soviet Buildup
Wednesday, 9 June 1943, Moscow. Associated Press reports:

Soviet reconnaissance planes operating in the rear area of the enemy
report frequent big troop movements during the last few days. Large transports were identified. New reserve formations of the Red Army are now
available, among them armored divisions on their way to the front or already deployed. There is great tension presently along the Eastern Front,
expressed by many violent clashes between patrols, particularly in sectors
having large concentrations of troops.

Presentation of New German Weapons
Thursday, 10 June 1943, Berlin. The DNB reports:

Following his statements in the Berlin Sportpalast, the Reichsminister
for Armaments and Ammunition, Speer, invited the ministers and secre-
taries of state to a presentation of new German weapons at a training area
in northern Germany.

From the OKW War Diary
Wednesday, 16 June 1943:

Army Group Center: Army Groups Center and South have been no-
tified that the final order for "Citadel" (X-8) can be expected any time after
18 June.

From the OKW War Diary
Friday, 18 June 1943:

Army Group South: No unusual action. The Army Group has submitted a comprehensive estimate of the enemy that identifies enemy reinforcements at its front, buildup of strong army reserves and stronger enemy

operational groups, and reinforcement of their air force. This profile of the enemy and the previously discovered stockpiling of ammunition and fuel are signs of a buildup for an offensive against the area before Kharkov.

Peace Rumors
18 June 1943, Moscow. The Associated Press reports:

Moscow state radio broadcasts: On behalf of the Soviet government we assert that an article appeared in the pro-German Swedish newspaper *Nya Dagligt Allehanda* stating that peace negotiations between the Soviet Union and Germany had recently taken place in Stockholm. These negotiations supposedly broke down because of differences on territorial questions. The Soviet Union hereby refutes the entire report as totally ridiculous and complete nonsense.

From the OKW War Diary
Saturday, 19 June 1943:

The end of a partisan operation in the area of Army Group Center: liquidation of captured suspects

Army Group Center: The Army Group presents an estimate of the situation which discusses possible enemy operations. An enemy offensive must be expected in any event. The best countermeasure would be Operation "Citadel."

German-Soviet Peace Talks?
19 June 1943, Berlin. The DNB informs:

The Swedish newspaper *Nya Dagligt Allehanda* published a sensational, false report about alleged German-Soviet peace talks in Stockholm. This report is a complete fabrication. Stating that such peace talks took place and any conjecture associated with them are rumors that the enemies of the Axis routinely spread.

From the OKW War Diary
Sunday, 20 June 1943:

Army Group Center: The commanders of Army Groups South and Center have been issued a Fuehrer directive concerning "Hornissen-Abtlg." (hornet detachment) as well as 7.5 and 8.8 pak (antitank guns) which are to be employed as defensive weapons in Operation "Citadel."

Invasion of Greece?
Monday, 21 June 1943, London: A correspondent of the *Svenska Dagbladet* reports:

Now that London's attention has been focused on Sardinia and Sicily for weeks, the press recently has been discussing the possibility of an invasion of Greece. In the *Observer,* Liberator is considering the advantages of an assault in Southeastern Europe. The *News Chronicle* printed a report from Berlin today, stating that Allied fleets are supposedly off the coast of Syria, ready to sail into the Aegean Sea.

An Imminent German Offensive?
Tuesday, 22 June 1943, Moscow. Reuters reports:

On the occasion of the second anniversary of the German invasion of the Soviet Union, STAVKA presented a comprehensive survey of the military events of the first two years of war. It can now be reported that very strong Soviet armies are in readiness at the fronts, among them the newly formed Shock Army, the core of which are ninety-one guards divisions. This Shock Army is completely motorized and equipped with most modern Soviet and Allied war materiel. In its structure are several elite Siberian divisions.

The Moscow High Command calls attention to German preparations and stresses that the next two weeks are a critical period that will decide whether Germany will launch a summer offensive or confine itself solely to defense. There are, however, good reasons to assume that Hitler will try to paralyze the Soviet Union by a tremendous blow within the next two weeks. Nevertheless, the Soviet Union is considering this possibility calmly and confidently, believing fully that it will also be able to cope with this offensive.

Radio Bermuenster (Switzerland)
Friday, 25 June 1943:

The general war situation is notable in that no battle has been fought anywhere for one and a half months. The fronts are static. Neither of the opposing armies has mounted an offensive this season although it is climatically and meteorologically favorable for major operations. Just recall briefly what military turnabouts had already transpired by this time last year. . . .

The first six months of this year have already passed; in four months the armies will have to adapt again to winter warfare.

Intercession Service in Moscow
25 June 1943: The Associated Press reports:

On the commencement of the third year of war, an intercession service for the victory of Soviet arms was conducted in the Moscow Cathedral. A message from the Patriarch, Sergius, the head of the Orthodox church in the USSR, was read in which he beseeched God to bless the Soviet commanders, army, and people.

From the OKW War Diary
Saturday, 26 June 1943:

Army Group Center: The Army Group submits an endorsement of the estimate of the situation by Group Weiss of 20 June. A Russian assault is probable, considering the present tactical distribution, only against the center and left flank of Group Weiss, and the right flank and center of the Second Pz. Army. This means that for the time being no major operational assault is to be expected but only holding attacks. Just the same, the concentration of Russian forces could entail serious reverses. Therefore, the Army Group requests once more that assault gun detachments be brought up from the Gomel area and proposes to mount its own attack quickly as the best solution under the present circumstances.

Fighting Partisans
Thursday, 1 July 1943, Berlin. The DNB reports:

According to the latest German observations, Soviet troops are concentrating in the central sector of the Eastern Front. In the same sector on the German side, apart from other measures that are secret, the fight against partisans is continuing. The fourth mopping up action in the last few weeks in the rear area of the Central Front sector has been concluded in the second half of June. German troops have destroyed 65 Soviet camps and 833 positions.

de Brinon's Return
Saturday, 3 July 1943, Vichy. OFI (Office Français d'Information) informs:

Ambassador and Secretary of State de Brinon has reported to Minister

In the rear area of the Central Front Sector, the end of June 1943 partisans on their way to new missions unimpressed by German mopping-up actions

President Laval on his trip to the Eastern Front as president of the Central Committee of the "French Voluntary Legion against Bolshevism."

Behind the Scenes

In the highest military commands—in the Fuehrer's headquarters in the forests of East Prussia and in STAVKA, the Soviet headquarters—has now begun a race against time, the worst enemy of strategic planning.

As early as 3 March 1943, the Amt Fremde Heere Ost (Foreign Armies Section East) in charge of reconnaissance reported in its Enemy Intelligence

Smolensk area, the end of June 1943, a VIP inspection of the "Legion des Volontaires Français contre le Bolchevisme" (L.V.F.). From right to left: SubLt. Servant, Ambassador de Brinon, Col. Puaud, Commander of Inf.Regt. 638 (L.V.F.)

Estimate No. 28: "The transfer of Stalingrad divisions into the Kursk area has been identified."

On Thursday, 4 March 1943, Marshal Zhukov noted: "The enemy offensive is to be caught in deeply echeloned defensive systems, worn out and then crushed in a counteroffensive." Most of the members of the Supreme War Council in Moscow thought that an offensive against German units preparing for an assault would be more effective and more promising. Zhukov, however, was opposed to this, probably because he wanted to avoid a confrontation of large armored formations in a mobile battle at this point.

On Friday, 5 March 1943, the OKH issued Operation Order No. 5 for conducting the war on the Eastern Front during the next several months.

A few days later, on 13 March 1943, Hitler and the chief of the General Staff of the Army, General of Infantry Zeitzler, arrived at Army Group Center (FM von Kluge) in Minsk. At that time it was decided that the situation on the inner flanks of the Second Army (General of Infantry Weiss) and the Second Panzer Army (Colonel General R. Schmidt) had to be stabilized. After that, an assault group was to be formed from the forces of the Ninth Army (Colonel General Model) in order to launch the planned operation in the direction of Kursk in early May.

Following the conference, Hitler issued the first operation order for Operation "Citadel." He endorsed the decision to mount an offensive against the Soviet forces in the Kursk area as early as the beginning of May. With

60

this directive Hitler fully met the wishes of his generals. In addition, they planned to reduce the Kuban bridgehead (Gotenkopf position), to leave Army Group South (FM von Manstein) in its linear defense, and at the same time form in its northern sector a strong Panzer group whose mission was to cut off the Kursk Salient in cooperation with another assault group at the southern flank of Army Group Center.

By mid-April 1943, Army Group South was directed to assemble a strong assault group in the Belgorod area and Army Group Center another south of Orel. In addition to the forces being brought in without critically denuding other sectors of both Army Groups, nine divisions were no longer needed following the conclusion of Operation "Buffalo Movement"—the evacuation of the Rzhev-Vyazma Front salient in the spring of 1943. More divisions from France and two from the Kuban bridgehead were promised as reinforcements. All assault divisions were to be fully reconstituted and reinvigorated as quickly as possible at the expense of other formations on the Eastern Front. With this decision to mount an offensive, the OKH, however, ignored the relative combat proportions at the Eastern Front, thus miscalculating Soviet potential and misinterpreting their intentions. This was a gross error that would have to be paid for later.

At the same time, OKH made another grave mistake. It thought it could deceive the Soviets about the preparations for the offensive, keep the directions of the main effort secret, and thus take advantage of the element of surprise. But STAVKA built a reserve front disguised as a steppe military district (Colonel General Konev), something it had been contemplating doing as early as the beginning of March.

In addition, the thaw began unusually early this spring in the Kursk area. In spite of the morning frost, the roads were in poor condition and the clay and black soil were sodden. STAVKA soon became aware of the German buildup and conducted violent harassing attacks against the movement of the Army Group from March 1943 on. Soviet planes bombed the supply line Smolensk-Bryansk night after night and also tried to destroy the important railroad repair workshops at Roslavl. Train stations along this stretch were bombed for sixty kilometers, communication lines were disrupted, and the siding important for the operation of this one-track line was destroyed. Therefore, this junction was blocked for days. The Red Air Fleet also was able to bomb the ammunition dump spotted by the partisans in Bryansk.

During the night of 20/21 March 1943, partisans blew up both of the railroad bridges over the Desna at Vigonitishi on the Minsk-Bryansk route of approach. Two days later, the commanders of this partisan unit gave a description of the mission on Moscow radio.

During the last weeks of March 1943, STAVKA's knowledge of German intentions became more and more extensive. Stalin, who appreciated good intelligence information, was kept up to date on the latest OKH preparations for the summer offensive. The intelligence reports submitted to the dictator revealed daily—like single pieces of a mosaic—a clearer picture of German intentions.

All the threads met in the office of Lieutenant General Onyanov, the officer in charge of German reconnaissance in the Main Reconnaissance Section of the General Staff, Glavnoye Razvedivatelnoye Upravleniye, GRU.

Kursk area, April 1943, a Guards Rifle Division at the Central Front saluting the flag

Military intelligence reports were collected here daily, evaluated, and subsequently submitted to Stalin, who decided which information would then be passed on to STAVKA. These reports resulted from the work of many Soviet agents in occupied Europe and the intelligence work of partisan groups located directly behind German lines. A substantial part of the secret information was gathered by the field troops of the Red Army or air force, through information gained from prisoners or turncoats, captured documents, scouts, air reconnaissance, and radio monitoring.

By the beginning of 1943, STAVKA already had established five special radio battalions. They were to jam enemy radio traffic and simultaneously protect Soviet radio transmissions. The 129th, 130th, 131st, 132nd, and 226th Special Radio Battalions were called the "first units for transmitting electronic interference." The General Staff hailed their formation as a significant achievement in the development of electronic warfare in the Red Army. Following necessary training, each battalion was assigned to a major front line command in the Kursk Salient.

Each of these special units had equipment for concealment of traffic, radio deception, radio reconnaissance, and direction- and position-finding operations. Moreover, each unit had eight to ten mobile jamming stations, eighteen to twenty receivers to intercept secret transmissions, and four sounding devices. Captured German radio equipment was used for disinformation operations. The favorite objects of the monitoring assaults of these special radio battalions were the operational and tactical communications of German intelligence transmission systems at army, corps, and division levels. The goal was to try to gain information about the main and reserve frequencies of individual radio stations and the position as well as the strengths of enemy forces, their displacements, and armaments.

According to the latest research it is certain that, despite many publications on the background history on the Battle of Kursk, reports from the Soviet spy ring of Alexander Rado ("Dora") in Switzerland did not decide the outcome of Operation "Citadel." This group of Soviet agents in Geneva, known as "The Red Three" or "Dora," was not in a position to gather valuable information for the Soviets because it did not have any contacts within the German staffs. Although Rudolf Roessler ("Lucy") delivered some interesting information to a Rado informant by the name of Christian Schneider ("Taylor"), this only caused confusion at the Moscow GRU headquarters.

Roessler was an exiled German journalist who possessed a large library of militaria and a press-clipping archive. He was a layman when it came to expertise about the German Wehrmacht, and combined the information he secretly obtained from a member of the Swiss Secret Service with that from his own archive. The main Swiss sources were the interrogation records of German deserters and internees. Through Mr. Schneider, Rado had this information radioed to Moscow without realizing its true origin. Here it ultimately landed on Lieutenant General Onyanov's desk. As Red Army reconnaissance and that of the Soviet air force became increasingly more effective, Onyanov was amazed at the discrepancies between their reports and Rado's radio messages, particularly regarding the disposition of German troops on the Eastern Front.

The most reliable information on Hitler's Wehrmacht, however, did not come from Moscow's spies or partisans but from the British Secret Service, much despised by Stalin; more precisely from its MI 6 section (Military Intelligence 6). At British Prime Minister Winston Churchill's personal instructions, the latest reports from the British Secret Service's Ultra Operation on the German Eastern Front were flown to Moscow by special courier. This information from the most important Allied intelligence source was not merely second-hand, pieced-together spy reports, but original radio messages from the highest German echelons.[1] It took nearly a year before the British were able to duplicate the German coding machine "Enigma" and thus break the code. From 1940 on, they were able to read the intercepted German radio transmissions in the "absolutely undecipherable" code almost simultaneously with the Germans.

The history of this most secret of all British operations, with the fitting name of "Ultra," goes back several years. In 1932 a team of three young Polish mathematicians—J. Rozycki, M. Rejewski, and H. Zygalski—succeeded in cracking the code of Enigma while intensively studying the cycle theory in Warsaw. And a few months prior to the German invasion of Poland, in the summer of 1939, these three scientists produced the biggest coup of all by duplicating the Enigma machine itself. Having learned of this, Major G. Bertrand, head of the DY Section of the French Secret Service, visited the Polish capital on 24 July 1939, accompanied by British specialists Commander Denniston and D. Knox (a mathematician). The Polish Secret Service gave them two duplicate German coding machines. One was kept in Paris and the other brought to London, where at first it was received with great skepticism. In the fall of 1939, the cryptologists of the

Kromy area, the radio control point of AOK 9 (Armeeoberkommando = Army Headquarters), spring 1943, the radio operator (in the white circle) is coding messages on the "enigma" coding machine; the British Secret Service is monitoring

Secret Intelligence Service (SIS) set up their headquarters in Bletchley Park, a country estate north of London. This was the location of the great-grandfather of the computer which was supposed to help decipher—at first with a lot of effort—the intercepted Enigma radio messages.

In this way, orders from the German High Command of the Army, the Luftwaffe, and the Navy, as well as their subordinate commands, plus reports on operational plans, strengths of formations and their positions, the composition of commands, and other important secret intelligence fell into Churchill's hands. The British Prime Minister himself, as the highest authority, decided to whom this information was to be forwarded.

The Ultra secret was so well kept that the Germans did not learn about it until thirty years after the end of the war. It sounds paradoxical that the British had to obtain details about Soviet forces from the decoded Enigma Luftwaffe radio traffic material, because their Communist ally withheld from them information about his own troops, although the Anglo-Americans were supplying them lavishly with all possible equipment and materiel.[2] Worse yet, Moscow even refused to divulge details about captured German weapons to the other allies. With the decoded Enigma traffic the British had unmistakable evidence that the Germans had cracked the Soviet army code.[3]

Despite this unpleasant experience with the Soviets, from early July 1941

on, Lieutenant General Mason-McFarlane, head of the British Military Mission in Moscow, and from May 1942 his successor, Rear Admiral Miles, passed on Ultra information to the Soviet General Staff. At Churchill's instructions they were to be handed only to Stalin personally, or to the chief of the General Staff, Marshal Shaposhnikov, and after June 1942 to his successor, Marshal Vasilevsky.[4]

For security reasons, either "an unnamed high officer in the German Command," or "a well-placed source in Berlin," and sometimes even "a very trustworthy, coincidental person" was given as the source. London was careful not to pass on details—such as radio identification signals of the German units—known only from the decoded material. The only British condition was that the Soviets were to refrain from openly mentioning by radio that they were receiving secret information from British sources.[5] As a rule various little discrepancies in the German spelling of Russian cities and other geographical names were inserted in order to cover up any indication of the true origin of the reports.[6]

As early as August 1941, a special section of MI 6 under the direct supervision of the War Office was established in London for the purpose of cooperating with the Soviet Military Mission there.[7] From May 1942 on, the two unequal partners met regularly twice a week with no reciprocal results. Intelligence reports continued to flow only in one direction, from west to east. Even the personal intervention of the British ambassador in Moscow, who often met with Soviet Foreign Minister Molotov, did not change things.[8]

In early June 1942, Admiral Miles in Moscow learned from the Soviet General Staff that the Red Army in the Central Front had succeeded in capturing the key to the German "Auca" code used by the Luftwaffe ground-air radio traffic. The Soviets thus turned to the British for assistance in monitoring and evaluating this tactical code.[9] The Auca code was used for communications between aircraft crews and ground stations or Luftwaffe officers assigned to armored units for optimum air-ground attack support for the ground troops.

Ostrov, April 1943: Commanding General of the 13th Army, Lt.Gen. Pukhov, and Member of the War Council, Maj.Gen. Koslov, leaning over a map of future operations

Bryansk area, April 1943: Col. Puaud, Commander of Inf.Regt. 638 (L.V.F.) greeting a highly decorated L.V.F. master sergeant

On Monday, 22 March 1943, the British War Office received indisputable evidence that the Germans were preparing for a summer offensive in the Kursk Salient. By deciphering Luftwaffe Enigma transmissions, they learned that German Panzer divisions had been moved to the Central Front. They also picked up details about new movements in the operational zone of Luftflotte 4 (FM von Richthofen). The VIII Fliegerkorps had been transferred to Kharkov to support ground troops in the German offensive planned to begin at the end of April.[10] This vital information was sent to Moscow without delay.

On the same day, following notification by the War Office, Lieutenant General Gissard Lequesne-Martel, the former commander of the "Royal Armoured Corps," was appointed successor to Admiral Miles as head of the British Military Mission in Moscow. This change would influence the passing on of Ultra material to the Soviets in the future with regard to German Panzer forces. The new mission head was an armored specialist who had played a significant role in forming British tank forces.

On Friday, 26 March 1943, fighter squadron "Normandie" (Major de Tulasne) participated for the first time in fighting on the Eastern Front. The squadron was formed from former fighter pilots of the French Armée de l'Air in Ivanov near Moscow and equipped with Soviet fighter planes of

67

the type Jak-1. This was done at the initiative of General de Gaulle, the leader of the "Free French," in December 1942. The squadron was now employed to attack German troop concentrations and as air escort for Soviet bombers in attacks on German communication lines north of Orel.

While the fighters of the Free French were circling in the cloudy Russian March sky with their Jak-1 planes and looking out for German troop movements, only a few kilometers away other sons of France, these fighting for Hitler, were trying to track Soviet partisans or repulse the Red Army attacks at the Desna west of the Kursk Salient. These were units of the "Legion des Volontaires Français contre le Bolchevisme" (LVF). This unit came into being at the initiative of the "Three D": Doriot (founder of the Parti Populaire Français), Deloncle (Mouvement Social Révolutionnaire), and Déat (Rassemblement National Populaire), the French politicians cooperating with the Germans in occupied France.

With the consent of German military authorities in Paris and the blessing of Cardinal Baudrillart and other princes of the French Roman Catholic church, the LVF was formed on 5 August 1941. Wearing German uniforms, 181 officers and 2,271 NCO's and men took an oath to Adolf Hitler and were placed in the German Infantry Regiment 638 under the command of Colonel Labonne, the former French military attache in Ankara. On 23 November 1941, this regiment was employed for the first time with the German 7th Infantry Division (Major General Freiherr von Gablenz) near Dyukovo before Moscow. Here the LVF fared no better than Napoleon's Grande Armée 129 years before. By 7 December 1941, the regiment lost more than 50 percent of its combat strength and had to retreat to Smolensk following hard Russian counterattacks and temperatures of more than forty degrees below zero centigrade.

After rehabilitation in Dembiza, southern Poland, the LVF was transferred to the central sector of the Eastern Front in the spring of 1942. It spent the whole year fighting partisans with mixed results and secured German supply lines. In the spring of 1943, the LVF, now under Colonel Puaud (a foreign legion veteran who had made peace with freedom-loving Arabian tribes in the mountains of Morocco), was once more sent into action. A part of the 3rd Battalion under Captain Madec was participating in antipartisan actions in the forests around Bryansk. The bulk of Infantry Regiment 638 was located at the Desna and the 1st Battalion (Captain Bridoux) was trying to cooperate with German security units in getting the partisan problem in the Borisov area under control.

On Tuesday, 30 March 1943, after Army Group Center had ordered Colonel General Model to prepare for Operation "Citadel," AOK 9 (Armeeoberkommando 9, headquarters of the Ninth Army) was temporarily renamed Festungsstab. 11 (fortification staff) and moved to Orel.

General of the Army Rokossovsky: "The High Command of the front was convinced that our enemy would strike with strong forces. It instructed the troops as early as the end of March to complete the construction of defense positions. The commander of the engineering troops of the front, General Proshlyakov, had developed a detailed plan and did everything to finish the work conscientiously and by the deadlines."

Although the Soviet troops now sometimes went on the defensive along the entire front, the strategic advantages they gained continued to influence events favorably.

Even after Stalingrad, the Third Reich still remained a dangerous adversary for the Soviet Union, but combat proportions had changed fundamentally since the 1942/43 winter. Due to the growing economic, scientific, technological, and military superiority of the USSR—thanks in great measure to enormous allied deliveries within the lend-lease agreements—Hitler's plans for an offensive from spring 1943 on had little chance to succeed. The Red Army already had replaced completely their personnel and materiel losses by this time. New, large, operational formations, particularly armored and air armies, and numerous artillery units, some of which had gained experience in the Battle of Stalingrad, were ready.

The bloody purges of the Stalin regime among the older Red Army commanders shortly before the outbreak of the Second World War allowed a generation of dynamic young generals to rise quickly. Therefore, the average age of the Soviet commanders was nearly twenty years less than that of their German counterparts. The result of this rejuvenation was improved performance and increased activity in the work of the general staff and the tactical mobility of the troops.

The most recent war experience also influenced the tactics of the large Soviet formations. The structural development of the armored and mechanized corps aimed, for example, at giving them greater independence in operations by assigning them artillery and mortar sections. This was to im-

Sumy area, April 1943: German soldiers digging trenches: ". . . using defense measures to cover up preparations for an assault."

69

prove the operational capabilities of armored brigades and regiments, which were being equipped with more heavy and medium tanks as well as self-propelled guns. Even the scarcity of transportation, one of the Red Army's main problems, was now being eased by the increased deliveries of excellent, U.S. cross-country trucks. Moreover, millions of tons of high-quality U.S. rations began to alleviate the food supply problem. This historically had been the greatest difficulty in developing fully the Red Army's potential because of the poor road and railroad systems and the huge numbers of Soviet troops.

Operations at the Eastern Front were turning to static warfare at the end of March 1943. At the same time, a new military and political catastrophe of enormous dimensions was brewing for the Wehrmacht in North Africa. The defeat of the German and Italian forces, which the superior Anglo-American forces had now driven together on a narrow track of land in Tunis, was imminent.

As the Soviets were aware of the concentration of assault formations in the Kharkov area from early April on, they anticipated a large-scale operation. The German High Command tried to cover up their offensive intentions by the use of camouflage and various deceptive measures. For example, they constructed the rear area in depth with artillery positions on an extensive scale in order to give the impression that they had gone completely on the defensive. Marshal Zhukov: "In agreement with Chief of the General Staff Vasilevsky and the commanders of the front we ordered a thorough reconnaissance of the Central, Voronezh, and Southwestern Fronts. The front armies for their part also conducted air and troop reconnaissance in force in their own sectors. By early April we had enough material on the enemy buildup in the Orel, Sumy, Belgorod, and Kharkov areas."

On Saturday, 3 April 1943, STAVKA drew up a directive which stressed the necessity of "taking prisoners by all means to be able to keep track of the changes in enemy dispositions. We must conduct timely reconnaissance in those sectors where the Germans are concentrating their troops. We must pay particular attention to the armored formations." At the same time Marshal Vasilevsky ordered the Reconnaissance Section of the General Staff (Lieutenant General Ilyichov) and the Central Staff of the Partisan Movement to determine the strength of the German reserves, their composition and dispositions, to include the arrival of new troops from France and other countries.

On Monday, 5 April 1943, AOK 9 (Colonel General Model) moved to his new headquarters in Kiskinka near Orel.

On Thursday, 8 April 1943, Marshal Zhukov submitted his plan to Stalin. He proposed to wear out the German formations attacking at Kursk and their armor with an active defense. Then he would smash them with fresh reserves in a counterattack. Zhukov: "I consider it pointless to let our troops go on the offensive in the near future to beat the enemy to it." Stalin approved the plan. Fresh formations were transferred to the Kursk area. One of them was the Steppe Military District (Colonel General Konev). They were STAVKA's strongest strategic reserves in the Second World War. The

Steppe Military District (later called Steppe Front) was committed east of Kursk and was to be ready either to defend or attack.

Also on 8 April 1943, at Moscow's urging, Rudolf Roessler ("Lucy"), the top agent of the "Red Three" (Rado), reported the latest news on the Kursk offensive from Lucerne. It had been postponed "until early May." In reality, Hitler did not decide until a week later, on 15 April 1943, to launch Operation "Citadel"[11] on 4 May 1943.

On Friday, 9 April 1943, Colonel General Model submitted his proposal for conducting "Citadel." In it, the commander of the Ninth Army wanted to thrust forward with two Panzer corps directly from north to south at Kursk, with one Panzer corps supporting the right flank and an army corps the left. The objective was the high ground east of Kursk. In Model's words, "it is the key for controlling the entire east-west zone of operations."

On Saturday, 10 April 1943, Stalin instructed his General Staff to prepare at STAVKA a conference on the plan for the summer offensive. In particular they were to get the opinions of the front commanders as to the expected direction of the thrust of the German attacks. Those on the Central and Voronezh Fronts (General of the Army Rokossovsky and General of the Army Vatutin) were convinced that the enemy would attack in the direction of Kursk.

The firing range at the Maintenance airfield in Dembiza, Southern Poland, April 1943: both 37mm Fla-Kanonen 18 antiaircraft guns of a Ju 87 G-1 from the 10th (Pz) SG 2 are being adjusted for antitank combat.

Sevsk area, April 1943: waiting to be transferred to prepared positions. In the background a PzKpfw V Panther

Marshal Zhukov: "On 11 April, I arrived in Moscow late at night. Vasilevsky informed me that Stalin wanted to have a situation map plus the necessary data and proposals submitted by 12 April. . . . As there was general agreement, everything was finished by evening. Antonov (the deputy chief of the General Staff) had a deserved reputation as an excellent officer, and while we were drawing up the draft for the report for Stalin, he quickly drew a situation map and a deployment plan for the fronts in the Kursk Salient. Therefore, as early as mid-April, headquarters had reached a preliminary decision on a defense plan. We kept it operative until the end of May and early June 1943, when the final decision was confirmed. At this

stage, the enemy's intention to launch a powerful attack using Panzer groups equipped with the new Tiger tank and self-propelled gun, Ferdinand, against our Voronezh and Central Fronts was known to us in detail."

On Monday, 12 April 1943, Army Group Center's own draft for Operation "Citadel," which General Model suggested on 9 April, was passed on to the OKH. Among other things planned, "Ninth Army breaks through enemy positions between Trosna and Maloarchangelsk with the combined forces on both sides of the Orel-Kursk railroad line and thrusts nonstop with the main group . . . to the high ground north and east of Kursk to take Kursk. . . . They are to link up as soon as possible with Army Group South formations attacking from the south via Oboyan toward Tim. . . ."

On the same day, 12 April, STAVKA held a conference on the plans for the summer offensive. Present were Stalin, Zhukov, Vasilevsky, Antonov, and Lieutenant General Shtemenko, chief of the Operations Section of the General Staff. At the conference on the evening of 12 April, all participants, following a thorough analysis, agreed that the enemy's most likely objective of his summer offensive would be the encirclement and annihilation of the main forces of the Central and Voronezh Fronts in the Kursk Salient. A temporary and active defense presented the best possibility of bleeding the Wehrmacht's attack formations white and creating favorable conditions for the mounting of a large-scale Soviet summer counteroffensive.

Subsequently the General Staff and the commanders of the Central and Voronezh Fronts received from STAVKA a directive to prepare for defensive operations in the Kursk Salient. At the same time, plans were drafted for a counteroffensive in the direction of Orel and Belgorod-Kharkov. The attack toward Orel was given the code name "Kutuzov." The troops to mount this attack were from the left flank of the Western Front (Colonel General Sokolovsky) and the Bryansk Front (Colonel General Popov) as well as the right flank of the Central Front (General of the Army Rokossovsky). The troops of the Voronezh Front and the Steppe Military District in cooperation with those from the Southwestern Front were to smash the German forces in the Belgorod-Kharkov area. The code name of this operation was "Polkovdets Rumyantsev."

On Tuesday, 13 April 1943, Enigma radio traffic revealed that the German Luftwaffenkommando Ost (Air Force Command East) had received instructions to move forward its elements standing by for the summer offensive. The British Secret Service thus learned for the first time the code name of the planned operation "Citadel." Churchill relayed this information immediately to Moscow, too.[12]

On Thursday, 15 April 1943, Hitler issued Operation Order No. 6 for Operation "Citadel" as this year's first offensive. The decisive Kursk offensive was to give the Germans the initiative for both spring and summer. Hitler: "The victory at Kursk must be a signal to the world." Following the success of Operation "Citadel," Hitler wanted to turn the attack to the southwest as soon as possible (Operation "Panther") in order to take advantage of the Russians' confusion.

The operations plan of "Citadel" was the classic "cutting off" of a salient with a pincer attack at its base. The grave weakness of this scheme was that the vital element of surprise to make such an operation feasible was practically zero. This could only be ameliorated by a surprise initial attack, the fury of the assault, and the enemy's ignorance of the focal point. The plan offered a second solution, counterattack after letting the Red Army have the initial initiative against strong field fortifications.

OKH and the two commanders of Army Group South and Center, Manstein and Kluge, favored a mobile defense, wanting to strike the Soviets with a counterblow as soon as the Soviets had committed their assault forces.

Рис. 1. Общий вид и разрез участка «маск-ангара».

From a Red Army service manual on camouflaging the terrain in the rear area of a front: a perfect deception of the enemy

In this way, the superiority of German leadership and better troops could be successful in an open battlefield. They preferred this to fighting with heavy losses through the strong Soviet defense system and holding fast rigidly along an overextended front. Hitler, however, thought differently, choosing a first strike. He shied away from any loss of ground and thought that Stalin had no need to do him the favor of launching an offensive. Germany had no time to lose, considering the impending invasion in the west.

Hitler's idea was to encircle and then annihilate strong Soviet forces located in the Kursk Salient with concentric attacks by Army Group Center from the area south of Orel and Army Group South from the region on both sides of Belgorod. The OKH hoped to be able to force the breakthrough to Kursk by stripping other, secondary front sectors, radically shortening the breakthrough sectors—2.8 to 3.3 kilometers per division—and committing the new Tiger and Panther heavy tanks with a concentrated density of thirty to forty tanks per kilometer of front.

General of Infantry Zeitzler, chief of the General Staff of the OKH, supported this plan but imposed the condition that the assault be launched as quickly as possible in April. If it occurred later, the Soviet defenses would become too strong. Hitler did not approve of this timing at all. He wanted to wait until the Panther and in particular the Tiger tanks arrived. They would give the troops enormous incentive to perform well on the battle-

75

Airfield near Akh-
tyrka, April 17,
1943: a tactical re-
connaissance aircraft
Focke-Wulf FW189
prior to take-off

field. The biggest disadvantage of the whole plan, however, was that the
Soviets were expecting an offensive in the Kursk Salient all along.

Manstein wanted to strike in a war of movement, an operation in the
open field. He saw the Kursk Salient as a Soviet bastion that could be taken
only with much effort and great losses.

The date for the assault was set for 4 May 1943. At this time the fortification work was fully in progress on the Soviet side. Lieutenant General
Moskalenko, commander of the Fortieth Army of the Western Front (Colonel General Sokolovsky): "All our soldiers became engineers. We dug
hundreds of kilometers of trench lines and communication trenches; built
cover for tanks, guns, motor vehicles, and horses; and roofed dugouts for
the soldiers which even a 150mm shell could not damage. Everything was
adapted to the terrain to such an extent that ground and air reconnaissance
could recognize little."

General of Panzer Troops von Knobelsdorff, commanding general of
the XLVIII Panzer Corps of Army Group South (FM von Manstein): "Hand
in hand with bringing up new forces the adversary was building extensive
and carefully conceived field fortifications with great rear echelonment. Enemy field fortifications in the Corps' front sector reached a depth of 20
kilometers. Once again the Russians showed that they were masters in
choosing, constructing, and consolidating their fortification system, camouflaging it from view from the air or ground."

76

Oboyan area: local
inhabitants helping
the Red Army to
build roads

Lieutenant General Dragunsky, commander of the 1st Mechanized Brigade of the First Tank Army attached to the Voronezh Front (General of the Army Vatutin): "For each tank, gun, and machine gun, firing positions were prepared, firing sectors and orientation guides fixed, the initial firing orders prepared as well as main, reserve, and sham positions planned."

General of the Army Rokossovsky, commander of the Central Front: "Soldiers and commanders were confident and convinced of the strength of the fortifications they had built. Since they had already successfully defeated enemy attacks in this line in February and March, they were confident of their experience." The Germans could not imagine the strength of the Soviet defensive line that was being built.

There were about eight bunkers per kilometer of front. A network of communication trenches leading to all the bunkers and cover crisscrossed the centers of battalion defensive positions. There were on average 3.8 kilometers of trenches for every kilometer of front. Most heavily fortified were the main defensive zones. Here were numerous interconnected, continuous trenches together with barbed wire obstacles, mine fields, tank ditches, bunkers and dugouts, countless machine-gun nests, innumerable antitank barriers, artillery emplacements echeloned in depth, and dug-in tanks. These formed a defensive system that could not be pierced with one stroke.

The artillery had several alternate emplacements so well camouflaged that they could only be discerned with difficulty. The tactical defensive zone consisted of main and secondary defensive belts. This was between 15 and 20 kilometers deep. About 20 to 30 kilometers behind the main defensive position was a continuous, rear defensive belt manned by reserves. Each army had three consolidated defensive lines held by troops. In addition the Central and the Voronezh Fronts had set up three defensive lines and the Steppe Military District east of the Kursk Salient had organized a defensive line between Rososhnoye and Beli Kolodes. The operational-tactical positions of both fronts were manned by troops to a depth of 70 kilometers.

All told, the depth of the eight defensive belts and lines ranged between 250 and 300 kilometers. This system of defensive trenches was without parallel on the Eastern Front. In only the sector of the Central Front and the Voronezh Front nearly 10,000 kilometers of trenches had been dug. There were 83,912 defensive emplacements, machine gun and antitank positions, as well as 17,505 dugouts and bunkers. In addition, 637,500 tank and infantry mines had been laid and 593 kilometers of wire fencing erected. In weaker sectors, barriers were erected between these defense lines. Even the reserve Steppe Military District, concentrated in the hinterland behind the Voronezh and Central Fronts, built a defensive line at the Kshen.

In order to be able to coordinate better the different formations and to simplify tactics, the strong points were oriented toward antitank defense. The density of antitank guns was 12 to 15 per kilometer of front in the most vulnerable directions. In comparison, the defense of Moscow had only a density of five guns and Stalingrad at the most six to eight guns per kilometer. General of the Army Rokossovsky: "Highest priority was given to building various types of antitank obstacles. Before the first line and in the directions threatened by tanks there were continuous zones of such obstacles. They consisted of mine fields, tank ditches, antitank teeth, dams to flood the terrain, and tree barriers."

In contrast to the Battles for Moscow and Stalingrad, antitank defense in the tactical defense zones was organized according to a uniform plan for its entire depth (120 to 150 kilometers). The backbone of this system was with company antitank defense strong points, battalion antitank centers, division and army antitank areas, plus mobile obstacle sections. Lieutenant General Moskalenko, commander of the Fortieth Army of the Western Front: "In the most important sectors we dug tank ditches and built steep banks along the rivers. Even in the forests we set up tree barriers with explosive charges."

The basis of this antitank defense system was first, antitank areas organized within regimental sectors, echeloned in depth and incorporated in the deployment of companies and battalions; second, the early and carefully positioned artillery antitank defense reserves; third, tank obstacles, an organic part of the overall system. The fundamental idea was to draw attacking tanks into an ambush of enfilade fire. These strong points were sited to correspond to the combat organization of the infantry units.

In each rifle regiment, there were antitank defense points of varying strength organized by sector. In divisions, average densities of antitank weapons were eleven guns and up to ten other antitank weapons per kilometer of front. In addition, regimental and divisional commanders had very mobile, motorized antitank defense reserves available. Fire plans of antitank defense centers were coordinated with artillery fire from both open and covered emplacements and with the fires of antitank defense reserves.

78

At Maloarchangelsk in the Central Front Sector, mid-April 1943: Red Army soldiers at work. On the average there were 3.8 km of trenches per kilometer of front

Important elements in antitank defense with a depth ranging between 30 and 35 kilometers were the motorized obstacle sections formed in the spring of 1943. A typical section was a truck-dispatched mobile engineer unit equipped with antitank mines, melinite petards, and portable obstacles that could be sent immediately to areas where armor attack was imminent.

Antitank riflemen were positioned in platoons or groups in areas threatened by tanks. Following similar principles, the infantry developed fire plans in the second and rear defensive belts. To combat the new German Panther and Tiger heavy tanks, antitank strong points were supported by 85mm antiaircraft guns and 152mm howitzers. All antitank strong points were able to communicate with each other. The guns in strong points were often emplaced for direct fire. For example, armored and assault gun regiments allocated to rifle divisions were planned to be employed in a direct fire role or as ambush weapons in directions threatened by tanks. These tactics were used in the Sixth Guards Army (Lieutenant General Chistyakov) and the Seventh Guards Army (Lieutenant General Shumilov) of the Voronezh Front.

Tanks and assault guns were also assigned to antitank defense strong points and sited in such a manner that Tiger and Panther tanks with strong frontal armor could be destroyed by being hit laterally. This antitank defense system was especially important to STAVKA, because Soviet troops still lacked experience in fighting the heavy German tanks and particularly "Ferdinand," the heavy assault gun.

General of the Panzer Troops von Knobelsdorff (XLVIII Pz. Corps): "The enemy built parallel fortifications with vast and tactically very cunning mining of the terrain. This focused on the Donets, the Rasumnaya lowlands, and the Belgorod area."

Lieutenant General Batov, commander of the Sixty-fifth Army: "Expansive mine fields stretched from the front line far into the rear area of the army. They were so extensive that we had to post warning pickets and mark the mined sectors with signs."

Lieutenant General Moskalenko, commanding general of the Fortieth Army: "In the sector of the Fortieth Army, 59,032 tank mines, 70,994 infantry mines, and 6,377 shells were laid. This was the first time that we used shells to a large extent as mine barriers. Roads and bridges were se-

79

cured with delayed-action mines. Most mines were placed in front of our positions and in the main defensive belt." Thus, there were approximately 1,500 to 1,600 tank mines for each kilometer in the Kursk Salient; nearly 400 percent more than were laid before Moscow and 250 percent more than Stalingrad.

Antitank defense was even stronger in areas where the main German thrusts were anticipated. In the sector of the 81st Rifle Division of the Seventh Guards Army (Lieutenant General Shumilov) there were 2,133 tank and 2,126 infantry mines per kilometer of front. In addition, antitank artillery reserves from three brigades and two regiments were positioned near the front line. Lieutenant General Moskalenko: "Moreover, troops equipped with hand grenades, tank mines, and other explosives were trained to combat enemy tanks at any time they entered the positions of the rifle companies."

Artillery batteries, like all units, were integrated in the antitank defense system. From concealed positions, they were emplaced to fire preplanned barrages and concentrated fires at Panzer units in strength. All batteries were trained to use direct fire at tanks that had broken through to their positions. General of the Army Rokossovsky: "Although our plans did not envisage the use of rocket launchers to combat tanks, we decided to employ the Katyushas for this purpose."

In planning the company defensive positions, the foremost objective was to create impregnable curtains of fire. Depending on the terrain, the units were deployed in checkerboard formation in order to cover entire battalion areas with fire and be capable of conducting flank and oblique fire. In most battalions defensive positions, heavy machine gun fires and concentrated preplanned artillery barrages were plotted in front of advance positions and in depth in the battalion and regimental sectors.

Rocket and mortar units also registered their fire in defensive sectors and near the front lines. Communication trenches were arranged so they could be turned into blocking positions if desired. Battalion resistance centers were designed for all-around defense. General of the Army Rokossov-

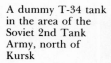
A dummy T-34 tank in the area of the Soviet 2nd Tank Army, north of Kursk

80

sky: "Artillery weapons were echeloned the entire depth of the armies. Planning included the maneuvering of fire and massing it in the directions of expected attack. To obtain uncomplicated and reliable fire control, a network of observation posts with dedicated communications was created."

The depth of the defense was from 120 to 150 kilometers in the front sectors, 40 to 50 kilometers in the sectors of armies. In contrast to previous defensive plans, antitank gun reserves in the Kursk Salient were of greater strength and were at every troop level. Antiaircraft regiments were required to take special courses in antitank gunnery. Air defense measures were as extensively developed. Many light and heavy machine guns and even antitank guns were sited to engage enemy aircraft.

Field headquarters were placed as close as possible to the troops to enable them to address tactical problems as they developed. STAVKA ordered two of its best men, Marshal Zhukov and the chief of the General Staff, Marshal Vasilevsky, to coordinate specific combat preparations of the fronts. They first increased the customary tight security. All communications means were subjected to extremely close control. Conversations over field telephones were reduced to a minimum. Radio communications were maintained only with those transmitting stations that had been employed before and, therefore, well known to German radio intercept. Any mention of troop preparations for the operation was categorically prohibited. Individual commanders were restricted in relaying combat and tactical assignments to subordinate commanders on a personal, face-to-face basis. Troop movements were permitted only at night.

Meanwhile, they tried to deceive German air reconnaissance not only by cleverly camouflaging the real defensive works but also by building many dummy positions. There were more than 1,000 kilometers of false trenches, emplacements, and observation posts, as well as 900 mobile dummy tanks. In addition, there were three ersatz tank disposition areas for large armored formations and thirteen airfields with more than 200 replicas of various types of aircraft. The terrain containing actual positions was camouflaged equally carefully by both engineer and line troops.

Besides working on the defensive works, the troops spent their time training and being educated politically. General of the Army Rokossovsky: "In addition to the defensive work, the troops were intensively occupied with combat training. At least one-third of the exercises took place at night. Intensive training was also conducted in staff procedures."

The tank crews practiced firing their weapons while moving and advancing in close formations. The infantry received thorough training in antitank combat in specially constructed training areas. Lieutenant General Moskalenko: "The riflemen learned how to use antitank hand grenades and incendiary bottles (Molotov cocktails) and destroy tanks being covered by advancing infantry. To train the soldiers to endure, we had T-34's roll over them in trenches from different directions. In this way they gained confidence that in a well-built trench they did not have to be afraid of a tank and even could destroy it if they knew its vulnerable points."

General of the Army Rokossovsky: "As we counted on the enemy using his heavy Tiger tank with 88mm guns, our soldiers and commanders had to become familiar with its tactical-technical data and methods of fighting it."

During those days, the political administration of the Central Front distributed leaflets to antitank riflemen, artillerymen, and infantrymen on how to fight tanks, including thousands of posters containing pictures of the new German tanks and practical advice on how to destroy them.

Approximately 500,000 railroad cars loaded with war materiel were sent from the heart of Russia to the Kursk Salient, providing the best proof of the tremendous number of heavy weapons that were concentrated in this sector. Even the local population was involved in building defensive works and airfields. All told, about 300,000 people, most of them women, children, and old men, worked on these projects. They also helped rebuild roads, trails, and railroad lines, and worked in field hospitals. Marshal Zhukov: "In the industrial centers of the front areas, tanks, aircraft, trucks, artillery equipment, as well as other heavy weapons and equipment were overhauled on a large scale. . . ."

All the villages and hamlets within the defensive system were evacuated completely, in some sectors even up to 150 kilometers behind the main defensive line. These built-up areas were turned into fortifications with security troops posted there in defensive posture. All larger cities, like Kursk, were turned into fortresses and provided with all-around defense. Tactical troops and reserves built huge supply depots and ammunition dumps with shellproof dugouts in the forests and gorges.

The size and strength of the defensive works in the Kursk Salient were the result of painstaking reconnaissance of the enemy, including the entire rear area from the Vistula to the front. The Central Front and Voronezh Front groups had, in addition to normal commanders' observation posts and artillery lookouts, more than 2,700 special observation positions for enemy reconnaissance exclusively. They conducted more than 100 reconnaissance in force operations and 2,600 night raids, in which they took 187 German prisoners, whose interrogations were a valuable supplement to information known about the enemy. Special Russian reconnaissance parties were sent into the depths of German rear areas. They operated in conjunction with the numerous partisan operations and with the Soviet Secret Service agents. For example, one of these special intelligence parties under First Lieutenant Bukhtoyarov detected seven airfields, thirteen ammunition dumps, and eight fuel dumps, and reported back with thirty prisoners. The

Lgov area, Central Front, mid-April 1943: a Soviet antitank position; riflemen with PTRD-41 type Degtyarev antitank rifles

82

information passed on to STAVKA included, in addition to particulars on the plans of the German High Command, reports on the strengths, armaments, and tactical dispositions of German formations of Army Groups Center and South.

Intensive air reconnaissance covered German concentration areas and provided further details on airfields, defensive works, strong points, and artillery positions. Marshal Zhukov: "The staff of the partisan movement was ordered not only to paralyze important communication routes in the enemy's rear area, but also to gather important information about the enemy and relay it to headquarters."

According to Zhukov there were more than approximately 500,000 partisans operating in the German hinterland. Their reconnaissance work was directed by commissars trained in intelligence work; many were members of the NKVD. Their reports usually were sent directly to the operations group in the staff of the partisan movement of the appropriate front sector. The information was analyzed here and then passed on to the operations section of the Red Army Front High Command, usually stationed at the same location. From there the intelligence documents were dispatched to Moscow by special courier using air transport and submitted to STAVKA on the same day. Here it was all finally evaluated. The results were radioed to the commanders of the front concerned, but only the commander himself was permitted to decipher the radio messages.

The leaflet from the reconnaissance section of the General Staff of the Red Army entitled "The Organization of the Reconnaissance of the Enemy's Rear Area" (author Colonel Surin) contains these words: "Only by performing continuous reconnaissance in the enemy's rear can we determine his strength in time, and thus spare commanders and troops alike unexpected, surprise actions of the enemy. . . . Partisans and the local inhabitants, whose reports are often very valuable, should be engaged broadly in a thorough study of the enemy situation in depth. There may be German spies in the partisan groups. Therefore, contact with partisan units may occur only after receiving express instructions from the reconnaissance officer." To simplify verification, the partisan staffs distributed checklists containing requested information on important strategic or tactical areas as well as a number of seemingly unimportant questions. From the answers the reconnaissance officer or the political commissar tried to deduce whether or not the truth was being told.

Bogdukhov, a Tiger detachment of the 4th Panzer Army prior to an exercise

One of the instructions for the reconnaissance missions of the Central Staff of the Partisan Movement contained a total of 172 questions divided into 21 fields. Since the lower partisan staffs added a series of questions that varied regionally and since the answers required local knowledge, they usually succeeded in uncovering even the most clever German agent. This guaranteed STAVKA that it was receiving mostly reliable information from German rear areas. At STAVKA's instructions, the Red Army supported by various branches of Soviet counterintelligence and the secret police conducted numerous deception operations. Their objective was to keep the OKH in the dark about Soviet plans and the operational situation. The intention was to disguise Soviet preparations for a counterattack in the Kursk Salient as purely defensive measures.

Based upon its huge system of fortification, the Red Army prepared to defend itself in a mobile manner in the Kursk Salient and to meet the Ger-

man attack with counteroffensives. One armored army each of the Central and Voronezh Fronts plus several armored corps were waiting to strike counterblows in three or four directions. Soviet armored forces had attained a high level qualitatively and quantitatively and were reinforced with several newly formed tank regiments and tank brigades. For the first time since the war began, there were armored armies available in addition to independent tank regiments, tank brigades, and tank corps. Their task was to repel the attacks of German Panzer formations on Kursk and to establish the necessary conditions for a counteroffensive.

These new armored armies were created to replace the large and unwieldy formations used with limited success in the past. As a rule, they possessed two tank corps and one mechanized corps plus troop units for reinforcement and security. These new armored armies under a new structure enabled the Soviet Command to concentrate large masses of tanks in a single area. They were under STAVKA's command, but operationally assigned to the fronts. Their standard equipment was T-34 tanks with improved treads and stronger engines plus SU-122 and SU-152 self-propelled guns. The SU-152 became a weapon most dreaded by the Germans. The Soviets' heavy 152mm rounds were able to penetrate the armor of any German tank.

Captain Rudel from the III Group of Stuka Squadron 2 "Immelmann" demonstrating the tactics of combatting tanks with Stukas (dive bombers) equipped with two 37mm Fla-Kanonen 18 antiaircraft guns: ". . . the ideal point to attack is the rear. This is where the engine is located. This power plant requires cooling thus permitting use of only a thin plate of armor"

To prepare for the heaviest artillery fire in history, STAVKA picked its foremost expert, already tried and tested in the Battle of Stalingrad, Marshal Voronov. Stalin ordered him to coordinate the employment of the artillery which was supposed to support the summer campaign of the Red Army. The number of artillery tubes that Voronov had at his disposal was three times as great as at Stalingrad.

The most important mistake of OKH's strategic planning and the subsequent course of the fighting was the erroneous estimate of the strength of the Red Army. A sudden increase in Soviet equipment was considered impossible and the enemy's potential to increase his striking power was disregarded in the planning. But the Soviet troops comprising the Central, Bryansk, and Western Fronts had been prepared since April for a German offensive by the Ninth Army (Colonel General Model) of Army Group Center against the front sector at Orel.

As early as Monday, 19 April 1943, Colonel General Model ordered commanding officers and General Staff officers of his Panzer divisions to his headquarters in Orel. To his amazement he discovered that the allocations for the Ninth Army hardly related to the missions he had been assigned. He immediately radioed Army Group Center: "More tanks! More officers! More artillery! Better training for the assault troops!"

Meanwhile, OKH hoped to have a wonderworking medicine to weaken the Soviets—Red Army defectors. In fact, by early 1943 about one million Russian "Hilfswillige" (volunteer helpers known in short as Hiwis) were serving in the German Wehrmacht. Every regiment had them working as medics, drivers, grooms, cooks, translators, or guides. Most of the prisoners, however, were in POW camps. Approximately 2.5 million of them died there of starvation, disease, or inhumane treatment.

On Tuesday, 20 April 1943, OKH issued General Order No. 13. The solution sounded simple and convincing: "The better the defectors are treated, the more that will come. The more defectors, the less enemy to fight!" The defectors were to "be given ample rations" (rations for workers doing hard labor). Tobacco goods, magazines, suitable reading material, and even musical instruments and motion pictures were to be provided. Officer defectors were assigned orderlies to help them. Missing clothing was to be replaced and they were to receive rapid medical attention. They were supposed to be allowed to "keep their personal effects, uniforms (even boots!)"—and "to take advantage of every possible convenient means of transport;" also "to be granted rest days." Each defector was to be given a week to consider joining the "Ost-Legion" (Eastern Legion), serving as a "Hiwi," or the "voluntary work force in the liberated eastern regions."

In every section of the army, volunteer collecting centers hastily were set up. All defectors from the different sectors first were brought to one of these centers and treated in accordance with OKH Order No. 13 by specially trained Russian attendants. At the same time OKH was planning a mammoth propaganda campaign in cooperation with Section Fremde Heere Ost (Foreign Armies East), code named "Silberstreif" (silver streak). During the night of 5 to 6 May 1943, the first action of Operation "Citadel"

Grundsätzlicher Befehl Nr. 13

des Oberkommandos der deutschen Wehrmacht über die Behandlung der auf deutsche Seite übergehenden Angehörigen der Roten Armee

Die große Zahl der freiwillig zu uns Übertretenden beweist, daß die einsichtigen Offiziere und Soldaten der Roten Armee nicht gewillt sind, sich auch weiterhin sinnlos für das Sowjetregime zu opfern. Alle Offiziere und Soldaten, welche ehrlich den Kampf aufgeben und freiwillig zu uns übertreten, sind daher als Gegner des Sowjetregimes zu betrachten und dementsprechend bevorzugt zu behandeln:

In Ergänzung und Erweiterung der bisher gegebenen Befehle wird daher angeordnet:

I. Als freiwillig zu uns übergetreten gilt jeder Angehörige der Roten Armee (Offizier, Politruk, Unteroffizier oder Mann), der sich nach Lösung aus dem

ПРИКАЗ № 13

Верховного командования Германской Армии.

О военнослужащих Красной Армии, добровольно переходящих на сторону Германской Армии.

Благоразумные солдаты и офицеры Красной Армии не желают дальше безсмысленно жертвовать собой ради сохранения советского режима, о чем свидетельствует большое количество военнослужащих Красной Армии, переходящих добровольно на нашу сторону.

Всех офицеров и солдат Красной Армии добровольно переходящих к нам следует рассматривать, как противников советской власти и в соответствии с этим, с ними обращаться.

Приказываю:

I. Каждого военнослужащего Красной Армии (офицера, политработника, бойца и др.) покинувшего свою часть и самостоятельно или в составе группы добровольно являющегося к нам, считать *не военнопленным, а добровольно перешедшим на сторону Германской Армии.*

General Directive No. 13 as a leaflet in Operation "Silberstreif" (Silver Streak) emphasizing how well defectors will be treated

was supposed to be the dropping of 400 million fliers, among them 200 million copies of General Order No. 13 in different eastern languages.

On the same day Rudolf Roessler ("Lucy") reported from Lucerne: "The launching of the German Kursk offensive had been postponed again from the beginning of May to a later date." In reality Hitler's previous order, according to which Operation "Citadel" was to start on 4 May 1943, was still valid.[13]

On Friday, 23 April 1943, STAVKA issued a directive to the Steppe Military District (Colonel General Konev) "to train primarily for offensive operations." One of the most important tasks of this military district was to use STAVKA's powerful strategic reserves in preventing a breakthrough from Orel as well as from Belgorod and increasing the impact of the assault while passing to the counteroffensive.

Two days later, on Sunday, 25 April 1943, STAVKA considered the situation at the Voronezh Front (General of the Army Vatutin). General Shtemenko: "The defense plan of the front is approved and 10 May is set as the date for completion of defense measures." At the same time STAVKA ordered General of the Army Vatutin to be prepared to attack by 1 June at the latest. The troops of the left flank of the Western and Bryansk Fronts plus the right flank of the Central Front were to mount an offensive in the direction of Orel by 20 May.

On Monday, 26 April 1943, Hitler reminded Army Groups South and Center once more to prepare carefully for Operation "Citadel."

On Wednesday, 28 April 1943, there was a conference in Munich on "Citadel" between Hitler and his commanders. Colonel General Model was the first to express his second thoughts. He voiced his doubts about the success of the planned offensive, pointing out that his Ninth Army had a shortage of 26,442 men and that it was common knowledge that the Soviets were consolidating their defense. It was necessary to build strong assault reserves for the Orel-Karachev Salient. Model requested two additional armored plus four fully refitted infantry divisions in addition to stronger support troops, heavy artillery, rocket launchers, self-propelled assault guns, and engineer units. Moreover, he suggested, as Field Marshal von Manstein already had done in March, to hold back forces concentrated for the offensive in the Orel Salient, wait for the Soviets to launch their offensive, and then turn the table and counterattack. Should OKW, in view of the Anglo-American activities in the Mediterranean Sea or Western Europe, withdraw troops from other fronts, there would be no choice but to evacuate the Orel Salient. In that case a defensive line should be drawn on both sides of the Desna and both sides of Karachev.

Hitler, however, did not let himself be swayed and only postponed the launching date originally set for 4 May 1943 because, as he said, "the assaulting divisions do not seem to have enough tanks, assault guns, and antitank guns to face the heavily fortified enemy defense system." The new date for Operation "Citadel" was now fixed for 12 June 1943, based on the prospective delivery of the heavy tanks and antitank guns.

Meanwhile, the number of partisan attacks had doubled compared to March, particularly along the approach route Minsk-Gomel. Blowing up the Besed Bridge on the Krichev-Unecha railroad line, the Ninth Army's only approach route, for example, cost ten entire days to enable effective repairs to be accomplished.

Early in the morning of 30 April 1943, the corpse of Major William Martin of the British Royal Marines and his briefcase were recovered from the Atlantic by fishermen off the Spanish port of Huelva. Documents, letters, and other articles left no room for doubt that this was a courier, on his way from London to the staff of the British Eighteenth Army Group (General Alexander) in Tunis, whose seaplane—as had already been reported—had crashed into the ocean a few days earlier. When a member of the Spanish General Staff, who had been entrusted with the case, managed to get the letters out of their envelopes without breaking the seals, it became immediately clear to him that these documents were military dynamite. One was a letter from General Nye, the vice chief of staff of the British General Staff, to General Alexander. In it Nye discussed various questions concerning the Allied Command in the Mediterranean area and referred quite

Belgorod area, Sunday, May 2, 1943: waiting for orders for a reconnaissance mission. The German attack "is expected at any time"—reports STAVKA confidentially

clearly to Greece as one of the two possible invasion points. Another letter was written in a personal style by Lord Mountbatten, the chief of staff of Combined Operations (to which the British commandos were assigned), to Admiral Cunningham, commander of the Allied naval forces in the Mediterranean area. It contained a similar allusion.

As soon as the courier's body was recovered, both the British vice consul in Huelva, Mr. Haselden, and the British naval attaché in Madrid requested, at first very discreetly and then with mounting urgency, the return of the deceased and all documents. The Spanish delayed the matter long enough to give German intelligence agents in Huelva an opportunity to exploit this fantastic stroke of luck. Then the courier mail was shoved intact back into the envelopes and the British request was granted.

The story of this imaginary officer is probably one of the most successful disinformation operations of the Second World War. Actually the corpse was planted off the Spanish coast by the submarine *Seraph* under Commander Jewell. Carried out under Churchill's personal orders, the operation's code name was "Mincemeat." In order to make the deception more credible and additionally to safeguard the actual plan for the landing in Sicily, one of the "secret items of information" slipped to the Germans with the corpse was that Sicily would be the landing point. This was done as a supposed cover story to conceal the "real" plans of an invasion in Greece.

Therefore, in case information about the actual invasion should leak to the Germans, practically unavoidable in an operation of this magnitude, it would have every appearance of being intentional deception and would corroborate the Germans' assumption that the documents were authentic. To make it even more plausible, it was stressed in the correspondence under "Personal and Most Secret" that the actual code name, "Husky," for the landing in Sicily was in "reality" the code name for the (alleged) landing in the Greek Peloponnesos. The hope was if German intelligence somehow came across the name "Husky," they would assume that the Peloponnesos was one of the two invasion points.

Also on 30 April, the head of the British Military Mission in Moscow passed on to the Soviet General Staff an extremely important operational report, the Enigma report on Operation "Citadel" decoded on 25 April, signed by the commander of Army Group South and directed to the OKH, Foreign Armies East Section. It contained a detailed outline of the Soviet forces in the Kursk Salient in the area of Army Group South plus an estimate of their effectiveness and the presumed schedule for the actions of individual large Red Army formations. In the second part of the Enigma report, operational intentions of both German Army Groups in Operation "Citadel" were provided.[14] With this report, STAVKA learned two facts that were to be decisive for future actions: first, the definite German plans for the Kursk Salient and the German Command's intelligence of Soviet forces located there. With such knowledge any experienced General Staff officer could perform wonders.

On Sunday, 2 May 1943, STAVKA sent the commanders of the fronts in the Kursk Salient a radio message with the urgent warning that the German assault "is to be expected at any moment." This was the first of three similar STAVKA warnings that preceded Operation "Citadel," causing much excitement in subordinate major units.

On Tuesday, 4 May 1943, Marshal Stalin ordered that ". . . attacks against railroad trains and raids on motor vehicle columns are the most important tasks of the air force." The war councils were instructed "to destroy enemy aircraft on the airfields and in the air, to disrupt railroad transports, and harass motorized movements on the roads." The German commanders used the lull for a short home leave. Field Marshal von Manstein was with his family and had Field Marshal Freiherr von Weichs stand in for him as commander in chief of Army Group South.

Field Marshal von Manstein: "On 4 May I wanted to return to my headquarters because the mounting of 'Citadel' was expected to be in mid-May; at the latest at the beginning of the second third of the month. On 3 May my chief, General Busse, came to me in Liegnitz (Legnica) to report that we were supposed to be in Munich at a conference with Hitler on 4 May." Field Marshal von Kluge, commander in chief of Army Group Center, and the inspector general of the Panzer Troops, Colonel General Guderian, as well as the chief of the General Staff of the Luftwaffe, Colonel General Jeschonnek, and the Minister for Armaments Speer participated in this conference.

Orel area; Airfield Karachev, early May 1943: following an attack by Soviet ground-attack bombers on the base of Stuka Squadron 2 "Immelmann"

When they arrived in Munich, they learned that Colonel General Model had already reported to Hitler. Model, who enjoyed Hitler's special confidence, aired his doubts, as he had done already on 28 April 1943. He discussed the operation's chances of success, stressing the difficulties they would face breaking through the heavily fortified enemy positions. This led to a sharp difference of opinion between Hitler and Model. Model, who was to lead a northern spearhead against Kursk, could now demonstrate, on the basis of comprehensive reconnaissance data, in particular aerial photographs, that the Soviets had built an extraordinary fortification system echeloned in depth in exactly those sectors of the front against which the main efforts of both army groups were planned. Moreover, troop movements indicated strong enemy reserves in the Kursk Salient.

Model emphasized that the Ninth Army was up against very heavy odds with this Russian defensive system and pointed out that according to German intelligence reports the Soviets had developed a new antitank rifle capable of penetrating the armor of the "Panzer IV." Field Marshal von Manstein: "These remarks apparently made a deep impression on Hitler. He feared that our assault would not break through or at least not rapidly enough to lead to a successful encirclement. Field Marshal von Kluge, who obviously felt slighted by Model reporting directly to Hitler, declared in his usual temperamental manner that Model's estimate of an enemy fortification system twenty kilometers deep was exaggerated, since aerial photographs also showed all the abandoned trenches from previous operations. Furthermore, Kluge pointed out that if the Germans waited much longer they could fall into a disadvantageous position and perhaps be forced to withdraw forces from the "Citadel" front.

Finally, Hitler wanted to hear the opinions of field marshals von Manstein and von Kluge on postponing Operation "Citadel." Both strongly advised against a later offensive. The chief of the General Staff, General Zeitzler, also shared this opinion. Nevertheless, Hitler considered a postponement necessary in order to reinforce the Panzer forces, perhaps even doubling the number of tanks in the attacking forces. In Hitler's opinion, this weakness in armor could be alleviated by 10 June by bringing up assault guns, Panther and Tiger tanks, and a detachment of extra-heavy Ferdinand assault guns. The Panzer IV and the self-propelled assault guns were to receive lateral aprons to protect them against Soviet antitank rifles.

Colonel General Jeschonnek urged mounting the attack soon, because it would be impossible to keep secret the preparations for the offensive much longer. Moreover, every further postponement only would benefit building up Soviet defenses. Both the OKH and the forward headquarters expected the assault to be a success, however, provided that it was launched before mid-June.

Colonel General Guderian contradicted all the participants and declared that an offensive at Kursk would be futile. The expected great tank losses would undoubtedly be irreplaceable. In addition, it once again would spoil his plans to refit the Panzer formations. Guderian emphasized that the tanks on whose use Colonel General Zeitzler set such a great store still had a lot of deficiencies. Instead, he felt that OKW should be thinking about saving armored reserves for the Western Front in order to be able to counter the Allied invasion troops, which definitely could be expected to be composed of mobile formations in 1944.

Reichsminister for Armaments and Ammunition, Speer, supported Guderian's arguments to postpone the offensive. The other generals were even more undecided. Manstein, for example, believed that the most opportune date for an assault, April, was past but considered another postponement impossible. Speer called attention to the many mechanical problems in the new tanks, particularly in the Tiger, and added that the planned monthly output quota of 250 Panthers could not be met because of growing difficulties in obtaining materials.

General of Artillery Jodl, chief of the Army Staff in the OKW, was in favor of giving up Operation "Citadel" altogether in view of the dubious overall situation.

Despite some uncertainties in assessing the situation, the majority of those present were basically in favor of a summer offensive. Delaying the operation would help the Soviets in preparing their defenses. However, even the Fuehrer could not make up his mind, although he certainly wanted the troops to have the new Panther tank. General Busse, chief of staff of Army Group South, urged that a decision be made for or against the plan or the optimum date would be missed.

Zmiyevo area south of Orel, May 3, 1943. Although waiting for deployment, always busy: A tank crew of the 9th Panzer Division engrossed in learning to identify the enemy

93

Hitler, unconvinced by either of his general's basic arguments, again put off his final decision, making the starting date of the offensive dependent on the activation of new Panzer units that would be equipped with the Panther and Tiger tanks. He saw a surprise massive attack by these tanks as one of the decisive prerequisites for a victory at Kursk. Field Marshal von Manstein: "Hitler then repeated his argument for a postponement until 10 June. As for the greater number of tanks on both sides, he said that the greater number of Soviet tanks would be offset by the technical superiority of the additional Tigers, Panthers, and Ferdinands. However, he would not be able to provide additional infantry divisions."

At the end of the conference, Hitler proclaimed: " 'Citadel' must not fail!"

On Thursday, 6 May 1943, German air reconnaissance brought back the first pictures of dug-in Soviet tanks at numerous points in the Kursk Salient. On the same day the Red Air Fleet conducted their first massive raids against German airfields. Six air armies participated in these operations: First Air Army (Lieutenant General Gromov) of the Western Front; Fifteenth (Lieutenant General Naumienko), Bryansk Front; Sixteenth (Lieutenant General Rudenko), Central Front; Second (Lieutenant General Krasovsky), Voronezh Front; Seventeenth (Lieutenant General Sudiets), Southwestern Front; and Ninth of the Southern Front. The German offensive in the Kursk area was anticipated between 10 and 12 May. The Red Air Fleet had the mission of destroying a great part of the Luftwaffe on the ground even before the battle began. Air Marshal Novikov was placed in charge of the operation.

In the early morning hours of 6 May 1943, Soviet bombers attacked seventeen German airfields of Luftflotte 4 and 6 from Smolensk to the Sea of Asov, a section about 1,200 kilometers long. The Soviet operation was prepared using the utmost secrecy and was known only to a small number of people. Transmissions of any messages concerning this operation in writing, over the telegraph, or by telephone were strictly prohibited. The Soviet losses amounted to only twenty-one aircraft.

In the morning hours of 7 and 8 May 1943, the Soviets repeated their raids on German airfields but with less success. The Germans had moved some of their aircraft to airfields in the rear. Those remaining were well camouflaged and were given added fighter protection. STAVKA terminated the missions three days later. These attacks would be called the greatest operation of the Red Air Forces in the Second World War. In three days 1,400 missions were flown with more than 500 German planes destroyed. Soviet losses totalled 122 aircraft.

On Saturday, 8 May 1943, the General Staff of the Red Army received alarming news from its secret service, a second false report, as it turned out, that German assaults in the directions of Orel-Kursk and Belgorod-Kharkov were to be launched between 10 and 12 May. A few hours later, STAVKA sent Directive No. 30123 by radio to the commanding generals

of the Bryansk, Central, Voronezh, and Southwestern Fronts. All troops in the first defensive line and reserve formations were to be fully combat ready by 10 May. In particular, the air force had to be able not only to ward off enemy air raids during the offensive but also seize air supremacy from the outset. Marshal Vasilevsky: "The directive to the commanding general of the Steppe Military District ordered us to speed up reinforcement of the Military District's troop units. All available elements of the Military District had to be ready to conduct defensive as well as offensive operations by 10 May."

Orel area, in the photographic interpretation section of a short range reconnaissance squadron, May 6, 1943: buried Soviet tanks are discovered for the first time

Monday, 10 May 1943, was also significant for German armor. Inspector General of Panzer Troops, Colonel General Guderian: "On 10 May, Hitler was in Berlin and I was called to the Reichschancellery for a conference on Panther production, because the industry was unable to meet the production dates originally fixed. As compensation, however, a greater number of tanks are to leave the assembly line, instead of 250, the more respectable total of 324.

"Following the meeting, I held Hitler's hand and asked him to permit me to speak frankly. He agreed and I implored him to give up the planned assault on the Eastern Front. I told him that he could see the difficulties with which we already had to struggle, that we could be certain that the

95

great effort would not pay off, and that defensive preparations in the west would have to suffer considerably. I closed with the question: 'Why do you want to attack at all in the east this year?' Here Keitel got involved in the conversation: 'We have to attack for political reasons.' I replied: 'Do you think that anyone knows where Kursk is? The world could care less whether or not we have Kursk.' I repeated my question: 'Why do we want to attack at all in the east this year?' Hitler answered: 'You are quite right. The thought of this assault gives me a peculiar feeling in my stomach.' I replied: 'Then you have the right feeling about the situation. Don't touch it!' Hitler assured me that he had in no way bound himself and that the discussion was over."

Nevertheless, Hitler was not really thinking of giving up the attack on Kursk. He would only postpone the launching date of Operation "Citadel" once again—now to 12 June 1943. This was supposed to make it possible to bring the not yet battle-ready Panther tanks and the Ferdinand assault guns directly from the assembly line to the front.

On the Soviet side, when nothing happened in the Kursk Salient during the night of 12/13 May, the front commanding generals were certain that STAVKA had fallen victim to another false alarm.

On Thursday, 13 May 1943, the remnants of the German Africa Corps capitulated on the Tunisian peninsula of Cap Bon. With this, North Africa was finally in the hands of the Anglo-Americans. Consequently, Operation "Citadel" had to be postponed again. Hitler was not sure whether Mussolini would be able to keep Italy on a pro-German course after this defeat, so he considered giving up the operation completely. He quietly planned to move his six best Panzer divisions from the Eastern Front to Southern Europe. Not to have to face this burdensome problem, Hitler put off Operation "Citadel" again—this time until the end of June in order, as he said, "to wait and see how things developed on the Apennine peninsula."

Meanwhile German preparations in the Kursk Salient were in high gear. In order to deceive the enemy intercept stations into believing there was a buildup of large armored formations, Colonel General Model had tape recordings made of tank exercises and then had them played in the nearby woods. The Soviets, however, were not misled by this trick. Their air reconnaissance had already established by this time that there were more than 900 tanks and approximately 580 aircraft on 16 airfields concentrated in the Orel-Komy area.

On Friday, 14 May 1943, the OKH believed it knew where the western Allies would strike following the victory in North Africa, probably in Greece. On this day the authenticity of the secret documents found on the drowned British courier near Huelva was confirmed by the staff of the High Command of the German Navy (Admiral Dönitz): "A thorough examination provided these conclusions: 1) The authenticity of the obtained documents is indisputable. Investigation whether they were intentionally slipped to us—which is not very probable—and the question whether the enemy has learned that we have obtained the documents or simply of their loss at sea is still being pursued. It is possible that the enemy does not know that we have

Near Bychki, May 12, 1943, in the Central Front Sector of the Soviet 70th Army, at a rocket launcher emplacement, the dreaded Katyushas, also called Stalinorgel: a multi-rocket launcher that could shoot up to 30 of these missiles over an area of 6 km, accompanied by an infernal noise

obtained the documents. . . ." This analysis corresponds exactly with Hitler's own estimate of November 1942 of Allied Command intentions in the Mediterranean Sea.

The fact that an invasion was imminent in the Balkans or elsewhere in the Mediterranean area additionally shook the confidence of the German Command and made an offensive operation in the Eastern Front secondary. But the Soviets were also not clear on what course to follow at this time. Marshal Zhukov: "Stalin was wavering on whether our troops should wait on the defensive for the enemy's attack, or should strike a preventive blow. He feared that our defense was not strong enough for a German assault, as had been the case repeatedly in 1941 and 1942. On the other hand, he was not sure that our troops would be able to defeat the enemy in our own preemptive offensive.

"After many discussions, Stalin finally decided in mid-May 1943 to meet the Fascists' offensive with a deeply echeloned defense, powerful air attacks, and counterattacks by operational and strategic reserves. The plan was to exhaust them this way; then to smash them with an enormous counteroffensive in the direction of Belgorod-Kharkov and Orel and subsequently to push spearheads deep into their most vulnerable position areas."

Although the mud period was over, both of these gigantic armies opposing one another seemed to be in a passive mode with hardly any patrol activity in the sector of the Kursk Salient. German flyers only were on missions day and night without letup. General of the Army Rokossovsky: "In May and June Luftwaffe activities increased. They attacked railroad junctions, stations, and bridges to prevent us from bringing up troops, equipment, ammunition, and fuel to the front. The Fascists bombed objectives far behind the front at night with flights of twenty to twenty-five aircraft. During the day they attacked objectives near the front line with fewer bombers escorted by fighters. Sometimes they attacked only with single planes."

A general of the Central Front has described his highly personal and unfortunate experience. Major General Antipenko, chief of Rear Services of the Central Front: "One day as I drew close to the village where the command post was situated, I saw an enemy aircraft approaching two or three times. The village was a terrible sight. The house in which Rokossovsky was quartered was demolished completely and his adjutant was laying wounded in the ruins. Our joy was great when Rokossovsky came to-

97

This He 111 bomber of Bomber Squadron Group "Boelcke" 27 looks like a prehistoric monster here at the edge of the forest

ward us. He had been having breakfast in the mess hall about 100 meters away from his quarters and in this way had escaped unharmed. He wanted to know immediately what I had to say. In the staff meeting I informed him that the enemy had attacked the railroad line Kastornoye-Kursk without any interference and even hit trains and locomotives at night. More than 400 bombs had fallen on this line in two months."

Meanwhile the German Command was taking advantage of the lull and starting with Operation "Gypsy Baron" mounted a series of large-scale operations to counter the increasingly dangerous partisan menace in the huge forests in Army Group Center's rear area. In this forest and swamp region, about the size of the Rhineland Palatinate, several thousand partisans were operating. These irregular troops kept the rear areas stirred up. They blew up railroads and bridges, attacked villages, and ambushed small units and men on leave as well as transport and hospital trains. They were a major threat to getting supplies to Ninth Army troops.

The commander of the XLVII Panzer Corps (General of the Pz. Tr. Lemelsen) was assigned the task of searching out the partisans and destroying them. For this operation he had a colorful mixture of security troops composed of Russian Ostverbände (eastern formations), Hungarian security troops, a Flemish battalion, and part of the French III Volunteer (LVF) Battalion. In addition, he had a cavalry unit and major units from Army Group Center such as the 4th and 18th Panzer Divisions, the 10th Panzer Grenadier Division, and the 7th and 292nd Infantry Divisions.

Belgorod area, May
15, 1943, a mine-
field of artillery
shells in the sector
of the 168th Inf.Div.
The Russians con-
tinue to demonstrate
defensive intentions

By 15 May 1943, the preparations for this operation were completed.
The large swamps with their jungle-like, wooded areas and dense under-
brush infested with billions of mosquitoes made it extremely difficult and
an unusual and physically taxing effort to fight in the area. The many tricks
of partisan fighting with the paths mined with undetectable wooden mines
and booby traps turned Operation "Gypsy Baron" into a suicide mission.

The ever-vigilant Soviet Secret Service meanwhile was convinced that
the Germans finally would launch Operation "Citadel" in the second half
of May 1943. And for the second time within ten days—the last alarm came
on 8 May—STAVKA was warned. This time the Germans would attack, in
the words of the message, "with the highest probability." General Shtemenko: "On 19 May 1943, the General Staff received new and we believed
reliable information that the enemy would attack between 19 and 26 May."
Once again STAVKA sent the commanders of the fronts in the area of the
Kursk Salient a directive to be in a state of increased combat readiness during the coming weeks.

On Friday, 21 May 1943, Hitler returned to his mountaintop farm in
Berchtesgaden. The following day he signed secret instructions for Field
Marshal Rommel who was working on plans and schedules for secretly in-
filtrating four German divisions into northern Italy. When Hitler gave the

99

code word Operation "Alarich," at least eighteen more infantry and Panzer divisions under his personal command were to follow from the Eastern Front and occupied Europe. Meanwhile time was going by and Hitler still hesitated on ordering the launching of "Citadel." He feared that the Italian generals might desert from the alliance with Germany or the western Allies might mount their invasion ahead of schedule.

But, on Saturday, 22 May 1943, the Luftwaffe commenced its heaviest bombing of strategic targets in the Kursk Salient in preparation for "Citadel." The main objective was the railroad junction at Kursk. Soviet fighter planes of the Second and Sixteenth Air Armies and the 101st Fighter Division of the National Air Defense Command had the mission of intercepting the attack of the approximately 170 bombers. The two German assault armies, planned for mounting the offensive from the areas of Orel, north of Kursk, Belgorod, and south of Kursk, now had attained a strength of about 500,000 men. The Luftwaffe formations with some 1,200 aircraft were also in a state of advanced readiness.

Wednesday, 26 May 1943, the day that STAVKA warned that the Germans would mount their offensive, passed without anything special occurring. As the senior Soviet officers took these warnings seriously, they did not suspect a false report but thought something else was to happen. Marshal Vasilevsky: "When nothing occurred, the War Council of the Voronezh Front believed that the enemy had given up their offensive totally. Therefore, it was requested that Stalin consider our own preemptive attack against the enemy. Stalin immediately seemed to favor this suggestion. It took a lot of effort for Zhukov, Antonov, and me to talk him out of it."

At the end of May 1943, the OKH stated in a situation estimate that the Germans could well expect a surprise Red Army offensive.

For weeks, the German troops had been waiting in prepared positions for the order to attack. The concentration of forces and the care taken in the preparations were unparalleled in the eastern campaign. Army Groups Center and South had approximately 1,500 and 1,600 tanks and assault guns, respectively. All told, German forces here with approximately 3,000 tanks and 1,800 aircraft were equipped in their relatively confined front sector with about the same quantity of materiel as in the invasion of the Soviet Union on 22 June 1941. At that time they had had a total of 3,580 tanks and 1,830 aircraft in a front of approximately 3,000 kilometers stretching from the Baltic Sea to the Black Sea.

More than two-thirds of the German Panzer and motorized infantry divisions at the Eastern Front were to be committed to the Kursk Salient offensive. Because much of the artillery was lost at Stalingrad, the assault formations lacked sufficient heavy artillery to be able to direct strong concentrated fire into the depth of the Soviet defense. And the Army Group did not have sufficiently strong infantry forces.

In early June 1943, the Soviets were not only superior in ground troops, the Red Air Fleet now had more than thirty air corps with approximately

10,000 planes at its disposal. Its aircraft and other equipment were of a remarkably high standard. The German air formations in the east were predominantly flying Messerschmitt Me 109 F's because most of the Focke-Wulf FW 190's were committed to the defense of the Reich. In contrast, Soviet fighter squadrons were equipped largely with modern aircraft such as the MiG, Jak, or LaGG. The Luftwaffe had forfeited its strength simply by flying too many missions. Only remnants of the once-powerful German bomber formations were left at the Eastern Front, and they rarely flew operational missions.

Shatalovka airfield, southeast of Stary Oskol, May 28, 1943, the base of Stuka Squadron 1: one of the 7th Squadron Group's planes (Capt. Stoll-Berberich) is being made ready for a mission

On Wednesday, 2 June 1943, the Luftwaffe flew an even stronger day-time attack with 543 aircraft (424 bombers) on the Kursk railroad junction. Two hundred eighty Soviet fighters of the Sixteenth and Second Air Armies of the Central Front and 106 fighters of the 101st Fighter Division of the National Air Defense intercepted the German planes. Lieutenant General Moskalenko: "Our fighters were not able to intercept all the German bombers coming from so many directions. Approximately 100 were able to complete their bombing missions."

On Thursday, 3 June 1943, a large-scale "Citadel" map exercise took place in Kharkov, directed by Field Marshal von Manstein. At this time the participants were informed that turncoats, who were expected to defect en masse at the beginning of the German assault, were to be employed to form a Russian liberation army.

Meanwhile, the deceptive British Operation "Mincemeat" took its toll. Convinced that the Allies planned to land in Greece in the near future, at Hitler's express orders the German High Command transferred some of the Panzer forces so urgently needed for "Citadel" to the distant Peloponnesos. Colonel General Guderian: "The OKW had the peculiar idea to send the 1st Panzer Division to the Peloponnesos to prevent a British landing. This division had just been replenished and equipped with the first Panther tank detachment. It was our strongest reserve. . . . My infuriated objections were lost among Keitel's grotesque arguments. He maintained that it would be impossible to supply a mountain infantry division, which I considered far more suited for Greece, with the necessary forage, because this would require too much transport space. . . . We in Russia soon sorely would miss the 1st Panzer Division."

At dusk on 3 June 1943, at 2000, 168 aircraft, mostly He 111 and Ju 88 of Bomber Squadrons KG 3, KG 4, KG 27, and KG 100, took off. The objective of this Luftflotte 4 mission (FM von Richthofen) was the Molotov-Avrozavod combined works in Gorky, one of the largest Soviet tank production sites this side of the Urals. The four-square-kilometer target lay just barely within the range of the bomber formations transferred into the Bryansk area. The new optical sight "Lotfe 7D," which had just arrived, was expected to make bombing more precise. As a navigational aid the crews were using Radio Moscow. Coming from the south they made a wide circle around the Soviet capital in order not to come within the range of Moscow's antiaircraft artillery barrier.

The 149 planes that reached the objective dropped 24 tons of bombs at midnight. Five of these aircraft were shot down by the Soviet air defense. In a quick series of night raids the Luftwaffe tried to eliminate the Molotov Works which supposedly produced 800 of the famous T-34 tanks a week before Operation "Citadel" began.

On Friday, 4 June 1943, the London *Times* duly reported the death of Major W. Martin. This was planned to be additional "evidence" to prove the authenticity of the documents found on the corpse off Huelva. German intelligence officers carefully read and evaluated English newspapers as soon as they arrived in Madrid or Lisbon.

During the night of 4/5 June 1943, 128 German bombers dropped 179 tons of bombs on the factories in Gorky. Two planes did not return.

On Saturday, 5 June 1943, Operation "Gypsy Baron," the large-scale antipartisan action, was terminated. In the evening the participating Panzer divisions returned to their former billets north of Orel following two night marches. The infantry divisions were emplaced as reinforcements between the front line divisions in their prepared positions.

During the night of 5/6 June 1943, the Luftwaffe again attacked Gorky. This time 242 tons of bombs poured down on the Molotov Works. Of 154 aircraft in the raid, one was lost. But during the night of 7/8 June, only 20 planes flew this fourth mission to the factories of Gorky. They dropped 39 tons of bombs. According to information from agents, these raids caused the Gorky Molotov Works to be paralyzed for six weeks. (In reality the combined works never stopped working.)

On Tuesday, 8 June 1943, the Free French fighter squadron "Normandie" (Major de Tulasne) participated in the operations of the Soviet First Air Army (Lieutenant General Gromov) attached to the Western Front (Colonel General Sokolovsky). This fighter squadron based at the airfield in Kationka was assigned to the 303rd Rifle Division (General Tsakharov) and integrated into the 18th Guards Rifle Regiment (Colonel Golubov).

On the evening of 8 June 1943, the Red Air Fleet launched a major strike to prevent the Luftwaffe from bombing Gorky. Their main objectives were the German airfields in Seshcha, Bryansk, Karachev, Orel, and Borovskoye. For this operation the forces of the First, Fifteenth, and Second Air Armies of the front air forces plus formations of strategic bombers of the 8th Long-Distance Flying Corps were used. According to Soviet sources ". . . a total surprise could not be achieved in this operation. The enemy had learned a lesson from the air operations in May. His air defense was totally prepared."

During the night of 8/9 June 1943, 132 German bombers (Ju 88 and He 111) took off to bomb the synthetic rubber works in Jaroslav. Soviet

Dimitrovsk-Orlovsky area, June 8, 1943, in the sector of the 72nd Inf.Div.: pursuing partisans in an armored personnel carrier

103

antiaircraft fire was so intense that only 109 planes were able to penetrate to the objective, dropping 190 tons of incendiary and high-explosive bombs. With this last raid, the strategic commitment of the Luftwaffe practically ceased on the Eastern Front in 1943.

On the evening of 10 June 1943, the Red Air Fleet repeated its attack on the 28 identified German air bases. The Soviets reported that 223 German aircraft were destroyed on the ground.

On Monday, 14 June 1943, OKH issued the final orders for Operation "Citadel." The following day, the commanding general of Army Group

Bobrik area, June 15th, 1943, in the sector of the 20th Panzer Division: a battery of "Wespen" (wasps)—105mm light howitzers on the chassis of Mark II's—being moved

Center, Field Marshal von Kluge, visited the XLI Panzer Corps. General of Panzer Troops Harpe: "We walked through the trenches of two divisions for hours, seeing individual observation posts in the open areas and troops resting in dugouts. There was one company deployed over 1 to 1.5 kilometers of front, with a single reserve battalion every 30 to 40 kilometers. Finally von Kluge said: 'This is sheer madness. How can you expect to hold this position? No support is available from Army or Army Group.'"

On Tuesday, 15 June 1943, the work in the Kursk Salient by the local population, under the supervision of the partisan organizations on the so-called national defense line along the left bank of the Don between Voyeikovo, Voronezh, and Boguchar, was completed. General Shtemenko: "A defensive zone of 300 kilometers in depth was created behind the fixed fronts in areas where the enemy was expected to attack. Here, our strategic reserves were to annihilate the enemy in case he managed a breakthrough." In the evening a deserter from the 3rd Battalion of Infantry Regiment 164 was brought to the headquarters of the Soviet Fortieth Army (Lieutenant General Moskalenko). He revealed that the mission of the German division facing the right flank of the Fortieth Army was to defend in place; that the assault was to be conducted "at some other more important sector."

On Wednesday, June 16, 1943, Hitler finally decided to begin Operation "Citadel" according to the plan already approved. He believed that he no longer had to worry about Italy's willingness to continue the war. The inspector general of Panzer Troops, Colonel General Guderian, believed that a refitting period past June urgently was necessary to restore the Panzer formations. The commanders of Army Groups South and Center, however, thought that the attack should occur by mid-June at the very latest. Hitler, however, refused to consider any of these opinions and once again reduced the strength of the Red Army in his mind. He saw the information collected by OKH reconnaissance as pure "exaggeration," despite the fact that what was seen clearly on the aerial photographs of the Kursk Salient was alarming enough.

South of Orel: mid-June 1943: FM von Kluge inspecting an armored group of the XLVII Panzer Corps

Friday, 18 June 1943, was an extremely significant day for "Citadel." The OKW War Diary noted that on this day the Fuehrer, although un-

derstanding "the misgivings of the Armed Forces Executive Staff," finally said that he was in favor of beginning offensive operation "Citadel."

Just three days later, on 21 June 1943, Hitler set 3 July 1943 as the date for launching the offensive. On the same day the OKH learned that air reconnaissance had discovered one of the strongest Soviet defensive lines north of Belgorod in Army Group South's axis of attack. Contrary to usual practice, the offensive was not to begin at dawn. Instead, the plan was to jump off late in the afternoon, the most unfavorable time of all, because all elements of surprise were forfeited. Strategically, Operation "Citadel" was turning into a great gamble, since German reserves would be committed in the most crucial operation of the year.

Meanwhile, OKH was already giving instructions for receiving the masses of defectors and prisoners anticipated during the first hours of "Citadel." They were—contrary to all previous instructions and promises in General Order No. 13 of 20 April 1943—to be transported immediately to Germany as cheap labor for the armaments industry and mines.

On Wednesday, 23 June 1943, Rudolf Roessler ("Lucy") reported from Lucerne "the very latest news from Fuehrer headquarters [an excerpt from his authentic radio message]: the German attack against Kursk, contemplated since the end of May, is no longer planned. . . ."[15]

On Friday, 25 June 1943, Hitler fixed the start of "Citadel"—this time once and for all—for 5 July 1943. It still was to run according to the original Operation Order No. 6.

Army Group Center

The operations plan contained a concentric attack from south and north toward Kursk. Army Group Center (FM von Kluge) was to attack with fifteen infantry divisions, six Panzer divisions, and one Panzer grenadier division from the sector west of Maloarchangelsk. Ninth Army (Colonel General Model) provided the main effort in its center. The XLVII Panzer Corps (General of Pz. Tr. Lemelsen) with the 6th Infantry Division and the 20th, 18th, 2nd, 4th, and 9th Panzer Divisions was to penetrate the Soviet position with a breadth of forty kilometers along the main thrust line, Orel-Kursk. They then were to drive forward rapidly between the road and railroad line toward Kursk to the high ground north of the city and link up there with Army Group South. Flank cover was to be provided on the right by the XLVI Panzer Corps (General of Infantry Zorn) with the 102nd Infantry Division, the von Manteuffel Group, the 258th, 7th, and 31st Infantry Divisions and on the left by the XLI Panzer Corps (General of Pz. Tr. Harpe) with the 292nd and 86th Infantry Divisions, the 18th Panzer Division, and the 10th Panzer Grenadier Division. Army Group Center had no general reserves at all. Each division was assigned only one reserve battalion. Luftflotte 6 (Colonel General Ritter von Greim) supporting Army Group Center allocated the 1st Air Force Division (Lieutenant General Deichmann) to Operation "Citadel" with three fighter squadron groups plus elements of the 4th Air Force Division. Elements of the Second Army (General of Pz. Tr. R. Schmidt) were intended for local attacks at the Western Front of the Kursk Salient.

Grayvoron area, June 24, 1943, final preparations: Panzergrenadiers (armored infantrymen) from the Division "Grossedeutschland" assembling before marching off to prepared positions

Army Group South

Army Group South (FM von Manstein) was to push forward from both sides of Belgorod with eight infantry divisions and nine Panzer divisions.

Fourth Panzer Army (Colonel General Hoth) was assigned the main effort on the north toward Kursk. It was composed of II SS-Panzer Corps (SS-Obergruppenf. Hausser) with the 167th Infantry Division, 2nd SS-Panzer Division "Das Reich," 1st SS-Panzer Division "Leibstandarte," and the 3rd SS-Panzer Division "Totenkopf"; the XLVIII Panzer Corps (General of Pz. Tr. von Knobelsdorff) with the 167th and 332nd Infantry Divisions, 11th Panzer Division, Panzer Grenadier Division "Grossdeutschland," 3rd Panzer Division, and "Panther" Brigade Decker; and the LII Army Corps (General of Infantry Ote) with the 25th and 57th Infantry Divisions. Fourth Army's objective was to link up as rapidly as possible with Ninth Army attacking from the north.

At the same time, the Kempf Army (General of Pz. Tr. Kempf) was to attack to the south of Belgorod. Under General Kempf's command were XI Army Corps (General of Pz. Tr. Raus) with the 320th, 106th, and the 198th Infantry Divisions; and the III Panzer Corps (General of Pz. Tr. Breith) with the 168th Infantry Division and the 6th, 7th, and 19th Panzer Divisions. The Kempf Army was to cover aggressively the right flank of Hoth's Fourth Army. Both of these armies were concentrated in the area north of Kharkov.

Fourth Panzer Army's main thrust—Oboyan to Kursk—was to be twenty-five kilometers wide, while the secondary attack by the Kempf Army toward Belgorod-Korocha was planned to be about fifteen kilometers wide.

All told, twenty-three infantry divisions and sixteen fast-moving formations were to participate in Operation "Citadel." Of the infantry divisions, six (two with Army Group South, four with Army Group Center) were to be kept in reserve when the operation began to follow later as the assault made progress.

The Luftwaffe committed all of Luftflotte 4 (General of Air Force Dessloch) in the sector of Army Group South. Included in its formations were Kampfgeschwader (KG) 3, 27, and 55; the 3rd Group of KG 4; the 1st Group of KG 100; Schlachtgeschwader (ground-attack squadron) 9; and the Jagdgeschwaders (fighter squadrons) 3 and 52. The units of Luftflotte 4 and 6 comprised more than two-thirds of the total of all the air force formations at the Eastern Front. The planners for Operation "Citadel" had at their disposal 900,000 men with nearly 10,000 guns and mortars, approximately 2,700 tanks and assault guns, 1,200 tactical and ground-attack aircraft, and 700 fighter planes.

At this stage, according to Soviet information STAVKA was aware of the dispositions and strengths of German formations assembled in the Kursk Salient area, thanks to the Special Signal Battalion. The Russians, therefore, had built up an invincible defense for the battle as well as all that was necessary for the planned counteroffensive. About 40 percent of all the operational formations of the Red Army were available. Among them were five armored armies concentrated in the Kursk area.

Army Group Center under FM von Kluge was stretched over the entire 132 kilometers of the Central Front. Kluge had three armies in the first line and one armored army with two independent tank corps in the second. His main effort was on the right at Orel. Two more armies were deployed

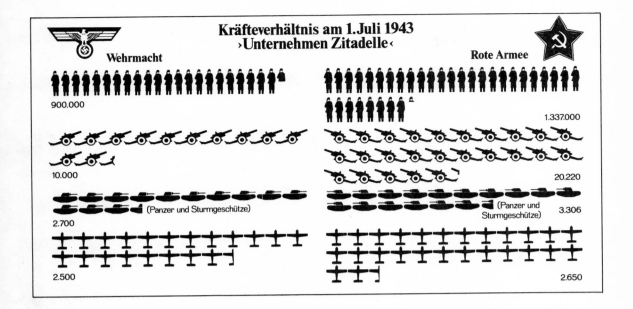

Kräfteverhältnis am 1.Juli 1943
›Unternehmen Zitadelle‹

Wehrmacht

Rote Armee

900.000

1.337.000

10.000

20.220

(Panzer und Sturmgeschütze)
2.700

(Panzer und Sturmgeschütze)
3.306

2.500

2.650

Relative Combat
Proportion on July
1, 1943
(According to Russian information)

for secondary thrusts. Three corps and heavy artillery batteries were deployed in depth in their rear.

On the Russian side, the Kursk Salient was defended by the Central Front (General of the Army Rokossovsky, Major General Telegin, and Chief of Staff Lieutenant General Malinin) and the Voronezh Front (General of the Army Vatutin, Lieutenant General Khrushchev, and Chief of Staff Major General Ivanov). They had at their disposal approximately 100 divisions containing about 1.3 million men, nearly 20,000 guns and mortars, 3,600 tanks and self-propelled guns, and 2,600 aircraft. The Central Front had the mission of defending the northern sector of the Kursk Salient, from Alexandrovka to Korenevo, a distance of nearly 360 kilometers. Emphasis was given to the right wing (Thirteenth Army under Lieutenant General Pukhov and Seventieth Army under Lieutenant General Galinin), where the main thrust was anticipated along a defensive line of 95 kilometers. In the Thirteenth Army sector, General of the Army Rokossovsky concentrated about 60 percent of his artillery brigades and 33 percent of his armored brigades and regiments.

Opposite Army Group South (FM von Manstein) lay the southern section of the Kursk Salient, from Korenevo to Volchansk. In a 244-kilometer defensive line the Voronezh Front had three armies on the front and two armies in reserve, one of which was a tank army. The center and left wing in the sector of the Sixth Guards Army (Lieutenant General Chistyakov) and the Seventh Guards Army (Lieutenant General Shumilov) were positioned to defend against the expected German main effort. Their reserves consisted of one rifle and two armored corps. Prepared for action east of the Kursk Salient was the strategic reserve of the Steppe Military District (renamed Steppe Front on 10 July 1943, under Colonel General Konev, Lieutenant General Susaikov, and Chief of Staff Lieutenant General Zakharov) consisting of five armies and five independent corps. Three air ar-

111

Belgorod, June 26, 1943, a delegation of Turkish officers under the Chief of the General Staff, Col.Gen. Cemil Zahit Toydemyr (center) at a not quite successful demonstration of the Tiger (*Right front*) FM von Manstein

mies and elements of long-range air force formations with more than 3,000 aircraft were assigned to support the Central and Voronezh Fronts. They were to be reinforced with additional forces when the offensive was to be launched.

The Steppe Military District, behind the Central and the Voronezh Fronts along the defensive line Izmalkovo-Livny-Kshen River-Beli Kolodes, was given the mission of holding enemy breakthroughs on these fronts and then be prepared to mount the counteroffensive.

This deployment of Soviet forces had a decisive influence on the summer campaign of 1943. In contrast to the Battle of Stalingrad when there had been one Soviet division per 35 kilometers of front and 0.7 tank and assault gun plus 2.5 guns and mortars per kilometer, in the area of the

Central Front there was one division for only 6.9 kilometers and 26.5 cannons and mortars plus 4.7 tanks and assault guns per kilometer. The greatest mass of materiel and troops of the entire war was concentrated here in the Kursk area, one-third of the personnel and aircraft, half of all the tanks and self-propelled guns, and more than one-quarter of the guns and mortars.

Colonel General Konev: "Our High Command presumed that the Fascist Wehrmacht had no reserves and would be able to attack in only one strategic sector. In order to do this they would have to form a sufficiently strong strike group. . . . If the enemy did not attack soon thereafter, our troops were to be the first to attack. For this reason, we concentrated strong strategic reserves at the Tula-Yelets-Stary Oskol-Rososh line. In these areas were formations that had participated in the Battles of Stalingrad and Leningrad and had fought in other sectors of the Soviet-German Front."

During the evening of 25 June 1943, a commission of five Turkish officers under the command of the chief of the Turkish General Staff, Colonel General Toydemyr, landed at the North Kharkov Airport. Accompanied by Field Marshal von Manstein, the foreign guests were shown various German weapons, including the Tiger tank.

On Monday, 28 June 1943, Hitler informed Reichsminister Speer that according to reports from the front all the "Hornet" antitank assault guns could not be deployed because their muzzles lacked sufficient support brackets, making driving impossible. As the Hornet was particularly important to Operation "Citadel," the problem had to be solved immediately. However, Allied air raids impeded production and repeatedly caused delays in delivery of weapons to the front, especially of the newer types.

At this point, therefore, Model's Ninth Army had only two companies of Tiger tanks in his heavy Panzer Detachment 505. Army Group South had forty-five Tigers in heavy Panzer Detachment 503 plus Tiger companies with these heavy tanks in Panzer Grenadier Division "Grossdeutschland," 1st SS-Panzer Division "Leibstandarte Adolf Hitler," 2nd SS-Panzer Division "Das Reich," and 3rd SS-Panzer Division, respectively. Each of these companies had about fourteen tanks. With this handful of heavy tanks, still plagued with mechanical problems, Hitler intended to force the Soviet army to its knees.

The end of June 1943, machine-gun position of an advanced outpost at the front line of the Kursk salient

General of the Panzer Troops von Knobelsdorff: "It was disquieting to know that despite all our painstaking training, our thorough studies of warfare, and the bitter experiences of the past year, the General Staff of the Army was about to blunder into a risky venture that would jeopardize our last reserves."

During this time the STAVKA reserves were being continuously reinforced. The Steppe Military District (Colonel General Konev) order of battle included the Fourth Guards Army (Lieutenant General Kulik), Fifth Guards Army (Lieutenant General Zhadov), Twenty-seventh Army (Lieutenant General Trofimienko), Forty-seventh Army (Major General Kozlov), Fifty-third Army (Lieutenant General Managarov), Fifth Guards Tank Army (Lieutenant General Rotmistrov), and Fifth Air Army (Lieutenant General Goriunov), plus a rifle, three tank, three mechanized, and three cavalry corps. Including the air forces, 537,000 men were present for duty. The new Steppe Front had 3,397 guns, 4,004 mortars (82- and 120mm) as well as 1,551 tanks and assault guns.

On Wednesday, 30 June 1943, Marshal Vasilevsky was ordered by Stalin to concentrate on preparing the troops of the Voronezh Front for combat. Marshal Zhukov was to coordinate the operations of the Central, Bryansk, and Western Fronts. The commander of the air force, Marshal Novikov, and his deputies, Generals Vorosheykin and Khudyako, were responsible for coordinating air force missions.

On the same day, Colonel Teske, in charge of transport in Army Group Center, reported that in June partisan activities behind the German lines were the highest since the beginning of the war. In all, 298 locomotives, 1,222 railroad cars, and 44 bridges had been destroyed. Each day railroad tracks were being destroyed in thirty-two different places on average.

The situation at sea had also grown better for the Allies. In the first quarter of 1943, German submarines had sunk ships carrying a total of 1.5 million GRT; now in the second quarter only 0.7 million GRT had been sunk. Simultaneously, many more submarines had been lost than in previous times.

In the meantime, the Red Army had completed work on its defensive lines in the Kursk Salient. From April to June 1943, 5,000 kilometers of rifle and communication trenches were dug and 400,000 mines and built-in explosive charges laid. General of the Army Rokossovsky: "One hundred twelve kilometers of barbed wire obstacles were erected, 10.7 kilometers of it electric, and more than 170,000 mines laid in only the sector of the Thirteenth and Seventieth Armies." The number of automatic weapons and tanks the Soviet troops had at the front were nearly doubled between April and June. Marshal Zhukov: "In the summer of 1943 we had more than 6.4 million men, nearly 99,000 guns and mortars, about 2,200 artillery rocket launchers, more than 9,500 tanks and assault guns, as well as some 8,300 combat aircraft." Major General Fomichenko: "As our troops prepared to repel the enemy offensive at Kursk in the summer of 1943, they did a masterly job of camouflaging their positions. German reconnaissance planes flying over at an altitude of less than twenty meters could see only empty fields. Entire regiments with artillery, mortars, and tanks were hidden in this seemingly deserted country."

115

Voronezh area, an airfield of the Soviet 5th Air Army, early July 1943: an already obsolete medium bomber type Tupolev SB-2 (with M-103 engines) being made ready for an intelligence mission

General von Knobelsdorff: "It was a matter of course to conduct intensive reconnaissance in the other front sectors of the corps. Particularly interesting was the Mtsensk area. However, there was no sign of any enemy offensive intentions anywhere."

On Thursday, 1 July 1943, Hitler returned from Berchtesgaden to his headquarters, Wolfsschanze, in East Prussia. That very same evening he received all the army commanders of the Eastern Front and the commanding generals participating in Operation "Citadel" at his teahouse. Coming directly to the point he told them: "I have decided to fix 5 July as the date for launching Operation 'Citadel.' " He outlined the situation and explained in detail the planned operation and remarked: "Our allies are to blame for our failures. The Italians have let us down dismally. Germany needs the captured regions; without them it cannot exist in the long run. We must gain the hegemony of Europe. We stay where we are!" According to Hitler "Citadel" had to be postponed because there had been a possibility of an Anglo-American landing on the Italian coast. Had this happened, it would have become necessary to transfer some of the forces assembled for "Citadel" to that theater.

During the last hours of 1 July, the Soviet intelligence service believed it had unmistakable evidence that the Germans in the Kursk Salient would attack during the next few days. Marshal Vasilevsky: "The reconnaissance service informed the General Staff during the night of 2 July that it was

116

certain that the enemy would go on the offensive soon, no later than 6 July. I immediately reported this to Stalin and requested permission to inform the fronts without delay." Lieutenant General Batov, commanding general of the Sixty-fifth Army: "Since 1 July we had been waiting anxiously for the offensive which could begin at any moment. We were sure that the Fascists would attack at daybreak. Nobody could sleep during these short summer nights. The officers did not leave their observation posts for even an hour. We forbade our soldiers to go more than 100 meters away from the dugouts. All the radios were tuned in to specific frequencies."

During the same night German engineer units received an order to tape paths for the spearheads through the mine fields. They were to clear paths and mark them for the Panzer divisions and the artillery and vehicles of the individual units that were following.

Lieutenant General Moskalenko: "The next night we learned that a German soldier of the 168th Infantry Division in the Kondiryev area, five kilometers north of Belgorod, had been captured by the Sixth Guards Army. He confirmed the information already thought to be true. According to his statement, the assault was to open northwest of Belgorod during the night of 5 July. The German soldiers already had received their cold rations and, as usual before an attack, spirits. Moreover, they had engineers with them to clear mine fields and remove wire obstacles."

On the morning of 2 July 1943, Field Marshal von Manstein flew directly from East Prussia to Bucharest. The visit to Bucharest already had been announced on the radio and in the press. Manstein presented the Romanian dictator Antonescu the golden "Krimschild" (Crimean coat of arms) at a ceremony commemorating the anniversary of the capture of Sevastopol and quietly flew back to his headquarters in Cherkasy a few hours later. This was part of a deceptive plan designed to keep STAVKA in the dark about impending German operations. If the commander of Army Group South were in the capital of Romania, one might think that there would be no danger of an attack.

The War Office instructed a representative of the British Military Mission in Moscow to report to the Soviet General Staff and to inform them again of German Secret Service activities behind Soviet lines. In particular, the Germans were still breaking the Soviet army codes. The British learned this from its Ultra operation.[16]

Budapest, July 2, 1943, FM von Manstein leaving his plane: a flying visit prior to launching Operation "Citadel"

117

4 July–11 July 1943

First

Army Groups South
Soviet Defense
in the Northern and
of the Kursk

Phase
and Center Attack Lines Penetrated Southern Sections Salient

FM von Manstein in Bucharest

Sunday, 4 July 1943, Berlin. The DNB reports:

Representing Adolf Hitler, Field Marshal von Manstein presented the Romanian head of state, Marshal Antonescu, the golden "Krimschild" (Crimean coat of arms).

From the OKW War Diary

Monday, 5 July 1943:

Front situation: Early on 5 July, Operation "Citadel" commenced according to plan in the areas of the Kempf Army, Fourth Panzer Army, and Ninth Army. In the remainder of the Eastern Front only reconnaissance missions were carried out. Despite the unfavorable weather, the Luftwaffe gave strong support to our offensive operations.

The Battle North of Belgorod

Early in the morning on July 5, 1943, Operation "Citadel" begins according to plan: a battery of M-18, 149mm field guns open fire on the Soviet main defensive position

. . . The Soviets had prepared positions built to a depth of up to sixty kilometers. These positions were shaped by the natural obstacles of open terrain. Intermediate fields were not empty areas but reservoirs packed with reserves and mobile battle groups. Behind them echeloned in depth were operational forces composed of several armored and mechanical corps.

In spite of the bombs and mortars hailing down on them early in the morning on 5 July, the troops in the first Soviet defensive line held on

stubbornly. The guards rifle divisions dug in here believed that they were safe in their strong fortifications echeloned in depth. They were aware that swampy hollows and valleys, wide mine belts, wire entanglements, flamethrower barriers, and tank ditches were in front of them. They also could see that they were deployed in a labyrinth of trenches and bunkers, antitank positions, rifle pits, and mortar emplacements. Behind them a network of small strong points and defensive works were spread over the countryside. Solid barriers of fifty to sixty dug-in tanks were emplaced like knots at some positions.

The divisions of the German army proceeded against this sophisticated system of defensive works. Grenadiers and tanks penetrated the main fighting line after several hours of hard combat, made breaches here and there, widened them, and rolled up the positions in hand-to-hand fighting. The air was filled with mine explosions, detonations by engineers, and the angry screaming of shellfire.

In the midst of the heaviest fire, troops cut wire obstacles and levelled tank ditches, permitting the tanks to make their way through the narrow paths. Before the Soviet tank reserves behind the main battlefield could enter the action, German formations already had fought their way through the gaps in the front and flooded the open terrain.

The evening of the first day of combat was not yet over when reports came in from the shock divisions that the first line had been penetrated, all three kilometers of it.

Völkischer Beobachter, July 1943

Heavy Fighting

Tuesday, 6 July 1943. The German High Command announces:

The successful local offensive operations of German infantry in the Belgorod sectors developed into heavy fighting in the air and on the ground extending to the area north of Belgorod due to strong Russian counterattacks and are growing ever more violent.

From the War Diary of the OKW

6 July 1943:

Front situation: In Operation "Citadel" the Southern Group gained eighteen kilometers and the Northern Group ten kilometers in distance. The enemy knew the time when the attack was scheduled. Therefore, no operational surprise was achieved. On the remainder of the Eastern Front only local skirmishes were reported. The Luftwaffe supported the assault operations strongly. During the course of 5 July, the enemy lost 432 aircraft compared to our losses of 26.

A Tank Battle

By SS-war correspondent Robert Krötz:

Diving out of the hatch, we roll backwards and press ourselves behind the tracks. Blow by blow the shells of the Bolshevist armored platoon tear into our willow-covered tank, which miraculously does not burn. What are

122

we going to do? The Obersturmfuehrer (lieutenant), very calm even now, looks around, points with his hand to a little woods on the right, and is the first to jump up. He leaps ten times, throws himself down, jumps up again, and crawls on. The second one to move is the gunner. With more than forty tanks, heavily armed artillery platoon, and machine-gun posts, the enemy holding the high ground in front of us running along the main railroad line Belgorod-Kursk has seen the men escape and covers them with dense fire.

The driver and I are the last to leave. We run for our lives. The 150 meters through hell seem endless. My heart stops. How do we know the little woods is clean? We have left our own spearhead three kilometers behind us in our tank reconnaissance mission. Has the enemy infantry left or are they still sitting in their bunkers in the woods? We hardly give this a thought though it is obvious. Our nerves are on fire and our legs want to give up. But the hissing of the exploding shells and clouds of dust rising from the machine-gun bullets wildly hitting the ground around us hound us on. Twenty or thirty seconds later we drop exhausted into deserted enemy rifle pits dug in the southern tip of the green band of woods. Here the trees suddenly stop growing and form a border for the green steppe.

We press our hot faces into the cool earth and try to catch our breath for a few minutes. The Obersturmfuehrer orders observation to the north, crawls to the edge of the woods himself, and glances back at our tank, still standing in a hail of shells. Bullets are hissing through the trees. A good thing the stragglers of Bolshevists don't realize how weak we are: that we five men have only one pistol among us and only the will to get through.

Not until we have calmed down do the events of the morning roll over us once more like a movie. How did it happen? At 0300 we had decamped, moved to the north, and then in a small formation evaded the concentration of Bolshevist tanks in order to strike them in the left flank. Driving for half an hour we swerved far to the west, reached a little village with the infantry, and continued north again from there. The fighting started 800 meters in front of the railroad tracks. We were looking into the sun and had trouble making out who and how strong the enemy was. Two heavy American tanks on the right flank had been set ablaze after a short exchange of fire. Three or four T-34 tanks already were burning at this time on the high ground in the shadows of the houses of a small settlement. But the enemy fire didn't let up. We were hit by heavy-caliber shells which caused the instruments welded to the walls to fly all around us. We remained calm, aimed, fired, changed position, and fired again. We saw the flashes, but we couldn't make out the enemy tanks.

Then, already pretty shot up, we discovered the heavy armored platoon hidden behind some trees. We then received a direct hit on the gun barrel, disarming us. Nevertheless, the Obersturmfuehrer, leading three cover tanks, ordered them to attack. Meanwhile the other three tanks were rolling through the hollow into the village to the railroad line. Racing forward, we had been badly hit in our left tread. Obviously our driving gear also had been smashed after the first fifty meters. With a jolt the tank came to a standstill. We were thrown against the walls, shaking from the increasing impact of the heavy shells above us.

Did we think of death for one second? If anything, we cursed our bad luck and could have cried for our beautiful tank that had already shot down so many of the enemy. For half a second the commander struggled to make a decision. Then he had us dismount. We threw back the hatch and jumped out head over heels behind the tank. What happened next I have already tried to describe. Are we safe now? We were still sitting in the rifle pits in the woods and peering toward the railway embankment.

From the little village the din of the tank battle echoed over us. We felt alone and thought we had better not remain there for the enemy infantry to start hunting us down. Following the Obersturmfuehrer we leaped out into the open steppe separating us from the vanguard of our own infantry by two kilometers. Once again we were racing with death. We threw ourselves on the ground, crawled, jumped up again, and covered 500 meters

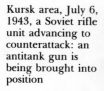
Kursk area, July 6, 1943, a Soviet rifle unit advancing to counterattack: an antitank gun is being brought into position

124

when we saw two Tigers coming over the high ground. They could be our rescuers. We jumped on the first tank and squeezed ourselves behind the turret and tried to calm down. Our pulses were racing. We winced when enemy artillery fire impacted against the turret and hull. One kilometer more, 500 meters more. Finally we reached the high ground and moved into the covered flat valley. The shelling could not reach us there.
Völkischer Beobachter, July 1943

The Battle of Kursk
6 July 1943, Moscow. A special STAVKA communiqué reports:

Since the morning of 5 July, Soviet troops in the Kursk-Orel and Belgorod sectors have been conducting heavy defensive operations against strong Fascist infantry and armored forces which, supported by many aircraft, have taken the offensive.

The enemy assaults were repelled with heavy losses to the aggressor. Some small German formations managed to penetrate our positions, but only at a few individual points. Incomplete information indicates that 586 German tanks and 203 aircraft were destroyed on the first day of fighting. The fighting is continuing. The start of the German offensive did not surprise the Soviet High Command.

de Brinon about His Trip to the Eastern Front
6 July 1943, Paris. The Office Français d'Information reports:

Ambassador de Brinon described his impressions to the representatives of the press: "As soon as I arrived in Russia, I was struck by the simple fact that two wars are being fought there, one at the front and one in the rear area. Actually not all the villages and not even all the cities are occupied. Only the major railroad and road junctions and their suburbs are defended by a well-consolidated defensive system against partisan activities."

De Brinon then described the activities of the Soviet partisan groups that the German forces were combatting so intensively. Subsequently he declared that the French Legionists were filled with a burning desire to participate in the fighting in the east. The German High Command was satisfied with their combat operations. He added that he did not know if new operations were to be expected in the near future, but one thing was certain, that the Germans did not need to conquer more territory. Their supply situation would be completely secure and preparations had been made to meet any eventualities.

From the OKW War Diary
Wednesday, 7 July 1943:

Front situation: In the Kursk area our assaults were continued with success. The penetration of the second enemy position has been accomplished. In the sector of the Northern Group, the enemy counterattacked with armor, using strong operational reserve forces. Our tank losses from enemy mines are considerable, particularly in the area of the Kempf Army.

Near Pushkarnoye, July 6, 1943, in the sector of the II SS-Panzer Corps: Tigers advancing in the front of a machine gun nest to protect the terrain already gained

Along the rest of the Eastern Front, only local clashes were reported. The Luftwaffe supported the ground fighting as on previous days despite bad weather. They flew some 3,200 missions and shot down 205 enemy planes, while losing 15 of their own aircraft.

The Tank Battle of Belgorod
By SS-war correspondent Gauss:

. . . It is 1100. Since early morning the infantry has been attacking, supported by strong Stuka dive bombers and ground-attack formations. They

126

have reached the first Bolshevist reserve position which is holding up the advance after the penetration of the front-line enemy barrier. Along the high ground stretching to the northwest there are enemy earth bunkers and trench positions echeloned. Artillery has been positioned on the reverse slope and is shelling our attacking formations. The Stukas continue to pour out their deadly loads onto the enemy positions. One enemy battery after another is knocked out. In the cornfield behind our tank-assembly area, an artillery detachment has been emplaced and has taken the enemy positions under fire. Our infantry is slowly working its way forward. Behind a thin screen of high steppe grass, the soldiers crawl forward and break into the Bolshevist trenches and bunkers. . . .

This is the hour of the tank. We are advancing along the valley floor with the Tigers flanked by medium and light companies. Our field glasses search the horizon, grope in the smoke of the battle draping the ridge containing the enemy bunkers like a theater curtain.

The leader of the Tiger half of the company, an Obersturmfuehrer from the Rhineland whose calmness ennobles us, gives the order to attack. The tank engines begin to howl as we load the guns. The heavy tanks slowly roll into the battle zone, but after 200 meters the enemy starts shooting an antitank gun. With one round, we lift it off the ground.

. . . It is now 1200. The sun is burning hot, so we have opened our hatches and are peering into the battle area. We do not receive effective fire until an hour later when we see a couple of T-34s waiting on the dominant elevation to the north. Their first shells land near us. Then hits splatter against our frontal plate. Load, unlock, shoot! A hit! We pursue. The first T-34 is burning. Our neighbor has destroyed the second, which is on fire.

The others move behind the high ground. After we have moved forward another 500 meters, about forty enemy tanks appear on the horizon. They advance past the two burning wrecks, stop, shoot, roll again, and shoot in rapid succession. Rounds splatter against our frontal plate and hull, but the shells don't do us much harm. We move forward a little again to a favorable firing position and open fire. The tank battle has begun. Approximately 1,000 meters apart on two opposite slopes lie the opposing forces facing each other like figures on a chessboard. Both want to sway fate with each shot. All the Tigers are firing now. The fighting is rising to a climax, but the men who drive and operate these fighting machines must remain calm.

They aim quickly, load quickly, respond to orders quickly. They drive a few meters forward, move to the right, then to the left, maneuver themselves out of the enemy's cross hairs, and get him into their own fire.

We count the burning torches of enemy tanks that will never again fire on German soldiers. After one hour, twelve of the T-34s are ablaze. The other thirty are circling back and forth, firing whatever they have. They shoot well, but our armor plating is very strong. We no longer wince when a steel knuckle knocks on our tank. We wipe the chipped-off slivers of paint from our faces and reload, aim, and shoot. After four hours, the first phase of the tank battle which we anticipated after breaking through the second Russian fortification line has ended victoriously.
Völkischer Beobachter, July 1943

(Left) A caricature
from *Pravda,* July
1943, entitled: De-
feated Wild Animals.
Caption: Back and
forth

(Right) "After one
day of battle, two fo-
cal points of the
German offensive
can be seen: the
burning Tiger"

The Tigers are Burning

7 July 1943, Moscow. The Sovinformburo reports:

The news that the German offensive had begun was received quite calmly
and with the greatest confidence by the military authorities and the population. Although the objectives of the offensive have not yet materialized,
from their dispositions, we can conclude that the enemy's plan is to cut off
the salient south of Orel.

Following one day of fighting, two focal points of the German offensive, Orel and Belgorod, can be identified. At both sites Hitler's troops attacked with strong tank, infantry, artillery, and air formations. These two
cities were stormed by Fascist Panzer Troops.

After the High Command of the Red Army did some regrouping under the protection of darkness, our armor and infantry formations counterattacked yesterday morning and seized the two cities from the enemy, and
pushed him further back in the course of the morning. A dogged, bloody
battle ensued, the outcome of which is still in doubt. Toward noon, however, we have learned that the Germans have brought up new reserves to
balance the Soviet superiority during the morning hours.

Our antitank defense concentrated its fire on the backbone of the German offensive thrust, the Tiger formations, which suffered heavy losses.
At least 250 of these big tanks burned out on the battlefield on the first
day. Dogged air battles were fought during the whole day along the front.
The "stormoviks" cooperated without letup in combatting the German Panzer assault, as did our new ground-attack planes firing new armor-piercing
shells.

128

Belgorod Front: Following heavy artillery preparatory fire which lasted more than an hour and which was far more intense than the one preceding the opening of the offensive, Hitler's Panzer formations followed by several divisions of motorized infantry and assault artillery attacked along a front of fifty kilometers. The impact of these mechanized formations was so violent that our units had to be withdrawn in several places in order to avoid a breakthrough. The troops, however, only withdrew to a prepared position lying about six kilometers behind the original line. This position had been consolidated and manned very carefully.

Shortly before midnight, a radio report arrived in Moscow saying that the Soviet army in the threatened front sectors had launched another counterattack and was making good progress. New, heavy, German attacks were expected on Thursday as it was learned that more reserves were on their way to the front. Last night the tactical Soviet Air Fleet again was engaged in the fighting, bombarding the concentrations of materiel and troops in the enemy's rear areas.

According to incomplete information that has just come in, the Germans have lost 520 tanks, 70 of them Tigers; 229 aircraft; and approximately 5,000 men killed today in the Battle of Orel-Belgorod. The total losses that the Hitler Wehrmacht has suffered in three days of fighting is thus increased to 1,539 tanks, 649 planes, and more than 20,000 soldiers killed. Statements from prisoners unanimously confirm that Field Marshal von Kluge is the commanding general of the German offensive.

From the OKW War Diary
Thursday, 8 July 1943:

Front situation: Heavy tank fighting is in progress in the Kursk area. Since the launching of Operation "Citadel" (5 July), a total of 460 enemy tanks have been destroyed. There has been no significant fighting on the remainder of the Eastern Front. The Luftwaffe supported the ground fighting with 4,000 missions and shot down 193 enemy aircraft.

German Successes in Shooting Down Enemy Planes
8 July 1943, Berlin. The DNB reports:

During the course of 7 July, according to preliminary reports, Luftwaffe fighters and antiaircraft artillery shot down 140 enemy planes in the

The Soviets for their part report 649 German aircraft shot down and 1539 tanks knocked out. The Germans report that within two days 637 Soviet Aircraft Downed, 300 Soviet Tanks Knocked Out

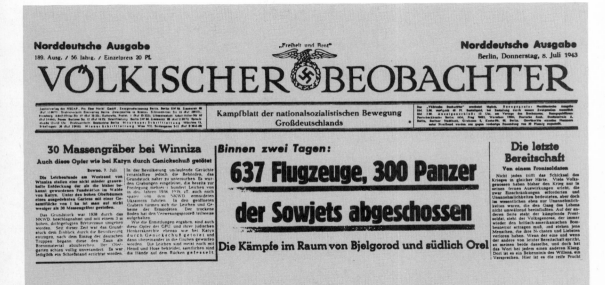

Near Muravl, south of Orel, July 1943, a Soviet rifle company on a mission: "The enemy turns every little wood into a fortress"

Belgorod operational area and south of Orel. Eight of our own planes were lost. This makes 777 Russian aircraft shot down, with only 49 of our planes lost between 5 and 7 July in this area.

Every Woods a Fortress

Soviet artillery fire which already had been surprisingly fierce was now taking on hurricane dimensions. The enemy had turned widely scattered villages and each little woods into fortresses. Rifle companies have been hidden in the ripe cornfields, dozens of heavy tank destroyers stood behind the sparse hedges, and endless swarms of tanks; T-34s and "General Lees;" and new, heavy self-propelled guns were crawling over the low ridges. Yet in our Tigers they met not only their equal but a superior adversary. . . . The third day of fighting was the hardest. Here, however, the German soldier showed he could be just as tough in attacking as the Bolshevist was in defending. He pushed back the forces in his way with sheer superhuman effort and neutralized them. With that the second line was also smashed. *Völkischer Beobachter,* July 1943

Only Insignificant Gains in Terrain
8 July 1943 Moscow. The Sovinformburo reports:

The third day of the Fascist offensive, continually growing in size due to the commitment of new reserves, brought the German formations only insignificant gains in terrain. Their successes must be rated against the heavy losses they have cost.

In contrast to the Orel Front where there are no significant changes, the Germans were able to widen somewhat their breaches at Belgorod. Toward evening our troops were back at their old front-line positions nearly everywhere and the units that were cut off temporarily by the tank breakthroughs could be relieved.

German tank losses in this sector of the front come to more than 220, of which 40 were Tigers. During the entire day there was dogged air fighting, but neither of the two adversaries was able to seize air supremacy.

130

The Greatest Battle of Matériel
8 July 1943, Berlin. The Italian agency Stefani reports:

The battle in the Kursk sector has continued to take a very satisfactory course for the German troops during the last twenty-four hours. The initiative now lies in their hands, as Berlin has established, and they are proceeding forcefully in the decisive sectors. In Berlin the fighting at Kursk is considered the greatest battle of men and matériel that has been fought in the East so far. The Russians literally had to endure a hurricane of fire and steel in their positions that they had built so elaborately since the end of the winter campaign. The Germans report innumerable obstacles, fighting positions, bunkers, wide tank ditches, and deep mine fields. Both sides have very strong tank formations.

According to a Berlin report, 20 percent of the destroyed Soviet tanks have come from the U.S.A. The Russian tank losses, by the way, are said to be very high; they came to 400 yesterday alone. This would mean that the Russians had lost approximately 700 tanks since the beginning of the battle. Significant also, according to the Berlin account, is the superiority of the German Luftwaffe. It has gained air supremacy over the battlefield, so that the Stukas and ground-attack planes effectively can support the ground troops and reinforcements can freely move forward. Military circles in Berlin have established that the operations have not yet reached their climax, so it can be deduced that the German advance may be continued in the next few days. The intentions of the German Command are top secret, of course.

The confidence that the fighting at Kursk favors the Germans has, if anything, increased since yesterday. The press continues to take pains in exercising restraint, but its tenor is quite unmistakable. It points out that recently the German soldier is proving to be superior to his Russian counterpart. The optimally trained, independent thinking and acting lone fighter is winning: the superior European against the spiritless human being of Bolshevist breeding.

In the Kursk salient, July 1943: German infantry mopping-up in the already captured terrain

131

From the OKW War Diary
Friday, 9 July 1943:

Front situation: The enemy is trying to stop the German assault in the Kursk area by committing strong armored forces. He has succeeded partially. Ninth Army's attacks were not able to penetrate the enemy's line of resistance.

In the zone of Fourth Panzer Army, 195 enemy tanks were destroyed on 8 July. At the remainder of the Eastern Front there has been no significant fighting. Strong elements of Luftflotte 4 and 6 supported the German offensive. One hundred ninety-four enemy aircraft were shot down and 13 of our planes were lost.

Heavy Soviet Counterattacks
9 July 1943, Berlin: The DNB reports:

Operations in the Kursk Salient were marked by heavy counterattacks by the Soviets, who tried to check the penetrations achieved by the Germans the day before. The fighting has been so heavy that it is now called the "Double Battle of Orel and Belgorod."

The headline in the *Nordmährische Grenzbote* (the North Moravian Frontier Courier) on July 10, 1943: *Enormous Tank Battle Between Orel-Belgorod* (*Bottom*) as this landser (private) can only confirm at his post during a lull in the fighting

The New Tactics of the German Panzer Forces
9 July 1943, Moscow. The Sovinformburo reports:

The territory captured by the Fascist invaders in the Belgorod sector in four days of fighting is only a fraction of what the Germans had gained on the first day of all their previous offensives. In these four days our troops have defended themselves successfully so that the Soviet High Command has had sufficient time to take countermeasures. The troops that have been held in reserve are now on their way forward. And the stormoviks, against which the Germans have no defense, are proving their worth once again. Hundreds of these aircraft with their armor-piercing bombs pour from the sky to attack the German tanks.

The heavy German tank losses seem to have led to a change in the tactics of their Panzer divisions. When German tanks come upon a mine field they bypass it immediately and German aircraft try to clear the mine field by dropping light bombs. This tactic, however, results in higher aircraft losses.

Another new tactic is the speed at which the Germans are operating. As soon as the Panzers encounter strong resistance they back off, and immediately turn their attention to another sector, where they try to achieve a new breakthrough. Our defenses have not been caught off guard. Wherever enemy tanks have crossed our forward positions, our infantry has not given up, but has cut the following Fascist infantry off from the tanks, and left the destruction of the tanks to the stormoviks and the special forces in the rear areas.

Fernsprechanschluß Nr. 238

Blatt erscheint jeden Dienstag,
Donnerstag und Samstag.

Schriftleitung und Verwaltung
Schönberg, Wallgasse Nr. 1.

Postspark.-Konto Breslau
Nr. 47.211.

Bezugs-Preise:
Beim Bezug durch die Post
siehe Postzeitungsliste.
Beim Bezug durch den
Verlag:
Durch Austräger
vierteljährig . . . . RM 3.50
Durch Abholen
vierteljährig . . . . RM 3.40
Anzeigen werden nach dem
aufliegenden Inseratentarif
berechnet.

Einzelpreis 9 Pfennig

Nordmährischer
Grenzbote

78   Mähr.-Schönberg, Samstag, den 10. Juli 1943   69. Jahrgang

Gewaltige Panzerschlacht
zwischen Orel — Bjelgorod

Aus dem Führerhauptquartier. Das Oberkommando der Wehrmacht gibt bekannt:

Das große Ringen im Raum Bjelgorod-Orel hat mit gesteigerter Heftigkeit an. Seit vorgestern hat sich hinter dem durchstoßenen sowjetischen Stellungssystem eine gewaltige Panzerschlacht entwickelt, in der die Sowjets die größten Anstrengungen unternahmen, unsere stetig vordringenden Verbände aufzufangen. Hierbei verlor der Feind an hohen Verlusten an Menschen abermals 120 Panzer sowie eine große Anzahl von Geschützen und Salvengeschützen. Kampf-, Sturzkampf- und Nachtgeschwader der Luftwaffe griffen in die Kämpfe ein und bekämpften vor allem neu

Front situation: Operation "Citadel" is proceeding. The Kempf Army repulsed enemy attacks on the east flank and pushed south, turning in just north of Belovskaya and cutting off an enemy group. The Fourth Panzer Army attacked farther to the north and gained ten kilometers of terrain. The Luftwaffe supported the ground fighting at the critical points and shot down 119 enemy aircraft with only 8 of our planes lost.

Evacuation of the Partisan-Infested Areas
10 July 1943:

Order to the chief of the anti-partisan formations and the Higher SS and to the police chief, Ukraine and Central Russia.

1. The Fuehrer has decided that all the inhabitants of the partisan-infested areas of the northern Ukraine and Central Russia are to be evacuated.

2. The entire male population able to work will be assigned to the Reichs Commissar for Arbeitseinsatz (planned distribution of labor) according to policies that still have to be made. However, prisoner-of-war conditions shall apply.

3. The female population and all orphans will be placed in our collecting camps.

4. The evacuated areas are to be administered by the Higher SS and police chiefs as far as possible according to an agreement with the Reichs Minister for Nutrition and the Minister for the Occupied Eastern Areas. Details are yet to be worked out. The Kok-saghyz is to be cultivated in part of the area and, so far as feasible, they are to be exploited agriculturally. The camps for children are to be situated at the edge of the areas so that they can be used for labor.

signed Himmler

From STAVKA's Point of View
10 July 1943, Moscow. The Sovinformburo reports:

The Soviet High Command is becoming increasingly convinced that the strategic objective of the Fascist offensive is restricted to cutting off the

Bubny, Belgorod area, July 10, 1943, dangerous and thankless clearing mines in the terrain just seized

134

salient in the front at Orel-Belgorod. If their operations, however, go favorably, they can be expected to extend and expand their objectives.

The fighting along the entire front, particularly at Orel and Belgorod, continued all of yesterday. It is too early to be able to say the fighting is subsiding but it is not gaining in violence.

Orel sector: After the assaults of Hitler's troops south of Orel had been unsuccessful for four days, they attacked at an adjacent front sector yesterday morning and made minor progress. In the evening the fighting along the Maloarchangelsk-Ponyri-Lgov line continued.

Belgorod sector: General Rokossovsky conducted heavy counterattacks all day long against the wedge made by German Panzer forces here yesterday. According to the latest radio reports, elements of the German tank spearhead southwest of Novy Oskol were defeated in dogged fighting with our tank brigades and acute losses were inflicted on them. The reports from the Orel Front continue to be favorable. Heavy German assaults were repelled along the Orel-Kursk railroad line; the Red Army is counterattacking.

From the OKW War Diary
Sunday, 11 July 1943:

Front situation: In the course of Operation "Citadel," we were able to narrow the Russian sector and clear the front at Belgorod. The Ninth Army gained only two to three kilometers of ground because of dogged enemy resistance. As we were unable to achieve a rapid victory, it is now essential to inflict high losses on the enemy while keeping our own losses as low as possible. To accomplish this, we must begin to relocate our own reserves. The Luftwaffe supported the ground fighting as on previous days and destroyed 126 enemy aircraft.

Vacillating Fighting
11 July 1943, Moscow. Reuters reports:

The attacks and counterattacks follow each other in rapid succession in the Belgorod sector where the Germans are trying to consolidate the positions they have gained. The situation is difficult to assess. But no enemy gains in terrain have been reported since last Friday. German Panzer forces with Tiger tanks leading them have attacked at different points near Belgorod. Russian artillery is combatting these German tanks successfully.

Behind the Scenes:
Army Group South
Calm reigned for nearly 100 days. On Sunday, 4 July 1943, the weather first was hot and humid. Near Belgorod south of the Kursk Salient, final preparations for Operation "Citadel" were in progress at Army Group South. Field Marshal von Manstein: "On 4 July, the headquarters of the Army Group with a tactical operations staff moved close to the front to be able to command the operations of both its armies. Our command train was parked in a woods and served as our command post. It consisted of one railroad car each for living and working for

135

A Squadron of Ju 87D Stukas approaching their target: The "fire-brigade of the air," lightly armed and too slow, it hardly had a chance against modern Soviet fighter planes

the chief of staff and me. There were working and sleeping cars and a dining car for Section Ia (Operations section) and a reduced Section Ic (Enemy Intelligence section) and other people whose presence was absolutely indispensable. A telephone and radio car and cars for the staff guard and for 20mm air defense artillery also were present."

Exactly at 1450, screaming Stuka squadrons dove at Soviet fortifications. It suddenly started to rain and the Battle of Kursk began. Following the air attack, the artillery opened its fire for effect, then at 1530, the Fourth Army's divisions (Colonel General Hoth) attacked the southern part of the Soviet defensive line in the Kursk Salient between Belgorod in the east and the village of Rakitnoye in the west. Their objective was to seize the ridge in their front to obtain a better line of departure for the offensive, which was scheduled to begin the following morning. Approximately 800 Stukas, other bombers, and ground-attack planes, plus antitank squadrons supported the attacks of the Fourth Army's formations in their thrusts forward through the strong Soviet defensive line of the Sixth Guards Army (Lieutenant General Chistyakov). On their way to their assembly areas, one-quarter of all the Fourth Army tanks of Panther Brigade broke down with mechanical defects in the deep mud produced by the torrential rain.

The chief of the Soviet General Staff, Marshal Vasilevsky: "On 4 July, at 1600, the enemy conducted a forceful reconnaissance with approximately four battalions supported by twenty tanks and artillery and air forces over a wide sector of the Voronezh Front. All attempts to penetrate our first defensive line were defeated." Several tanks were immobilized by the fire of the Soviet artillery.

Meanwhile, the 11th Panzer Division (Lieutenant General Balck) and the Panzer Grenadier Division "Grossdeutschland" (Lieutenant General Hoernlein) pushed forward toward Butovo. On the right flank, the three combat groups of II SS-Panzer Corps (SS-Obergruppenf. Hausser) seized the high ground near Yakhontov and Streletskoye. The outposts of the Sixth Guards Army were thrown back to the main line of resistance and the antitank regiment of "Grossdeutschland" and the 11th Panzer Division stormed the ridge near Butovo with the mission of neutralizing its observation posts.

At 1645 German artillery observers began to direct fire from the captured high ground toward the Soviet defensive lines lying before them. In the assault section of the XLVIII Panzer Corps (General of the Pz. Tr. von Knobelsdorff) Panzer Grenadiers and motorized rifle units thrust forward. Supported by assault gun and combat engineer units, they rolled over forward enemy positions and reached Cherkaskoye southwest of Alexeyevka by evening. But the men of the Panzer Grenadier Regiment 394 of the 3rd Panzer Division (Lieutenant General Westhoven) were held up by the defensive fire of the Soviet 71st Guards Rifle Division (Colonel Sivakov) at the Gertsovka hills. They did not reach their objective until dark.

Army Group Center

Meanwhile, 200 kilometers farther to the north at Army Group Center's front near Orel between Maloarchangelsk and Trosna, the situation was still calm. The Ninth Army (Colonel General Model) was waiting for the order to take the offensive.

On that evening, General of the Army Rokossovsky insured that the mine fields in front of the main line of resistance of the Central Front were guarded very closely. Toward 2200, a Soviet patrol of the Thirteenth Army (Lieutenant General Pukhov) encountered a German minesweeper unit south of Tagino. Taken prisoner, Lance-corporal Bruno Fermella made the following statement: "Today, on 4 July 1943, the Fuehrer had our engineer unit fall in and ordered us to tape paths through the mine fields together with the privates." Fermella belonged to the engineer battalion of the Rhine-Westphalian 6th Infantry Division (Lieutenant General Grossmann). During his interrogation, this Slovak reported that the German troops would attack through the cleared mine paths in a few hours at 0330, following a short artillery preparation, and that the formations were in their attack positions. General of the Army Rokossovsky, commander of the Central Front: "There was only a single hour left. Were the prisoners' statements credible? If they were the truth, the planned artillery preparation fire would have to begin immediately. . . ."

In the evening of 4 July 1943, the major unit commanders of the Soviet army were all at their forward observation posts. General of the Army Vatutin of the Voronezh Front commenced prearranged artillery fire on the German dug-in positions at 2230. Meanwhile, other reports of Lance-corporal Fermella's statement arrived at Central Front headquarters where Marshal Zhukov happened to be located at that moment. Zhukov immediately decided to shell the German attack positions facing the Central Front.

During the night of 4/5 July 1943, Hitler's proclamation signed on 4 July was read to all the units: "Today you will engage in a great offensive battle, the outcome of which can be decisive for the war. Your victory must convince the world more than ever before that any resistance to the German Wehrmacht is ultimately futile. . . !"

At 0110, the Soviets surprised the Germans with fire of previously unheard-of intensity: artillery, volley-firing guns of every caliber, mortars, and other heavy weapons. All these arms were directed at the German main attack line, his second line, rear area, approach routes, and specific jump-off positions. The German infantry and Panzer formations preparing for the assault and the artillery batteries, observation posts, staffs, munition, and fuel dumps all experienced a horrific hail of fire. Some 2,460 guns, mortars, and Katyushas of the Soviet Thirteenth Army and Sixth and Seventh Guards Armies were engaged in the shelling. So as not to betray the positions of the Soviet antitank defense units, their artillery remained silent. It looked as though a major Soviet offensive was imminent. The shelling subsided after an hour, but it had inflicted heavy losses on the German assault positions. As a result, the German High Command had to postpone the offensive against the Central Front for two and one-half hours and against the Voronezh Front for three hours in order to regain control of their commands.

Army Group South

On Monday, 5 July 1943, at 0330, the assault of Army Group South with the Kempf Army (General of Pz. Tr. Kempf) plus the Fourth Panzer

Army (Colonel General Hoth) began with a total of seven infantry divisions, eleven tank divisions, and three assault gun brigades. The main effort was led by the German XLVIII Panzer Corps (General of Pz. Tr. von Knobelsdorff) and the II SS-Panzer Corps (SS-Obergruppenf. Hausser) with approximately 700 tanks against the Sixth Guards Army (Lieutenant General Chistyakov) along the main road to Oboyan. In the sector of the Seventh Guards Army (Lieutenant General Shumilov), the III Panzer Corps (General of Pz. Tr. Breith) and Special Duty Corps Raus (General of Pz. Tr. Raus) with approximately 300 tanks tried to push forward in the direction of Korotcha.

Using formations of the 6th Panzer Division (Major General von Huenersdorff) and the 168th Infantry Division (Major General Châles de Beaulieu), the Raus Corps attacked at Belgorod to the north toward Stary Gorod, with one combat group moving through to Chernaya Polyana. The 19th Panzer Division (Lieutenant General G. Schmidt) advancing from the Belgorod bridgehead to the southeast carried the attack to Mikhailovka. There, however, it got held up, but the 7th Panzer Division (Lieutenant General Freiherr von Funck) encountered weaker resistance and was able to build a bridgehead west of Dorogobushino, near Solomino. The part of Belgorod that lay on the western bank of the Donets already had been evacuated before the assault began.

Lieutenant General Katukov, commander of the First Tank Army: "Like probably everyone who knew of the impending offensive, I was not able to sleep on the night of 5 July. Driven by an inner restlessness I jumped out of bed and looked at the clock; it was 0230. I washed quickly and went outdoors. The grass was wet with dew. On the horizon the morning was dawning. The silence seemed infinite and indestructible."

When the German bomber group took off on 5 July 1943 at 0300, air reconnaissance reported 132 Soviet ground-attack and 285 fighter planes approaching the airstrips of the VII Air Corps of Luftflotte 4 (General of Air Force Dessloch). In this air battle which began at dawn, German fighters, including Fighter Squadron 3 "Udet," in a very short time shot down 120 Soviet aircraft, winning for VIII Air Corps air supremacy in the southern sector. During the course of the day, the Germans shot down a total of 432 aircraft, losing only 26 of their own planes. Lieutenant General Shtemenko, chief of Operational Administration in the Soviet General Staff: "Some of our fighter planes had been sent to the Kursk Salient with poorly trained pilots. From this report, Stalin concluded that all the fighter-plane crews were not up to standards. Fortunately, as it turned out, things were not as tragic as believed; the crews could be exchanged fairly quickly."

At 0330 the ground-attack and Stuka squadrons of the 1st Air Division attached to Luftflotte 6 (Colonel General Ritter von Greim) took off to attack Soviet defensive positions. Stuka Squadron 1 (Lieutenant Colonel Pressler) attacked the important junction of Maloarchangelsk, the largest city in the area being attacked by Ninth Army (Colonel General Model). Simultaneously, artillery fire began in preparation for the assault. In the cloudless morning sky, an endless stream of Stuka and bomber squadrons appeared, approaching their objectives with fighter escorts.

Army Group Center
At 0530, following intense artillery preparation and ground-attack air

Belgorod area, 3:30 A.M. on July 5, 1943: Army Group South launches its attack

Krasnaya Sloboda–
Verkhne Tagino
area, July 5, 1943:
German forces ad-
vance toward Olk-
hovatka

support, Army Group Center (FM von Kluge) launched the attack on Kursk
from the north with formations of Ninth Army from the area west of Maloarchangelsk. These forces were deployed over approximately forty kilometers. The focal point of the offensive was in the area of the Soviet Thirteenth Army (Lieutenant General Pukhov) and the adjacent Forty-eighth
Army (Lieutenant General Romanenko) as well as the Seventieth Army
(Lieutenant General Galinin) between Olkhovatka-Maloarchangelsk-Gni-
lets. The XLI Panzer Corps (General of Pz. Tr. Harpe) and the XLVII
Panzer Corps (General of Pz. Tr. Lemelsen) provided the main effort with
three Infantry divisions and two Panzer divisions. They attacked from the
Krasnaya-Sloboda–Verkhne-Tagino area toward Olkhovatka.

In order to widen the breach in the flanks, the XXIII Army Corps
(General of Infantry Friessner) thrust forward simultaneously against Maloarchangelsk with two infantry divisions and with three infantry divisions
of the XLVI Panzer Corps (General of Infantry Zorn) against Gnilets. In
the direction of Olkhovatka the Germans committed approximately 300 tanks,
among them heavy Tiger tanks and Ferdinand assault guns. Strong bomber
squadrons attacked the positions of the Soviet Thirteenth Army without
letup in order to prepare the way for the Panzer formations. Particularly
dogged resistance was shown by the soldiers of the Soviet Seventieth Army
made up of members of the NKVD and of frontier guard forces from the
Far East, Transbaikalia, and Central Asia.

At 0620 the formations of Ninth Army launched another attack in the
northern part of the Kursk Salient. After nearly one hour of artillery preparation, Tigers, Ferdinands, and Hornets rolled forward escorted by sev-

140

eral hundred Panzer IVs and infantry mounted on combat vehicles. They penetrated the positions of the 15th and 81st Rifle Divisions of the Thirteenth Army. Colonel General Model employed assault tactics on the northern front of the Kursk Salient different from those employed by Marshal von Manstein with his Army Group South. The infantry was supposed to force the breakthrough, not the tank formations.

Army Group South

In the southern part of the Kursk Salient, the Fourth Panzer Army succeeded, supported by the Luftwaffe, in gaining a few kilometers of terrain. The II SS-Panzer Corps even reached the intermediate zone, but it was unable to penetrate the second Soviet position. The 7th Panzer Division

In the Stary Gorod sector, July 5, 1943, a shot-up Tiger from the 6th Pz.Div.: "Even Tigers can't make headway"

141

(Lieutenant General Freiherr von Funck) of the III Panzer Corps crossed the Donets west of Dorogobushino. Then it pushed through Soviet field fortifications and reached Razumnoye. At that point, a strong Soviet counterthrust stopped their advance. Army Group South owed some of its successes to Stalin himself. On the basis of a Soviet Secret Service report, he believed that the German main effort would not come from the south, but from Ninth Army in the north. Therefore, Stalin ordered STAVKA to shift strong forces from the Voronezh Front (General of the Army Vatutin) to the Central Front (General of the Army Rokossovsky). Thus Vatutin did not have enough strength to resist the initial German onslaught.

Major General Popiel, member of the Headquarters Staff of the 1st Panzer Army: "The regiments were hardly in combat for an hour and already one-third of their guns were knocked out of action. The crews were decimated. The German Luftwaffe was more responsible for our losses than the Panzers." At 1200 the German 6th Panzer Division (Major General von Huenersdorff) reported: "A deep mine field supported by enfilade fire of sharpshooters and machine guns from gun slits permitted only a small force to penetrate in the vicinity of Stary Gorod. Even Tigers were not able to go forward. The advance discontinued. We withdrew our troops in the afternoon."

Army Group Center

In the northern part of the Kursk Salient, the Ninth Army pushed forward despite dogged Soviet resistance, forcing the Soviet 15th and 81st Divisions to retreat. Following hard fighting and heavy losses, the attack of Ninth Army, however, bogged down after approximately ten kilometers. Two-thirds of their tanks were already lost. Even the attempts of the engineer battalions to break through the Soviet positions were useless, so Field Marshal von Kluge ordered the assault to stop. General Lemelsen: "Here it must be pointed out once again that the Russians were masters of camouflage. Neither mine fields nor antitank weapons could be detected anywhere before the time the first tank had moved into the mine field or the first Russian gun unexpectedly had opened fire."

Army Group South

The attack of Fourth Panzer Army in the southern part of the Kursk Salient now lost impact. As the left-wing division of the Kempf Army was lagging, II SS-Panzer Corps had to swing part of its formations to the east to protect its flank. The XLVIII Panzer Corps (General of Pz. Tr. von Knobelsdorff) was held up until late afternoon a few kilometers in front of the first enemy position by a heavily defended, swampy brook area. The deep Soviet defensive system with numerous dug-in tanks, trenches, strong points, mine fields, and tank obstacles prevented the German assault forces from moving any faster than step by step.

The Panzer regiments hit the Soviet mine fields and defensive fire head on. Although the new Tiger and Panther tanks destroyed many Soviet tanks, no decisive breakthrough occurred in either northern or southern sectors.

Within a short time the attacking grenadiers were held down by Soviet machine-gun fire. The heavy tanks and assault guns also were unable to assert themselves as was hoped. This was the price for an oversight of the German designers: Ferdinand, the new super-heavy assault gun, a real

142

monster weighing sixty-eight tons, covered with practically invulnerable armor and armed with the reliable 88mm cannon, could be destroyed in close combat by any Soviet infantryman with an explosive charge. It had not been equipped with even a single machine gun to defend itself. So, the crews had to waste their precious 88mm shells on single attacking infantrymen. Colonel General Guderian: ". . . literally shooting sparrows with cannons."

Army Group Center

In the north, at Army Group Center, the XLVII Panzer Corps (General of Pz. Tr. Lemelsen) leading the main effort fought its way through up to eight kilometers of the Soviet defensive system, but was soon threatened on its flanks by Soviet formations. The XXIII Army Corps (General of Infantry Friessner) advancing to cover the left flank in the Maloarchangelsk line encountered strong resistance halfway there. General of the Army Rokossovsky: "I ordered the commander of the Sixteenth Air Army to reattack the enemy at the breaches. Rudenko immediately had 200 fighters and 150 bombers take off. Their attacks slowed the Germans' pace and made it possible to move the 17th Rifle Division, two antitank brigades, and a mortar brigade into this sector. With their help we were able to hold up the enemy's advance."

Army Group South

At Army Group South, the Kempf Army reached the crossing over the Donets south of Belgorod. Its troops penetrated a Soviet position lying at the railroad embankment three kilometers east of the river, while at the same time a Panzer division broke through the southern section. Major General Popiel: "The fighting was exceptionally hard. Within a few hours all that was left of our two antitank regiments were their numbers. But, these will be recorded in the history of the First Armored Army."

Meanwhile at Belgorod and north of the city, the German assault became bogged down in the fortress-like defensive system. The ensuing battle through the defensive line was extremely violent. The Soviets were resisting doggedly and obstinately everywhere. The insufficient number of infantry divisions caused serious consequences from the beginning when it came to fighting through the prepared enemy positions, particularly in Army Group South.

At Army Group South, the 6th Panzer Division (Major General von Huenersdorff) of the III Panzer Corps (General of Pz. Tr. Breith) reported at 1600 that it had discontinued its attack on Stary Gorod. He did this because the town could only be captured from the south at great sacrifice, disproportionate to its success. The XLVIII Panzer Corps (General of Pz. Tr. von Knobelsdorff), however, managed despite the tenacious resistance of 67th Guards Rifle Division to penetrate the Soviet lines and cross the Psel. Major General Popiel: "The German infantry bypassed our emplacements and infiltrated between the batteries. The tenacity of the Fascists bordered on insanity. They fought to break through our defenses and occupy the road to Oboyan no matter what the losses. The infantry at our first echelon was routed and the artillery regiments were smashed. The remaining infantry elements retreated to the north. All that was left at the emplacements were wrecked guns and dead soldiers."

The advance on Oboyan was in full progress. Field Marshal von Man-

South of Belgorod, July 5, 1943, steering clear of the fighting with what they have left of their belongings: the last wagons of a refugee trek

143

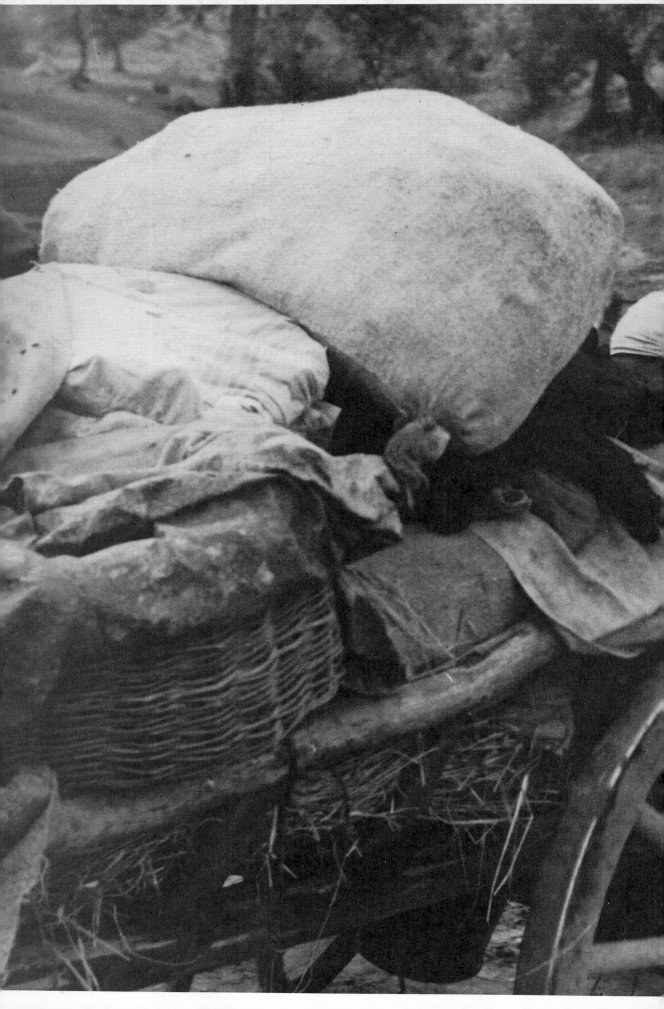

stein: "In the assault, the right-wing corps, the XI Army Corps (General of Pz. Tr. Raus) of the Kempf Army did not succeed in reaching the Korotcha sector, which was planned as the new phase line, but was able only to get to the hills west of the Koren sector."

Late in the afternoon on 5 July 1943, the II SS-Panzer Corps finally succeeded in breaking through the antitank defenses and the artillery positions of the 52nd Guards Rifle Division and penetrated twenty kilometers into the Soviet defensive system. Marshal Zhukov: "In the afternoon the enemy began a second advance with heavy Tiger tanks. This time he succeeded in breaking the resistance of the 52nd Guards Rifle Division under the command of Colonel Nekrassov. Several localities fell to the enemy. The adjacent 67th Guards Rifle Division of Colonel Baksov, being under great pressure, had to evacuate Cherkaskoye and withdraw to Krasny Pochinok."

Until sundown, German troops pushed forward, with enormous losses, some six to eight kilometers in the line of the main thrust in the northern sector. Colonel General Konev, commander of the Steppe Military District: "In the evening of 5 July the High Command of the Central Front decided to attack the following morning the main body of the enemy's troops advancing toward Olkhovatka west of the railroad line Orel-Kursk. To do this, three tank and two rifle corps were brought up."

On the evening of 5 July 1943, Luftflotte 4 could report a total of 303 Soviet aircraft shot down and Luftflotte 6 approximately 120, both with negligible losses of their own planes. During the night of 5/6 July 1943, the III Panzer Corps (General of Pz. Tr. Breith) positioned all his forces on the eastern bank of the Donets. The 6th Panzer Division (Major General von Huenersdorff) was moved behind the 7th Panzer Division (Lieutenant General Freiherr von Funck). The 168th Infantry Division (Major General Châles de Beaulieu) was ordered to advance with the 19th Panzer Division (Lieutenant General G. Schmidt) against positions on the high ground northeast of Belgorod.

Army Group Center

In the first morning hours of 6 July 1943, the fighting continued with undiminished vigor in the northern sector of the Kursk Salient. Stukas and other bombers appeared in the sky as early as 0230 to attack the approaching Soviet armored reserves. Lieutenant General Katukov, commander of

Podsoborovka area: during the night from the 5th to the 6th of July 1943, heavy rocket launchers supporting the German tank assault from the north in the direction of Kursk

146

First Tank Army: "Toward morning, the enemy succeeded in pushing back the 2nd, 67th, and 71st Rifle Divisions. But he did not suspect that our well-camouflaged tanks were waiting for him. As we later learned from prisoners, we had managed to move our tanks forward unnoticed into the combat formations of the Sixth Guards Army. At 0300 the enemy resumed his attack on Sixth Army. . . . Moreover, there was a secondary effort from the Belgorod area toward Korotcha. An endless stream of aircraft hung in the sky." Now Colonel General Model ordered 2nd Panzer Division (Lieutenant General Lübbe), 9th Panzer Division (Lieutenant General Scheller), and 18th Panzer Division (Major General von Schlieben) into the battle. The 4th Panzer (Lieutenant General von Saucken) and 12th Panzer Divisions (Lieutenant General Freiherr von Bodenhausen) with the 10th Panzer Grenadier Division (Lieutenant General A. Schmidt) continued to be held in reserve. Lieutenant General Katukov: "Clouds of dust darkened the early morning sky like an eclipse of the sun. In front rolled Tigers and Panthers like a steel shield, then came light tanks and behind them armored personnel carriers."

Following a bombardment by heavy artillery, the Central Front (General of the Army Rokossovsky) launched its counterattack at 0350. Covered by ground-attack aircraft, the XVII Guards Rifle Corps (Major General Bondariev), the 107th Brigade (Colonel Tielakov), and the 164th Brigade (Lieutenant Colonel Kopylov) of the XVI Armored Corps (Major General Grigoriev) attacked. They pushed forward out of the Olkhovatka area to the north and with the XIX Armored Corps (Major General Vasilyev) from Samodurovka to the northwest. This was meant to restore the situation at the left wing of the Thirteenth Army (Lieutenant General Pukhov).

In the northern sector of the Central Front, General of the Army Rokossovsky ordered some of the tanks to be buried for use as armored pillboxes. The other tanks were to be employed only against infantry and armored personnel carriers. This tactic held up the assault of the German Ninth Army for four days on the line Maloarchangelsk-Nikolskoye. General of the Army Rokossovsky: "The situation dictated this order. There had been cases of our tank commanders rushing at the Tigers in the heat of a counterattack and being thrown back with heavy casualties behind the infantry."

Yakovlevo area, July 6, 1943, the 1st SS-Pz.Div. "Leibstandarte Adolf Hitler" attacking: "100 tanks and assault guns per kilometer of front"

Army Group South

In the southern part of the Kursk Salient near Belgorod the XLVIII Panzer Corps (General of Pz. Tr. von Knobelsdorff) broke through the first line of the Soviet defensive system and penetrated the second line marked by heroic individual actions and enormous difficulties with the terrain.

On the morning of 6 July 1943, the II SS-Panzer Corps (SS-Obergruppenf. Hausser) assigned to Army Group South prepared for a new operation. All the Tigers of the 1st SS-Panzer Division "Leibstandarte Adolf Hitler" (SS-Brigadef. Wisch) just had been refueled and reloaded. They moved north toward the Psel knee. Simultaneously the 3rd SS-Panzer Division "Das Reich" (SS-Gruppenf. Krueger) pushed forward in the direction of Teterevino. Approximately 120 tanks of the II SS-Panzer Corps rolled along the Belgorod-Oboyan road.

Fierce fighting erupted in the Yakovlevo area, where the 1st Armored Guards Brigade and the 51st Guards Rifle Division were locked in battle with the 1st SS-Panzer Division "Leibstandarte Adolf Hitler." The Germans launched repeated, massive tank attacks. In some sectors the density reached 100 tanks and assault guns per kilometer of front. Lieutenant General Katukov: "The enemy had been attacking the XXXI Armored Corps without letup since 1000. Toward morning 160 tanks advanced in four columns, marching from the Chapayev-Shepelovka area and tried to force their way across the little river Pena. Here, however, the Fascists were subjected to the artillery fire of the VI Armored Corps, the 86th Independent Armored Brigade, and the 59th Independent Armored Regiment."

By 1100 German tanks had fought their way past the 155th Guards

Rifle Regiment's positions. Now they pushed westward toward the 151st Guards Rifle Regiment's sector. The last obstacle south of the Belgorod-Kursk road had been neutralized. Lieutenant General Dragunsky, commander of the 1st Mechanized Brigade: "At 1100, following artillery preparation and supported by hundreds of tanks, enemy infantry renewed its attack against the 67th Guards Rifle Division (Colonel Baksov) and the 52nd Guards Rifle Division (Colonel Nekrassov) of the Sixth Guards Army (Lieutenant General Chistyakov). At about 1500 the Fascists succeeded in pushing our divisions back after dogged fighting. Our men withdrew to the second defensive line, where elements of General Katukov's armored troops were positioned for defense."

Lieutenant Katukov: "Although it was noon, it seemed like twilight with the dust and smoke hiding the sky. Plane engines screamed as machine-gun bursts of fire rattled. Our fighter planes tried to drive the enemy bombers back and prevent them from dropping their fatal loads on our positions. Our observation post was only four kilometers from the forward line, but we were not able to see what was happening in front because a sea of fire and smoke cut off our sight."

After the regiment "Der Fuehrer" took the village of Luchki, the II SS-Panzer Corps was twenty kilometers deep in the defensive line of the Sixth Guards Army. Major General Popiel: "In front of us was a horrifying picture of the combat that had just ended. The ground was torn up with trenches and bomb craters. Columns of smoke were rising on the horizon. The remaining platoons, companies, and battalions gathered in the furrowed trenches." An enormous tank battle was developing in the south of Oboyan.

Near Luchki, July 6, 1943, a lull in the fighting in the sector of the II SS-Panzer Corps: "20 km deep into the defense lines of the 6th Guards Army . . ."

149

The ground was trembling from the bursting shells and bombs and from the din of the tanks. The smoke of the burning tanks changed the color of the sky and made the horizon disappear.

Army Group Center

In the northern part of the Kursk Salient the newly arrived Soviet reserves stopped the advance of the Ninth Army at Maloarchangelsk. The XLVII Panzer Corps (General of Pz. Tr. Lemelsen), however, managed to repel the Soviet armored corps and an infantry corps pushing forward from the Teploye-Olkhovatka area, but only after hard fighting. But, the XLI Panzer Corps (General of Pz. Tr. Harpe) linking up from the east gained ground.

On the afternoon of 6 July 1943, the Austrian 9th Panzer Division (Lieutenant General Scheller) entered the action. It attacked Ponyri which was being defended by the 307th Rifle Division (Major General Yenshin), but encountered hard resistance from Thirteenth Army (Lieutenant General Pukhov), which had been reinforced in time with Katyusha-rockets and antitank guns. In the sector of Army Group Center, it was possible to liberate German prisoners in the captured Russian positions. They had fallen into the hands of the Soviets at Stalingrad and told of hard labor and meager rations.

In the northern part of the Kursk Salient, the attack of the XXIII Army Corps (General of Infantry Friessner) failed at Maloarchangelsk. The posture of the Red Army clearly showed that the Soviets wanted to hold onto the Kursk Salient as a base of operations at all costs. At Ponyri a violent tank battle ensued. By committing strong operational reserves, STAVKA tried to stop the XLI Panzer Corps from breaking into the open. The XLVII Panzer Corps had moved forward about five kilometers, but the XLVI Panzer Corps (General of Infantry Zorn) on the right was lagging nearly five kilometers behind. An open flank was threatening to develop here. The XLI Panzer Corps was trying hard to seize the many villages around Ponyri. On the left the XLI Panzer Corps was engaged in hard defensive combat and was not making any headway.

Army Group South

On the evening of 6 July 1943, the second day of fighting, Army Group South had to commit nearly 30 percent of its tank forces—three Panzer divisions, in order to secure its flanks. This hindered Field Marshal von Manstein from striking a concentrated blow in his main effort. The Kempf Army met unexpectedly hard resistance, but was able, nevertheless, to advance slowly to the high ground between the Donets and the Koren rivers. The fiercest fighting was in the area of the second defensive line of the Sixth Guards Army (Lieutenant General Chistyakov) near Yakovlevo. The Kempf Army with its relatively weak forces was not able to advance to the east bank of the Korotcha River and simultaneously strike to the north to secure the east flank of the Fourth Panzer Army (Colonel General Hoth). The II SS-Panzer Corps took advantage of the momentarily lessening resistance and threw the Soviet troops out of Teterevino southwest of Prokhorovka.

All afternoon, strong Soviet armored formations had been harassing the flank of the II SS-Panzer Corps from the east. Lieutenant General Dra-

151

North of Sobrovka, July 6, 1943, a limbered 88mm Flak antiaircraft gun blocks a breakthrough attempt by Soviet tanks: "approximately 1000 tanks and assault guns in action on each side"

South of Zmiyevo, on the evening of July 6, 1943: the Panzeraufkla-rungsabteilung 9 (tank reconnaissance detachment) from the 9th Pz.Div. on the march

gunsky: "Individual groups of German tanks were able to break through our defenses and advance to the lines of the 3rd Mechanized Brigade only in the area of hill 247.2." At Yakovlevo-Luchki, formations of the II SS-Panzer Corps were able to penetrate the Soviet second defensive line in the sector of Sixth Guards Army.

To reinforce the Voronezh Front, STAVKA ordered the Fifth Guards Tank Army (Lieutenant General Rotmistrov) from the strategic reserves of the Steppe Military District (Colonel General Konev) to advance toward Oskol. This army had to cover great distances in a forced march. The weather was hot and the troops were marching on dirt roads. The heat and dust were very hard on the crews of the tanks, self-propelled guns, and personnel carriers of both sides.

Army Group Center

On the evening of 6 July 1943, heavy Panzer Detachment 505 (Major Savant) assigned to the XLVI Panzer Corps (General of Infantry Zorn) stormed Soborovka in the northern part of the Kursk Salient with its Tiger tanks. More and more Soviet tanks were thrown into the battle until approximately 1,000 tanks and assault guns were in action on both sides. The Germans tried to seize the crucial hills of Olkhovatka from the Soviets with hill 274 the central point. This high ground was the key to the city of Kursk and Army Group Center's objective.

At the same time Colonel General Model demanded the release of the 4th Panzer Division (Lieutenant General von Saucken) without which the breakthrough to Kursk was probably not feasible. But the primary reason that the strong, German armored assaults failed was the Soviet antitank defense. The fierceness of the fighting escalated visibly. The German Command tried to support its assaults with Stuka and bomber attacks, but the Luftwaffe, despite great successes, was unable to provide the army with effective support, operationally or tactically. Moreover, shortages and fuel scarcity made themselves felt increasingly. The fire did not subside until darkness. The Panzer crews had not slept for forty-eight hours and when they stopped the evening of 6 July, they dropped to the ground beside their tanks and fell asleep immediately.

Army Group South

The German assault in the southern part of the Kursk Salient on the right flank of the Voronezh Front (General of the Army Vatutin) defeated

152

II Guards Armored Corps of the front reserve, two rifle divisions of Sixty-ninth Army (Lieutenant General Kryuchenkin), and other mobile defense detachments at the Lipovy Donets.

Meanwhile, STAVKA began to commit its strategic reserves at the Voronezh Front sector. At 2300 the Fifth Guards Tank Army (Lieutenant General Rotmistrov) was ordered by the commander of the Steppe Military District, Colonel General Konev, to form up on the west bank of the Oskol River. Rotmistrov was assigned a deployment area thirty to thirty-five kilometers long. The Soviet XVIII and XXIX Armored Corps advanced on two roads. The V Mechanized Guards Corps moved forward as the second echelon. The 5th Independent Guards Motorcycle Regiment, the 53rd Guards Armored Regiment, the 689th Antitank Defense Artillery Regiment, and a battery of the 678th Artillery Howitzer Regiment had the mission of securing the Fifth Guards Tank Army's marshalling area, whose elements had a distance of nearly 300 kilometers to march.

Army Group Center

Hoping to achieve a breakthrough from the north via Olkhovatka toward Kursk, the Ninth Army (Colonel General Model) gathered its forces in this sector for a new thrust. The German Command did not suspect at this time that the Central Front (General of the Army Rokossovsky) was reinforcing the vulnerable boundary between Seventieth Army (Lieutenant General Galinin) and Thirteenth Army (Lieutenant General Pukhov) with the reserves of Sixty-fifth Army. Lieutenant General Batov, commanding general of Sixty-fifth Army: "We were afraid that the enemy might notice the partial withdrawal of our troops, so we planned to adopt operational camouflage measures on the morning of 8 July. All day we dispatched motor vehicles, tractors, and small-infantry columns from the rear area toward the front. Trucks dragged the tops of pine trees behind them, raising a lot of dust to give the impression of columns marching. Assuming that we were bringing up strong forces to the forward line, the enemy took the empty valleys, gorges, and woods under ceaseless artillery and mortar fire."

By relocating the artillery-antitank reserves of Thirteenth Army, the Central Front now succeeded in building up a tremendous concentration of antitank defenses for the battle for Ponyri—approximately seventy guns per kilometer of front. This was designed to stop the massive German Panzer assaults. General of the Army Rokossovsky: "On 7 July, at dawn, the

(*Left*) A Ju 87 G-1 type ground-attack aircraft, the "flying Pak" (antitank gun), of the 10th (Pz)/SG 2 (Lt. Koral) equipped with two 37mm Flak 18 anti-aircraft guns, taking off to combat tanks

enemy initiated the attack on Ponyri. The ground trembled from the detonations of the bombs, mortars, and mines; the thunder of the guns; the roar of the engines; and the clanking of the treads." At the same time the attack on Olkhovatka continued. Heated combat occurred at the second defensive line. In the Ponyri area the 307th Rifle Division (Major General Yenshin) repelled all attacks. Ferocious fighting spread along the entire front of Ninth Army. In spite of Soviet counterattacks, the German formations slowly gained ground southward along a front of ten kilometers.

Army Group South

In the southern part of the Kursk Salient, the German assault was directed against III Mechanized and the XXXI Armored Corps of First Tank Army (Lieutenant General Katukov). Particularly dogged fighting occurred in the sector of the 1st and 3rd Mechanized Brigade in the Syrtsevo area. Army Group South assigned Fourth Panzer Army (Colonel General Hoth) the task of capturing the high ground north of the road Prokhorovka-Oboyan. Even this was difficult to achieve, as Fourth Panzer Army clashed with approaching Soviet armored reserves earlier than anticipated. On the same day, Fourth Panzer Army was attacked from the east across the Lipovy Donets, from the northeast via Prokhorovka, and from the north and northwest from both sides of the Oboyan-Yakovlevo road by several armored and mechanized Red Army corps. The XI Army Corps (General of Pz. Tr. Raus) of the Kempf Army after a hard fight reached the high ground approximately six kilometers east of the railroad line Belgorod-Volchansk.

In the strip of woods on the west bank of the Korenye brook, XI Army Corps finally was forced to go on the defensive. Panzer Grenadier Division "Grossdeutschland" (Lieutenant General Hoernlein) became bogged down in the second Soviet line of resistance facing earth bunkers with dug-in T-34s, antitank guns, and flamethrowers, as well as strong artillery fire. Some of the Panzer Grenadiers were stuck right in the middle of the enemy's combat zone. Numerous tanks were knocked out by mines or Soviet ground-attack planes. General von Knobelsdorff: "Russian resistance rekindled even in the terrain that had already been won during the first days of the offensive." Nevertheless spearheads of XLVIII Panzer Corps (General of Pz. Tr. von Knobelsdorff) with 11th Panzer Division (Lieutenant General Balck) and Panzer Grenadier Division "Grossdeutschland" succeeded in pushing

(*Center*) A Soviet T 34/76B tank with smoke-candle containers on the rear hull, after being attacked by a Ju 87 G-1

(*Right*) Another burned-out Soviet tank: a T 34/76D, the victim of a Ju 87 G-1 attack

Oboyan road, July 8,
1943: killed by a
shell fragment, an
infantryman lying
somewhere along-
side the dusty sup-
ply line

forward along both sides of the road to Oboyan within ten kilometers of the town. Soviet Major General Popiel: "7 July was filled with dangerous moments. The enemy broke through our second defensive positions along the line dividing First Tank Army and V Guards Armored Corps. Our army now faced not only to the south but also to the east. This made its front lines ten kilometers longer than before. Our troop strength, however, had dwindled considerably."

Panzer Grenadier Division "Grossdeutschland" succeeded in reaching the crucial hill 230 on both sides of Syrtsevo. The Soviet infantry formations escaping in the direction of Syrtsevo and Gremuchi suffered heavy losses from German artillery fire, but the Panzer Grenadiers got bogged down at Syrtsevo in front of strong antitank gun and mine barriers. In attempting to cross the extensive mine field, the Panthers became engaged in fierce tank duels with Soviet tanks and suffered very heavy losses. Major General Popiel: "7 July was one of the hardest days in the Battle of Kursk."

Meanwhile the spearhead of Fifth Guards Tank Army (Lieutenant General Rotmistrov) reached the Protochino area to facilitate the deployment of the army. In the meantime, various improper decisions by Soviet commanders had negative consequences. Lieutenant General Rotmistrov: "During the battle some weaknesses in the Soviet antitank defense became evident. For example, up to 30 guns were concentrated at antitank strong points, which made fire direction very difficult. Moreover, splitting up several antitank brigades of the reserve and placing them at several antitank strong points was a wrong decision. This weakened considerably the striking power of the antitank formations of the Front High Command and made it difficult to shift these formations to other sectors."

Lieutenant General Dragunsky, commander of 1st Mechanized Brigade: "We were not able to halt the enemy that day. He continued to push on toward Oboyan. With superior forces and concentrations of tanks, he succeeded in breaking through our defenses and expanded his successes in the north and northwest. The 1st and 3rd Mechanized Brigades withdrew fighting. The 1st Guards Armored Brigade of our corps also fought doggedly."

On Thursday, 8 July 1943, the bulk of Fifth Guards Tank Army (Lieutenant General Rotmistrov) reached the assembly area on the west bank of the Oskol early in the morning after a difficult forced march. In less than three days the army covered 250 to 300 kilometers. In addition, the Voronezh Front received X Armored Corps as reinforcement from Fifth Guards Army (Lieutenant General Zhadov) and II Armored Corps from the Southwestern Front. With these heavy reinforcements, STAVKA hoped to stop the German attack on Oboyan and Prokhorovka and prevent a breakthrough of the second defensive line.

Rokossovsky believed that it was not the impact of the German thrust that was responsible for the German victories in the southern part of the Kursk Salient, rather the inept operational decisions of General of the Army Vatutin, the commander of the Voronezh Front. General of the Army Rokossovsky: "The Central Front definitely committed its forces better. It concentrated them at the vulnerable sectors which thus prevented the enemy from succeeding. The Voronezh Front, on the other hand, distributed its forces over all the defensive lines. Therefore, the enemy, like ourselves, was able to attack a narrow sector and penetrate relatively far into the de-

156

fensive system. They could only be stopped by committing many STAVKA reserves."

On the same day Fourth German Panzer Army (Colonel General Hoth) in the southern part of the Kursk Salient tried to force a breakthrough with their main effort along the Oboyan main road toward Syrtsevo-Greznoye. Major General Popiel: "Hoth did not want to lose an hour, not a minute. One has to admit that he was successful with this on 8 July. His tanks attacked before our brigade had concentrated for a counterattack."

Army Group Center

In the northern part of the Kursk Salient fighting continued to rage without letup on the right side of the Central Front in the Olkhovatka line. General Rokossovsky: "On 8 July 1943, at 0820, approximately 300 Fascist tanks, supported by artillery and mortar fire and Luftwaffe raids, attacked our positions northwest of Olkhovatka at the boundary between Thirteenth and Seventieth Armies and penetrated the infantry positions."

Army Group South

On 8 July, 6th Panzer Division (Major General von Huenersdorff), advancing to the north, was able to take Melekshovo in the southern sector of the Kursk Salient following a two-and-one-half-hour battle with newly deployed Soviet armored reserves. All day both the Luftwaffe and the Red Air Fleet attacked tank formations of the other side. The terrain was covered with wrecks of shot-down aircraft and burning tanks. Major General Popiel: "There were lightning-like clashes in the burning sky. It practically

157

(*Top*) Trosna area, July 8, 1943: a 15cm Nebelwerfer 41 (rocket launcher) in firing position. The Soviets dreaded the six explosive rockets weighing 31.8 kg, with a range of approx. 6 km for their area effectiveness, just as much as the Germans feared the Katyushas

was impossible to follow them or determine whether it was friend or foe crashing in a veil of smoke and fire. One of our stub-nosed Hawks tried everything to avoid landing among the enemy tanks. But it continued to lose altitude. There were no flames. In the last second, a trail of smoke became visible. He didn't make it and crashed in front of the forward Tigers. Enemy guns finished him off from a distance of fifty meters. Another one came down, burning like an oil-drenched rag, in front of our position. An airman jumped out of the plane and crept back to us. With his pistol in his bloody hand, this stocky pilot reported to Katukov. His uniform was torn and one could see his hairy chest. A large map case on a long strap was dangling at his knees."

While the II SS-Panzer Corps (SS-Obergruppenf. Hausser) was trying to thrust forward over the Psel into the rear of First Tank Army (Lieutenant General Katukov), General of the Army Vatutin ordered a tank task force of II Guards Armored Corps to counterattack into the deep flank of the II SS-Panzer Corps. This unit was securing the Belgorod-Oboyan road that was so vital as a supply link for the Germans. This Soviet buildup against the unsuspecting II SS-Panzer Corps was, however, crushed from the air.

It was the first time in the history of war that aircraft destroyed such a large tank formation. When Luftwaffe Captain Meyer spotted a concentration of Soviet armor at the flank of the II SS-Panzer Corps on a routine reconnaissance flight over the woods of Gostishchevo, he radioed his tank destroyer group in Mikoyanovka. In fifteen minutes the first of four squadrons appeared with sixteen planes. The tank-destroyer aircraft (Henschel Hs 129 B-2/R2) equipped with a 30mm MK 103 gun was a dangerous op-

(*Bottom*) Before Syrtsevo, July 8, 1943, Panzergrenadiers of the Div. "Grossedeutschland" during a lull in the fighting: in the background a captured Soviet T-34/76F with a Greek cross; in the foreground a light armored ammunition half track SdKfz252

158

ponent. These squadrons were supported by fighter aircraft. Within an hour the flying antitank guns crushed the Soviet armored formation. They destroyed fifty tanks, burned out or heavily damaged, which were abandoned on the battlefield.

On 8 July, there was also a tank battle north of Syrtsevo between Panzergruppe Strachwitz and approximately forty Soviet tanks of which ten were destroyed. Toward noon, following intense fighting, Panzer Fusilier Regiment of the Grossdeutschland Division in cooperation with Panzer Regiment 6 of 3rd Panzer Division (Lieutenant General Westhoven) took Syrtsevo. Major General Popiel: "When the artillery ceased firing and the smoke dissipated somewhat, we saw in the distance a large number of tanks. It was impossible to distinguish damaged tanks from those undamaged. The row began moving. Only a burned field a few hundred meters wide, nothing else, separated us from the enemy. Katukov didn't take the field glasses from his eyes. He mumbled: 'They are regrouping . . . advancing in a spearhead. . . . I think we have had it.'"

Army Group Center

In the northern part of the Kursk Salient, on the morning of 8 July 1943, Colonel General Model also committed 4th Panzer Division (Lieutenant General von Saucken) from his third reserve line. The grenadiers were welcomed by shells from dug-in T-34s and KW-1s, antitank guns, and infantry weapons. They reached the village of Teploye and were stopped there. Lieutenant General von Saucken: "We hardly had crossed the hill which provided cover than we were met by enemy fire. Artillery, mortars, Stalinorgans (rocket launchers), machine guns, and sharpshooters, but especially extensive antitank guns spewed fire and doom. Packs of enemy tanks with all muzzles ablaze sallied forth again and again to counterattack. In the open terrain our tanks, some of them Tigers, drove at full speed to make it harder for the enemy guns to hit them. We riflemen could not keep up this pace and hung far back. The enemy strong points that our tanks had rolled over resumed firing, forcing us to the ground. Some tanks had to turn back repeatedly to give us protection by fire."

Despite all these difficulties it seemed that the Germans would nevertheless succeed in breaking through. General of the Army Rokossovsky: "At the end of the third day of fighting, the reserves were engaged in the battle practically without exception and the Fascists continually were introducing new forces in the direction of their main effort. . . . What were we supposed to stop them with? I decided to try a risky maneuver and brought up my last reserves—IX Armored Corps under the command of General Bogdanov—to attack their main effort. It was situated in the Kursk area and was covering the city from the south. This completely fresh corps was our last hope."

Meanwhile Austrian 9th Panzer Division (Lieutenant General Scheller) and 18th Panzer Division (Major General von Schlieben) were trying to capture the strongly defended hill 253.5 and the village of Ponyri, to no avail. The 86th Infantry Division (Lieutenant General Weidling) also following up was unsuccessful. The extremely strong Soviet counterattacks and the pouring rain, which was turning the entire terrain into a swamp, made further operations impossible and Colonel General Model gave the order for all formations to halt.

In the evening, the 20th Panzer Division (Major General von Kessel) took Samodurovka, a neighboring village. Model now decided to wear out the enemy's matériel instead of trying to break through. The German formations gained ground north of Olkhovatka late in the evening, but their striking power was exhausted. All further attempts to take Olkhovatka and Ponyri were repelled by forces of the Central Front. Although nearly the entire Ninth Army was thrown into the battle, all its formations were unable to penetrate farther than five kilometers in any sector by 8 July.

In the southern part of the Kursk Salient, too, the Soviet Command was fearing the worst. Lieutenant General Katukov: "8 July was decisive for our army. Apparently the Fascist High Command had decided to stake everything on one card this time. Krivoshein reported, 'Individual tank groups have succeeded in breaking through the second defensive belt in the Ilyinsky area.' By his voice I could tell how worried he was."

Army Group South

In the afternoon elements of the III Panzer Corps (General of Pz. Tr. Breith) attacking to the north were able to push through the well-defended Soviet defensive system between the Razumnaya and Severny Donets rivers up to the Belgorod-Korotcha road. But here they were stopped from penetrating any farther by fresh Soviet armored reserves that had just arrived. Major General Popiel: "After he had brought in reserves and his men had rested, Hoth let his tanks advance once more. The sun had already begun to set. Dive-bombers were screaming again and the booming of detonations filled the air, glimmering from the heat. The fighting on the approach routes to Oboyan continued." The divisions of Fourth Panzer Army, however, were worn out after four days of combat and a temporary pause in the offensive was needed urgently in the Prokhorovka area.

The Soviet formations engaged in hard defensive fighting before Oboyan were also fatigued. The commander of 1st Mechanized Brigade, Lieutenant General Dragunsky: "Toward the evening of 8 July, one regiment had only ten tanks left. The adjacent brigade had to withdraw to another sector. Our tank regiment was no longer able to hold its position. Communications to the battalions was interrupted and we were running out of armor-piercing shells. Also, there were the many wounded. One would think we were on an island in the midst of a sea of fire. It was senseless to stay in this sector any longer. We had to make our way to the main forces of the brigade."

(*Top*) Sections of the III Panzer Corps advancing toward the Belgorod-Korocha road, July 9, 1943: in front a light SdKfz 250 half track with a Pak 37mm antitank gun

(*Bottom*) Orel area, July 9, 1943, in the rear area of the front: a meeting on the fringe of the big battle; in foreground a PzKpfw IV Model D with a short 75mm gun

The NS press continues to report successes:
Berlin, Friday, July 9, 1943
High Soviet Losses in Fierce Tank Battles

On that day the German Army Executive Staff submitted a report on the partisan situation between April and June 1943. It came to the conclusion that, despite considerably stronger countermeasures, partisan activities in the entire eastern sector had increased during the last three months. The number of attacks on railroads in June totalled 1,092 compared to 397 in January, the number of damaged locomotives 409 compared to 112, and damaged railroad bridges 54 compared to 22.

During the night of 8/9 July 1943, Fifth Guards Tank Army (Lieutenant General Rotmistrov) received an order at 0100 to move to the Bobryshevo-Vesely-Alexandrovsky area on the evening of 9 July and push back the advancing formations of Army Group Center. To do this the army had a front of 100 kilometers to cover.

On the morning of 9 July 1943, Field Marshal von Manstein's troops attacked with 500 tanks along a sector of ten kilometers. The 3rd Panzer Division (Lieutenant General Westhoven) was able to move forward on the left flank of the XLVIII Panzer Corps (General of Pz. Tr. von Knobelsdorff) west of the Rakovo-Kruglik road and thus gain a better position for an enveloping attack from the left against Berezovka.

Army Group Center

At Army Group Center (FM von Kluge), in the northern part of the Kursk Salient, Ninth Army (Colonel General Model) was able to gain a few kilometers following hard fighting and penetrate the third enemy position. But the drive was halted by enemy fire before the fortified high ground of Olkhovatka, about 18 kilometers from its starting point.

Army Group South

On the afternoon of 9 July 1943, formations of Army Group South assembled and advanced in the direction of Oboyan and Korotcha. The 35-kilometer German breach at Oboyan, and the 10-kilometer penetration at Korocha, confirmed General of the Army Rokossovsky's opinion that General of the Army Vatutin had made an error. He had misinterpreted Field Marshal von Manstein's intentions, precariously dispersing his forces along a front 164 kilometers long. This spread Sixth Guards Army, against which the mass of the German assault was directed, much too thin on much too long a defensive sector.

Major General Antipenko, chief of the Rear Supply Service of the Central Front: "The enemy directed a very powerful blow against the troops

The battle of equipment is continually demanding new sacrifices: The 320nd Inf.Div. burying its dead near Olshonets

(*Top*) Before Ber-
ezvka, on the eve-
ning of July 9, 1943:
German infantry-
men mopping up
the terrain just
gained

of the Voronezh Front with the main effort aimed at Sixth Guards Army
under the command of Lieutenant General Chistyakov whose defensive front
was too long. In four days the Fascists advanced 30 to 40 kilometers here,
which amounted to an operational breakthrough. Thanks only to the timely
help of the Steppe Military District could this dangerous situation be alleviated."

Despite this progress in the south of the salient, the dogged Soviet resistance forced Colonel General Hoth to give up his plan to break through
to Kursk by the shortest route via Oboyan. He had to change the direction
of the assault and shift it to Prokhorovka to get to Kursk by an alternate
route. The main elements of his Fourth Panzer Army were supposed to
attack with 700 tanks and assault guns from the west, the III Panzer Corps
(General of Pz. Tr. Breith) and the Kempf Army from the south. In this
way Field Marshal von Manstein planned to envelope the Soviet troops between the Lipovy Donets and the northern Donets rivers. After annihilating
these Soviet forces, the German armored formations planned to penetrate
the Soviet front and take Kursk from the southeast.

The Fifth Guards Tank Army (Lieutenant General Rotmistrov) of the
strategic reserves of STAVKA reinforced with II Armored Corps and II
Guards Armored Corps meanwhile had reached the assembly area north
of Prokhorovka. Its total strength included approximately 800 tanks and
assault guns.

The German assault in the southern sector of the Kursk Salient energetically supported by the Luftwaffe developed into an advance to the north.
The II SS-Panzer Corps (SS-Obergruppenf. Hausser) fiercely was fighting

(*Bottom*) Dangerous
mission: Soviet sap-
pers clearing a Ger-
man minefield prior
to a Soviet tank at-
tack

163

its way closer to Prokhorovka. The XLVIII Panzer Corps (General of Pz. Tr. von Knobelsdorff) pushed forward into the Kochetovka area and westward along the road to Oboyan.

In the meantime, during the night of 9/10 July 1943, tanks of the 3rd Panzer Division (Lieutenant General Westhoven) cleared Berezovka of enemy troops from the west. The Soviets, however, stopped them again from continuing the attack in the direction of Kruglik at the southern edge of a little woods north of Berezovka. East of the Oboyan road the tank battle group Graf Schimmelmann of 11th Panzer Division (Lieutenant General Balck) took hill 260.8. With this, the highest elevation before Oboyan was reached. In addition this was the deepest a German formation was able to penetrate the Soviet defensive line in the Kursk Salient during the entire Operation "Citadel."

On Saturday, 10 July 1943, shortly before sunrise the Anglo-American landing on the southern coast of Sicily (code name: Operation "Husky") under the command of General Eisenhower began. The new situation in the Mediterranean Sea, in the opinion of the OKH, called for a rapid and successful conclusion of the battle of the Kursk Salient.

Army Group Center

In the morning hours of 10 July, in the northern part of the salient, tanks of the German 2nd Panzer Division (Lieutenant General Lübbe) and 4th Panzer Division (Lieutenant General von Saucken) moved in wind and rain to their assembly areas. About the same time, German artillery opened

Only a map shows clearly how laboriously the German offensive proceeded in the northern sector of the Kursk salient

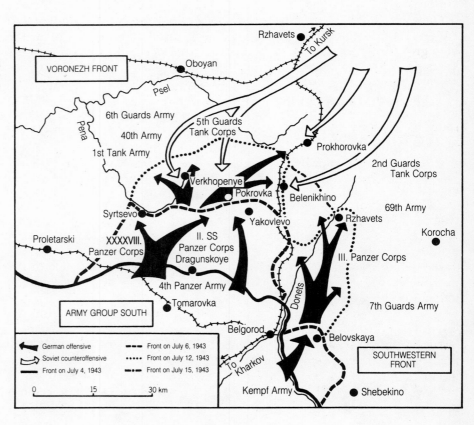

164

(*Top*) South of Orel, July 10, 1943: Just a week ago a brand new 24-t temporary bridge built by the Panzerpionierbataillon 86 (tank engineer battalion) from the 9th Pz.Div. stood here. In foreground a PzKfpw IV

a heavy preparation fire. The high ground of Olkhovatka containing Soviet positions and many dug-in tanks disappeared in the smoke of bursting shells. Stukas and He 111 planes bombed the objectives of the German Panzer divisions. The tanks rolled forward supported by the approaching bombers, while grenadiers were advancing over a two- to three-kilometer-wide depression without cover toward Soviet positions on the high ground. Despite the use of forward air controllers and prearranged signals, bombs repeatedly fell on German assembly areas causing casualties and damaging vehicles.

Field airbase of the Schlachtgeschwader 1 (ground-attack squadron), west of Belgorod, July 11, 1943: a FW 190F-8 type fighter from the II Schlachtgruppe (ground-attack wing) being loaded

The Soviets had come through the preparatory fire and air raids without any major losses and were now shooting at the Germans with every possible weapon. Although there was a total of 300 tanks from 4th and 2nd Panzer Divisions concentrated here to storm the last Soviet position, the high ground of Olkhovatka, their repeated attacks failed with considerable losses. The long, almost nude plateau (in some places one could see for kilometers) forced the tanks to attack, driving at full speed. The grenadiers had to follow on foot instead of riding in the personnel carriers as they usually did. After 100 meters they lost contact with the tanks. This made coordinating their tactics impossible. Many tanks had to turn back several times to rescue the grenadiers from the counterattacks that kept flaring up on their flanks. The Soviet close-range, antitank gunners hiding in the cornfields waited patiently for the tank spearheads to disperse before picking off the tanks one by one.

The 9th Panzer Division (Lieutenant General Scheller) took Snova, Bityug, and Berezovy-Log; crossed the Snova; and reached the northern part of Ponyri II. Despite murderous casualties and materiel shortages, the German divisions had managed to fight through the first half of the intricate Soviet defensive system. North of Olkhovatka they broke through both the main defensive and second defensive lines. But they gained only between ten and twelve kilometers in four days.

On the evening of 10 July, the German Ninth Army moved from the offensive to the defensive. Colonel General Model still hoped ultimately to break through the Soviet defense by committing all his forces after repelling the expected Soviet counterattack. This hope fast was becoming an illusion. The final advance of the right wing of 9th Panzer Division got as far as the ridge at Olkhovatka without, however, being able to surmount it.

165

Army Group South

On the same day, Panzer Regiment 6 of 3rd Panzer Division crossed the bridge over the Psel, the last natural obstacle before Kursk, accompanied by Panzer Grenadiers, assault guns, tank destroyers, and infantry. The Panzer regiments rolled southward toward the rear of the Soviet 71st Guards Rifle Division, which already had been attacked from the front by the German 255th Infantry Division (Lieutenant General Poppe) and the 332nd Infantry Division (Lieutenant General Schaefer). Several thousand Red Army soldiers had to surrender. Meanwhile the XLVIII Panzer Corps (General of Pz. Tr. von Knobelsdorff) continued to advance toward Oboyan. At the same time Panzer Grenadier Division "Grossdeutschland" was ordered to swing to the south and southwest and clear out the enemy forces on its left flank.

Supported by the Luftwaffe, the Panzer Grenadiers launched an attack against the high ground south of Kruglik and against the road leading north through Kruglik. In the meantime, the Fourth Panzer Army (Colonel General Hoth) and the Kempf Army began to attack in the direction of Prokhorovka. Elements broke through to the north along the Oboyan road. Major General Popiel: "On 10 July, one day before the last day of attack in the Oboyan direction, the enemy inflicted heavy losses on both of our armored brigades. We had a hard time of it."

In the first hours of the afternoon the "Grossdeutschland" Division reinforced with assault guns was able to push forward within one kilometer south of hill 247.0 to block the road north to Kruglik and then to storm that hill. Lieutenant General Katukov: "Although Manstein continued to throw masses of tanks and bombers into the action on 9 and 10 July, we felt that this was more a sign of despair than of strength."

How fierce the fighting was is shown by the fate of the 6th Panzer Division (Major General von Huenersdorff). It tried to cross a tank ditch that was secured by antitank guns. Only after sending in engineer sections were the tanks able to move over the obstacle. Then they rolled into an extensive mine field where they ultimately became stuck. This division which had had 100 tanks on the first day of the offensive only had 47 left on 10 July.

Lieutenant General Moskalenko, commander of Fortieth Army of the Voronezh Front: "The Germans wanted to be in Kursk in four days, but they were not able to break through even half of our defensive line." There

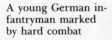
A young German infantryman marked by hard combat

168

was no longer any question of German success. The offensive to cut off the Kursk Salient had failed. Army Groups Center and South had achieved only minor successes in the four days. They penetrated approximately a breadth of 18 kilometers on one front with a distance of more than 20 kilometers in the north. In the south their front was approximately 50 kilometers with a distance traveled of 50 kilometers. The two German spearheads were about 120 kilometers apart when they finally were brought to a halt.

On 10 July STAVKA's strongest reserves, the Steppe Military District (Colonel General Konev), was renamed the Steppe Front. Although on this same day the western Allies had landed on the coast of Sicily, the OKW situation report said: "Operation 'Citadel' will be continued." The events at this front, however, soon would influence the fate of Operation "Citadel."

Army Group Center

During the night of 11/12 July 1943, Colonel General Model ordered the last reserves of Ninth Army, 10th Panzer Grenadier Division (Lieutenant General A. Schmidt), and 31st Infantry (Lieutenant General Hossbach) to attack in the northern part of the salient. The Panzer Grenadiers repelled a strong Soviet armored attack aimed at the train station of Ponyri. But a few hours later it became clear that there was practically no chance of achieving the anticipated victory at Kursk. The carefully planned Ninth Army attack against the high ground of Olkhovatka, which had received the greatest air support from the Luftwaffe, had failed. Yet Model intended to continue attempting the breakthrough of the Soviet positions. The latest was shifting the main effort to the XLVI Panzer Corps (General of Infantry Zorn).

Army Group South

On Sunday morning, 11 July 1943, Field Marshal von Manstein, having regrouped his forces south of Kursk in 24 hours, ordered the offensive to continue. Advancing from the west and the south on Prokhorovka, his troops initially were successful. A concentric attack by the III Panzer Corps (General of Pz. Tr. Breith) and the II SS-Panzer Corps (SS-Obergruppenf. Hausser) from the east, south, and west drove the defending Soviet forces together in the southern section of the river triangle. Suffering great losses, they started to withdraw to prepared positions at Gostishchevo.

The invasion of Sicily, so disastrous for Operation "Citadel," is only marginally mentioned here. The headline reads: *Major Battles at the Eastern Front and in the South*

South of Verkhne Olkhanets, July 11, 1943, the tank spearheads of the 6th Pz.Div. reaches the town. From left to right: PzKpfw III with a 5cm gun; a 75mm Sturmgeschütz 40 assault gun, model F, with additional armored plates on the sides. The so-called Schürzen (skirts) were necessary, because the new Soviet hollow projectiles went right through the armor of the PzKpfw III and the assault guns. On the right the trusty eight-wheel Büssing-NAG armored scout car with its frame antenna

From the southwest the three Panzer divisions of the II SS-Panzer Corps moved toward the northeast with more than 600 tanks. Their order of battle had on the left flank the 3rd SS-Panzer Division "Totenkopf" (SS-Brigadef. Priess), in the center the 1st SS-Panzer Division "Leibstandarte Adolf Hitler" (SS-Brigadef. Wisch), and on the right flank the 2nd SS-Panzer Division "Das Reich" (SS-Gruppenf. Krueger). The 1st SS-Panzer Division launched its attack between the railroad line and the Psel toward Prokhorovka. Very heavy tank combat developed in front of the positions of the Soviet XVIII Armored Corps (Major General Bakharev) and the XXIX Armored Corps (Major General Kirichenko). There was an impenetrable cloud of smoke over the battlefield.

In the meantime, in the area east of the Donets, the III Panzer Corps as the right wing of the Kempf Army together with 6th Panzer Division (Major General von Huenersdorff) were deployed as the forward echelon and the 19th Panzer Division (Lieutenant General G. Schmidt) and the 7th Panzer Division (Lieutenant General Freiherr von Funck) were behind them. The III Panzer Corps pushed forward from the south to the northeast toward Prokhorovka, which was already being threatened by the SS tanks. The "Totenkopf" Division built a bridgehead between Bogorodiskoye and Vesely on the northern bank of the Psel in the Oboyan area. At the same time the "Das Reich" and "Leibstandarte Adolf Hitler" Divisions were storming the stretch of land between the Psel and the railroad line near Prokhorovka.

On 11 July, the tank spearheads of the Kempf Army approached the banks of the northern Donets, twenty kilometers from Prokhorovka. The spearhead element led by Major Bäke of the 6th Panzer Division was crossing the upper Donets just as were the 7th and 19th Panzer Divisions with a total of 300 tanks and assault guns. On its thrust to the north the 6th Panzer Division was able to take Zhlyakhovo after hard fighting and advance to Verkhne Olkhanets.

With this the Soviet resistance facing the III Panzer Corps (General of Pz. Tr. Breith) between the rivers Rasumnaya and Donets collapsed. This left III Panzer Corps in the open. Lieutenant General Moskalenko: "Marshal Vasilevsky, the representative of headquarters, and Vatutin came to the conclusion following an estimate of the situation that to defeat this enemy thrust we would have to stop all attacks on Kursk from the south once and for all. But the Fascist formations that had broken through the line between Oboyan and Prokhorovka could be smashed only by powerful counterattacks by the front reinforced with strategic reserves." Meanwhile,

170

General of the Army Vatutin had an idea that, ultimately, would be decisive in the outcome of Operation "Citadel" but it incurred the anger of Marshal Zhukov and even of Stalin. In the end, however, the courageous commander of the Voronezh Front prevailed with the support of Lieutenant General N. Khrushchev, the member of the War Council of the Front who came from Kalinovka, near Kursk. In order to stop the III Panzer Corps and avert the threat to Oboyan, Vatutin decided to save the battered First Tank Army (Lieutenant General Katukov) from impending annihilation by ordering the armored corps to dig in with the rifle troops of Sixth Guards Army (Lieutenant General Chistyakov). The tanks were buried up to their turrets to form a powerful antitank defensive position and stop the Germans heading for Oboyan and Kursk. Nevertheless, Stalin's deputy, Marshal Zhukov, demanded that the armored corps be committed exclusively for mobile operations against the invading German formations. When Vatutin and Khrushchev did not agree, Zhukov complained to Stalin, who, without hesitation, ordered the Voronezh Front to counterattack with their armored formations.

It was only at the last minute that the War Council of the Voronezh Front succeeded in convincing the STAVKA representative of the soundness of its plan. He, in turn, was able to convince the dictator that this unconventional use of tanks was the right thing to do. If Zhukov had had his way, according to official Soviet history, ". . . in this case the counterthrusts of the Voronezh Front armored corps would have been ineffective. They would have resulted only in heavy losses in tanks and would have facilitated the breakthrough by the enemy in the line of Oboyan."

Army Group Center

Unexpectedly, in the course of 11 July 1943, the Soviets opened heavy surprise fire in the northern part of the Kursk Salient, east of Orel, in the area of the German Second Panzer Army (General of Pz. Tr. R. Schmidt). At first, this attack only involved units of battalion and regimental strength. Later, however, the counterattack became increasingly more massive. The German Army High Command considered them, on the basis of previous experience, as only harmless holding attacks and diversionary tactics to keep German reserves in the Orel Salient from joining the attack on Kursk. For this reason, even Field Marshal von Kluge attached no particular importance to these operations at this time.

Meanwhile, STAVKA decided to throw extra strategic reserves into the battle to strengthen the impending counteroffensive of the Bryansk Front (Colonel General Popov). This, however, presented difficulties. The reserves were located quite far from the front line, and bringing them up on the sodden roads caused repeated delays. Formations like the Eleventh Guards Army (Lieutenant General Bagramian), which had been in STAVKA reserve for three months, were supposed to go into action direct from their march order.

Another large formation of the STAVKA strategic reserve in the southern part of the Kursk Salient had a similar fate, as it, too, hardly had a chance to finish its preparations for combat. Lieutenant Rotmistrov: "While preparing for the counterattack, First Guards Tank Army and Fifth Guards Army, surprised by an unexpected attack by strong enemy tank formations and the Luftwaffe, were pushed back to Oboyan. Elements of Sixth Guards Army which were located at the left wing had to retreat to Prokhorovka."

Army Group South

On the afternoon of 11 July 1943, following a report of the successful advance of his troops, von Manstein decided to relocate his formations and all his reserves. He ordered a forced march to the Russian defensive sectors that had been broken through and a reattack at daybreak. In order to deceive the Soviet forces in the Prokhorovka area about its true intentions, Army Group Center launched an attack in the Novo-Oskochnoye-Rzhavets area against Sixty-ninth Army (Lieutenant General Kryuchenkin). The commander of the reinforced Soviet First Tank Army, Lieutenant General Katukov, found himself in a critical situation. STAVKA had ordered him to counterattack following the collapse of Sixth Guards Army to prevent the German Panzer formations from advancing to Oboyan. Marshal Zhukov: "Toward evening on this day a very dangerous situation arose at the Voronezh Front sector."

Army Group Center

On the evening of 11 July 1943, while the final preparations for the counterattack of the Bryansk Front (Colonel General Popov) and the left wing of the Western Front (Colonel General Sokolovsky) were still in progress, forward elements and tank spearheads of the Bryansk Front and the left wing of the Western Front were pressing harder and harder against the German Second Panzer Army (Colonel General R. Schmidt). These So-

ЗИМОЙ И ЛЕТОМ ОДНИМ ЦВЕТОМ

Зимний Гитлер: — Зато летом я буду наступать!

Итоги летнего наступления немцев.

(*Top*) A caricature from PRAVDA, July 1943.
THE SAME PICTURE IN WINTER AND IN SUMMER. Hitler in winter: For that I'll attack in the summer!

Caption And this was what his attack in the summer looked like

viet troops were supposed to defend Orel from the north and east, but they were already in heavy contact with these German vanguards. Behind the Soviet front lines the assault formations of both fronts were waiting for the order to attack. Events in this sector forced Army Group Center Command to halt the attack of Ninth Army on Kursk to allow it to provide reinforcements for Second Panzer Army as quickly as possible. Formations planned for the defensive battle in the Orel Salient had to be made available.

(*Bottom*) Deployed for the first time in Operation "Citadel": the light, explosive charge carrier "Goliath." This mini-tank that carried 75 kg of explosive charge was developed by Borgward and built by Zündapp.

173

Until sundown on 11 July 1943, German Panzer Grenadiers and other troops followed up in the southern part of the Kursk Salient. Then the entire III Panzer Corps (General of Pz. Tr. Breith) pushed forward into the area north of Sheino. Field Marshal von Manstein: "The way was open in unfortified terrain to engage the fast-moving formations of the enemy's operational reserves, which had been located east of Kharkov and now were moving rapidly here."

In the Prokhorovka line, the attack of the II SS-Panzer Corps gained only a little ground, yet the 3rd SS-Panzer Division "Totenkopf" was able to seize a bridgehead over the Psel. The XLVIII Panzer Corps (General of Pz. Tr. von Knobelsdorff) gained a big victory, the capture of 100 Soviet tanks. According to reports of the German command, the Russians were showing signs of fatigue. Colonel General Hoth was able to penetrate thirty-five kilometers into the Soviet defensive positions, but the situation of Ninth Army made this success questionable.

At dusk on 11 July, the Soviet Fifth Guards Tank Army (Lieutenant General Rotmistrov) with the XVIII and XXIX Armored Corps plus V Mechanized Guards Corps were ready for action. Up to now, the XI Army Corps (General of Pz. Tr. Raus) of the Kempf Army had established an effective defensive position and was able to hold it.

The III Panzer Corps had now reached the last Soviet defensive position. Within one week of fighting Army Group South, the Red Army lost 24,000 men as prisoners, 1,800 tanks, 267 guns, and 1,080 antitank guns. Field Marshal von Manstein was still holding the reliable XXIV Panzer Corps (General of Pz. Tr. Nehring) with the 17th Panzer Division and the 5th SS-Panzer Grenadier Division "Viking" (SS-Gruppenf. Gille = Lieutenant General) in reserve.

On the evening of 11 July, 1943, von Manstein received a report on the unsettling developments at Army Group Center. Nevertheless, he stuck to his decision to continue the offensive, but now with only a limited objective. The German Army Executive Staff, however, had doubts about the chances of success and on this day their war diary reads: "As a rapid victory could not be achieved, it is now essential to inflict great losses on the enemy while keeping our own as low as possible. For this purpose a relocation of our reserves has begun."

At this time the Soviet Fifth Guards Tank Army (Lieutenant General Rotmistrov) was moving to its assembly area for the counteroffensive with the II Guards Armored Corps and the II Armored Corps, which were located in the Belenikhino and Prokhorovka area. STAVKA was forced to remedy the situation as rapidly as possible. In the rear of this strong concentration of Soviet armor, the German III Panzer Corps was deployed. It could encircle and annihilate the Soviet formations in the Prokhorovka area once it linked up with Fourth Panzer Army (Colonel General Hoth). Lieutenant General Rotmistrov: "On the evening of 11 July, German formations reached the area immediately in front of Prokhorovka. My previous decision to mount a counterattack could not be carried out under these circumstances. Because of the withdrawal of our formations to Prokhorovka, the two-day-long artillery preparatory fire supporting the counterattack of Fifth Guards Tank Army had to be interrupted and a new assembly area had to be designated. Missions for our troops had to be changed and dis-

cussed again. The capture of Prokhorovka on 11 July forced me to commit two armored brigades west of Prokhorovka that evening to halt the enemy attack. The army had to be prepared for our counterattack all over again. There were only ten hours to do this; only three were left after daybreak. Under these circumstances the troops' combat preparations had to suffer. The corps and brigade commanders had no time to reconnoiter their new assembly areas and to designate the lines of their main effort."

Rotmistrov now ordered the 11th and 12th Mechanized Brigades of V Mechanized Guards Corps and the 26th Armored Brigade of the II Guards Armored Corps to advance against the German Panzer formations on the morning of the next day. Their orders were first to contain the forces of the III Panzer Corps with counterattacks in cooperation with the 92nd Guards Rifle Division and then to push them back. Major General Popiel: "Behind the front line everyone was preparing for the following day. In ravines and in the woods—any place halfway hidden from air observation—and beside the field hospitals, repair shops, field bakeries, and supply dumps were brand new, dust-covered T-34s. They belonged to Fifth Guards Tank Army of General Rotmistrov that had just arrived."

In the early hours of that night, the German 6th Panzer Division (Major General von Huenersdorff) was moved to the heavily fortified Rzhavets. In a surprise attack they were supposed to seize a bridgehead over the northern Donets and then advance to Provorot. The bulk of this division and the 19th Panzer Division (Lieutenant General G. Schmidt) were ordered to continue pursuing the defeated Soviet formations and simultaneously attack the left flank of Fifth Guards Tank Army (Lieutenant General Rotmistrov) and Sixty-ninth Army (Lieutenant General Kryuchenkin). Panzer Regiment 11 (Colonel von Oppeln-Bronikowski) and his two armored companies, one Panzer Grenadier battalion, and the rest of Tiger Detachment 503 started on their night march on Rzhavets. They were led by two captured T-34s at the head of the column under strict silence and no fire orders. The combat group moved toward the town ten kilometers away. After bypassing Kurakovska village, they were behind Soviet lines. The column threaded into the busy traffic on the main road and fell in line with Soviet units heading in the same direction. During a short rest, German and Red Army soldiers were sitting almost side by side without suspicion. One of the two captured T-34s unexpectedly stopped because of engine trouble and a Panzer IV pushed it into a ditch. At 0040 the head of the column reached the edge of Rzhavets and looked for the way to its bridge in the darkness between marching Soviet infantry and truck columns. In the village the combat group missed the turn to the bridge in their excitement and rolled past a column of twenty-two Soviet T-34s. Apparently the Soviet tank drivers had become suspicious, because they suddenly fell out of line and followed the Germans. Major Bäke and Lieutenant Zobel were able to knock out three of them in close-range combat with magnetic antitank charges, but now a batch of flares went up and machine guns began to rattle from all directions.

The combat group had not as yet reached its objective when a tremendous detonation blew up the bridge. The grenadiers and engineers, however, were able to reach the northern bank of the Donets over a footbridge and establish a bridgehead there. The surprised Red Army soldiers hardly put up a fight.

Belgorod area, July 11, 1943, a Panzer division advancing in a new front sector: in foreground one of the light Pzkpfw II (SdKfz 121), which were already rare at this stage

177

12 July–15 July 1943

Second

Prokhorovka: The
of the Second
Operation "Citadel"

Phase
Greatest Tank Battle
World War
Broken Off

Prokhorovka area, on the morning of July 12, 1943. Units of the II SS-Panzer Corps pushing foreward: "The tank battle has started"

Victories at Belgorod and Orel
Monday, 12 July 1943. The German High Command published the following:

In the battle between Belgorod and Orel our troops were able to encircle and annihilate a large enemy force. Several thousand prisoners were captured, 129 tanks knocked out, numerous guns and other weapons seized. All told, 220 tanks and 70 aircraft were destroyed yesterday. Attacks by the Soviets in the east and north of Orel were repelled. Since 5 July, the enemy has lost 28,000 prisoners, 1,640 tanks, and 1,400 guns.

In Sicily the British-North American landing troops have tried unsuccessfully to broaden the strip of coast they now occupy. German and Italian troops counterattacked according to prearranged plans at designated sites yesterday and threw the enemy back to the initial point of contact.

Great Battle of War Materiel
12 July 1943, Berlin. The DNB reported:

The course of the great battle of war materiel at the Eastern Front has been marked by the Russians' increasingly having to give way to the mounting pressure of German Panzer formations in the Belgorod sector. After the base of the German offensive was broadened and additional formations were brought up into the breaches during the past two days, Orel was attacked again from here and from the south. Thus both defensive and offensive operations are continuing according to plan along the entire line.

180

In mopping up the encircled Russians at Belgorod, 129 tanks were destroyed or captured and more than 4,200 prisoners taken. In order to regain the initiative, the Soviets are still trying to close the gaps at any price with additional reserves that are sent into action immediately without any rest. They attacked at several important points and at adjacent front sectors, but were repulsed everywhere.

With an Assault Gun in the Tank Battle at Prokhorovka
by war correspondent Nitschke:

. . . Even in the twilight we continued to fight with Bolshevist tanks and knocked one out. Dead tired we dug in under our assault gun and fell into a very deep sleep; no airplane could wake us.

It is 0330 now. In half an hour we have to be ready for action. The battery commander has just come back from the commander. The order: Panzer Grenadier Battalion X supported by a detachment of assault guns will take the village K. Just as the vehicles appear and are reloaded the order comes to depart. A few seconds later the battery commander's voice comes over the radio: "First battery ready? Battery forward!" Our eyes follow the proud row of heavy giants slowly churning out of the cornfield and heading to the assembly areas. . . .

In this tense second, Stukas sweep in from the north and dive at the village less than three kilometers away. In no time, a wall of smoke rises from it . . . We already can hear the commander's voice: "Battery forward! We are attacking!" All the field glasses are directed at the village, and hollow, and the hills on the far side. Behind us the Bolshevist strafing planes attack the tank assembly area.

The first shells burst among us . . . There in the hollow are six or seven dark dots. The commander spots them first: tanks, enemy tanks! A brief description of the target is given to the fire direction officer, then "Fire at will! Fire!" The shells roar from the muzzles. The tank battle has begun. Now other guns are firing too. The Bolshevists answer immediately. We see flashes of fire; we hear the shells whistling as they sweep over us; hunting fever consumes all our senses. We shoot, shoot . . . The field glasses pressed to our eyes, we stare—the rest of us completely enveloped in protective steel—over at the enemy. Then a bright reddish yellow flame bursts out of our first Bolshevist tank. "Hit" yells our commander, "Hit . . . !" resounds in our ears over the humming and buzzing interference that seems like the battle is being echoed in the radio. . . .

We barely hear any more the rattling of the machine guns that have entered the action; we pay no attention to the light clanking of the antitank shells that keep hitting our steel hull; only when a big shell strikes hard somewhere, a short, almost involuntary shudder runs through the vehicle. . . .

The battle is in full progress. The assault guns stand about in the bright sunshine like gigantic turtles incessantly spitting fire. We hear the final reports of other gun crews over the radio; we hear the commander's voice, his brief comments, his instructions. We roll on again, high above the ground, or so it seems to us when we look down at the grenadiers beside us jumping up, crawling, running, slowly inching forward. Hissing, screaming, whining, roaring shells of every caliber chase after us through the air. New enemy tanks continually are turning up. . . .

Here we sight another T-34. Too short . . . too far . . . missed to the right. The enemy is firing too. Clouds of smoke keep hiding him, yet he's barely 1,000 meters away; we knocked out the first enemy tanks at more than 2,000 meters! The next shot very nearly hits the Bolshevist. "Jammed," yells the gunner. That very second a terrible blow shakes us. Fragments fly about. Then another blow and a crash. "Out!" screams the commander. "Out, get out . . . !" Like lightning we are up and tumbling into the cool, wet grass, pressed flat, breathing in gasps. . . .

Another assault gun already is speeding toward us. We tear down the cables from our tank and hook them to our friend . . . We gain the hill

Prokhorovka area, July 12, 1943. The biggest tank battle of the war as seen by the commander of this tank through his periscopic sight: "All around us in the bright sunlight there are assault guns looking like gigantic turtles"

182

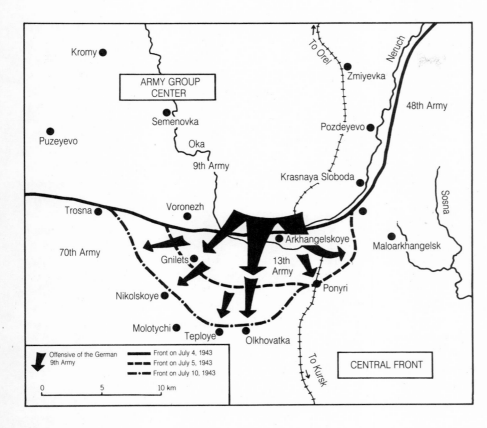

ARMY GROUP CENTER

Kromy

Puzeyevo

Semenovka

Oka

9th Army

Trosna

Voronezh

70th Army

Gnilets

Nikolskoye

Molotychi

Teploye

Olkhovatka

13th Army

Ponyri

Arkhangelskoye

Krasnaya Sloboda

Pozdeyevo

Zmiyevka

Maloarkhangelsk

48th Army

To Orel

Neruch

Sosna

To Kursk

CENTRAL FRONT

Offensive of the German 9th Army
Front on July 4, 1943
Front on July 5, 1943
Front on July 10, 1943

0   5   10 km

The German offensive is also unexpectedly slow in developing in the southern sector of the Kursk salient

and reach the armored tractor on the far side . . . For a second we can catch our breath. We share our last cigarettes and the remaining water in our field canteens. Beside us is our gun. We see the horrible wounds that the enemy shells made in it, but they weren't fatal. We look at each other with dirty, burnt faces; we look—and laugh . . . We are alive, alive . . . ! It's wonderful to be alive!
Völkischer Beobachter, July 1943.

The Greatest Tank Battle
Monday, 12 July 1943. Lieutenant General Rotmistrov:

Our tanks are advancing over the steppe in groups using the clumps of small trees and shrubs as cover. The gunfire becomes one mighty, continuous noise. The Soviet tanks run full speed into the German vanguard and break through their tank screen. The T-34s pick off the Tigers at short distances. At close quarters, their heavy armament and armor no longer are an advantage. The tanks of both sides are in the closest contact. There is neither time nor room to disengage, reestablish the battle order, and operate. The rounds fired so close penetrate the tanks' lateral as well as frontal plates. At this distance, the armor no longer protects and the muzzle length is no longer significant. Often the ammunition and the fuel explode and turrets are thrown many meters away.

Simultaneously, there is a dogfight above the battlefield. Both Soviet and German planes try to help their ground troops win the battle. Bombers, ground-attack planes, and fighters seem to be suspended in the sky above the front sector at Prokhorovka. One dogfight follows the other. Soon the heavens are covered with black smoke from the fires. On the black, scorched earth, the knocked-out tanks blaze like torches. It is difficult to determine which side is attacking and who is on the defense. The 2nd Battalion of the 181st Armored Brigade of the XVIII Armored Corps, attacking on the left bank of the Psel, runs into several Tigers that open fire on the Soviet tanks from a standstill.

The powerful, long-range guns of the Tigers are very dangerous, so our tanks have to shorten the distance between us as rapidly as possible in order to eliminate the enemy's advantage. The battalion commander, Captain P. A. Skripkin, orders: "Forward, follow me!" His first round penetrates the side of the Tiger. Immediately another Tiger opens fire on Skripkin's T-34. A round penetrates its side and a second hit wounds the battalion commander. The driver and radio man pull him out of the tank and bring him to a crater for cover. As a Tiger starts rolling directly at them, tanker Nikolayev jumps back into his hit, still-burning tank; starts up the engine; and storms toward the enemy. Like a blazing ball of fire, the T-34 rushes toward him over the field. The Tiger stops, but it's too late. The burning T-34 runs full speed directly into the German tank. The detonation shakes the ground.

Prokhorovka, July 13, 1943, this German light half track is scouting the forefield: "Soon the entire firmament is covered by the heavy smoke from the fires"

Day Report of Fourth Panzer Army
12 July 1943:

Estimate of the situation: On 12 July, the enemy attacked the Fourth Panzer Army along its entire front with elements of the IX Armored Corps and a mechanized corps, and several infantry divisions. The enemy's main efforts are aimed at our two flanks at and north of Kalinin, west of Prokhorovka, and west of Verkhopenye. For this, today the enemy committed two new armored corps (XVIII and XXIX) in the Prokhorovka area and apparently relocated X Armored Corps to the Novenkoye region. All attempts by the enemy to press into the flanks of the Panzer Army were repelled in heavy defensive fighting. Section attacks against the northern wing of the 167th Infantry Division, the bridgehead of the SS-Division "Totenkopf," the northern front of the XLVIII Pz. Corps, and LII Armored Corps south of Pena were warded off. Counterattacks against local breakthroughs are still in progress.

More Than 400 Tanks Destroyed
Tuesday, 13 July 1943. The Wehrmacht High Command discloses:

North of Belgorod the German assault supported by the Luftwaffe seized a large sector of terrain after having smashed two enemy armored formations. Soviet counterattacks by strong infantry and armored formations collapsed with very heavy losses. The Russians had deployed these forces from other fronts, bringing them up from the reserve echelon to confront our spearhead and the flanks of the German assault, resulting in fierce diverting attacks in the area east and north of Orel. Yesterday, formations of the army, the Waffen-SS, and the Luftwaffe destroyed another 400 tanks. One hundred three enemy aircraft were shot down in dogfights and by Luftwaffe antiaircraft artillery.

Red Army Counterattacks
13 July 1943, Moscow. STAVKA reports:

During continuous, furious artillery duels, our troops counterattacked locally in the Orel sector last night and this morning. They achieved some gains in terrain. New Fascist attacks have been repelled.

The attack that General Rokossovsky launched at midnight against German positions on the high ground north of Belgorod had favorable results. The Germans were thrown back at various points and had to move the front back several kilometers. More than 2,000 prisoners were captured as well as great amounts of all kinds of war materiel.

Hard Resistance
13 July 1943, Moscow. The Sovinformburo reports:

The battle between Orel and Belgorod is still in progress with undiminished severity. Our defenses have become more effective. After having made some local inroads in the Orel sector yesterday morning, heavy losses forced Hitler's troops to slow their attacks during the course of the afternoon. The Red Army counterattacked and recaptured the ground it had

Prokhorovka area, July 14, 1943, a German patrol taking cover behind a tank in "the merciless fighting surpassing human faculties . . ."

Maloarkhangelsk area, July 14, 1943, a Soviet tank soldier loading his tank: "The crisis of the battle east of Orel has passed its climax . . ."

lost during the morning. A thousand dead German Fascists and several dozen burnt-out tanks were left on the battlefield.

There was heavy fighting north and northeast of Belgorod on Monday. The enemy attacked along the entire front without letup from morning to night. The resistance of our Red Army soldiers grew even more stubborn and the German attempt to advance by counterthrust did not get far. This is the same attack that General Rokossovsky had driven back almost to Belgorod. Our Air Fleet flew continuous missions day and night against the German troops at the front and their communication lines.

From the OKW War Diary
Wednesday, 14 July 1943:

Front situation: Despite bad weather, attacks were continued successfully. The Fourth Panzer Army reached the Donets line and seized local bridgeheads. Strong counterattacks led by tanks were repelled. At the Second Panzer Army, the enemy kept up its fierce attacks with strong air and tank support in interior areas. The Luftwaffe attacked troop and railroad targets, as well as concentrations of tanks, and destroyed 103 enemy aircraft.

Decisive Hours at Orel
by war correspondent Wedel:

The large number of enemy forces committed in the offensive launched by the Soviets east of Orel that have come to light in the first forty-eight hours bear sober evidence of the dimensions of this action. We have identified two trench divisions, ten assault divisions, one artillery division, and two armored corps that have been committed by the Soviets in a limited area against the salient in the front sector extending farthest to the east in the Orel operational area. . . . The hours that have passed since Monday morning have seen more people die than sleep. . . .

In a few hours during the night, companies had to build up thin defensive screens without support from the right or the left. This new defensive line, receiving a couple of guns, assault guns, or antitank guns from other units, didn't have to rely on its own machine guns and antitank weapons. They constantly faced new enemy tanks rolling toward them followed

186

by masses of earth-colored Soviet infantry. Packs of strafing planes and other aircraft dove at them from the gray sky, trying to shatter their last remaining power of resistance with unhindered ground attacks using bombs, aircraft cannons, and machine guns.

Our soldiers have been in combat for days. They have disposed of their few belongings, their equipment, and everything in any way not essential. These were left in their old positions which were captured by the enemy. But they still have their weapons and ammunition, and are continuing to fight wherever their platoon or company has dug in; to resume resistance stubbornly and doggedly, without a thought as to how long they already have been engaged in combat, and how long it might go on like this, or how long they have been without hot food. . . . Who can judge what it means to be able to rise and counterattack despite desperate hopelessness and unrelenting combat beyond human endurance, with inadequate forces hoping to seize a few feet of terrain that just had been lost to the enemy's streamrolling tanks. . . !

The crisis of the battle east of Orel has passed its climax. The large-scale Soviet offensive, however, apparently has not been able to reach its goal, namely to penetrate the depth of the Orel operational area to check the German attack. The Soviets have not succeeded anywhere despite their superior forces. Thanks are due to the grenadiers and Panzer Grenadiers fighting in the eastern area near Orel, buying time until their leaders could undertake new operations.

Völkischer Beobachter, July 1943

German Offensive Discontinued
14 July 1943. The Sovinformbüro disclosed:

On the ninth day of the German offensive, Hitler's Field Marshal von Kluge almost had to discontinue completely his offensive operations at Orel. On the other hand, at the front at Belgorod, fierce fighting is raging on with undiminished severity.

Orel Front: The attacks of the German Fascist armored and infantry formations against Russian defensive systems at Orel continued to abate yesterday; they now are more like commando and patrol operations. Nevertheless, German artillery continues its counterbattery fire against our guns.

Belgorod Front: Although waves of German tanks and infantry have attacked our defensive lines, they have been repulsed everywhere. In some sectors the Soviet army was able to counterattack, leading to local shifts in the front. The battle is still very intense, but increasingly is turning into stationary fighting. In numerous towns there is bloody street fighting. The aggressors once more are suffering very heavy losses in their vain attempts to break through.

From the OKW War Diary
Thursday, 15 July 1943:

Front situation: In the Kursk area our offensive only gained ground slowly against very stubborn enemy resistance. Several enemy counterattacks were repelled. At the Second Pz. Army the enemy resumed his heavy tank attacks at the three penetration areas and gained additional ground.

At the other fronts there is only local fighting. The Luftwaffe supported our troops with approximately 3,000 missions during the day and night and shot down 212 enemy aircraft with 23 of our planes lost.

Kursk-Orel: A New Stage in the Battle
15 July 1943, Berlin. The DNB reports:

The situation at the Eastern Front is dominated by the new reserves and materiel that both sides have committed east and north of Orel. The Russians are concentrating on bringing up artillery units. With heavy artillery fire they are trying to stop the successful German counterattacks still in progress. It is quite obvious that the Soviet High Command is gasping for breath following its enormous expenditure of forces and materiel, and considers the fighting front north of Orel the right place to rest its troops. The Russian regrouping noticed yesterday now seems to be in full progress. With this, the overall battle is entering a new stage.

On the Battlefield
by war correspondent M. Lang:

. . . Trees destroyed, burned-out villages, fields furrowed by tanks, meadows pocked with craters, wrecked vehicles, and dead horses all mark the battle scene. The air is filled with constantly booming heavy gunfire, roaring rocket launchers whose missiles cross the sky like fiery dragons, and droning bombers and fighters. Human beings make themselves as small as possible and disappear into the earth, while the equipment celebrates orgies of destruction and seems to be triumphing over the living until the soldiers get up again and strike the annihilating blow.
Völkischer Beobachter, 15 July 1943

Counterattack at Orel
15 July 1943, Moscow. The Sovinformburo announces:

This evening the following special communiqué was made public: Our troops took the offensive in the north and east of Orel against German formations. The offensive was launched in two directions, from the sector north of Orel to the south and from the sector east of Orel to the west. In

Ponyri area, July 15, 1943, the infamous "rach-boom" (crashbang) 76.2mm division gun, Model 1942 (ZiS-3), one of the most frequently employed Soviet field guns, in firing position

189

the north of Orel our troops have thrust through the heavily fortified German defensive positions with a breadth of forty kilometers. They pushed forward forty-five kilometers in three days. Numerous enemy fortifications were destroyed.

German Troops on the Defensive
15 July 1943, Berlin. *Svenska Dagbladet* reports:

Military circles say that the Russians have stiffened their resistance in recent days. In fact one has the impression that the battle in the east is stagnating, with operations taking on a new aspect for the present. The Germans, who were attacking for a long time, have been forced to take up the defensive. In Berlin, however, it is believed that this is not disadvantageous, because the Russians have had to throw into battle reserves that had been designated for an offensive. Moreover, their losses have no relation to those of the Germans. The German Command apparently is assessing the fighting from the aspect of exhausting the enemy and seems to have let operational objectives become secondary to this goal. The fundamental idea apparently is to inflict great losses in materiel and personnel on the enemy while keeping friendly losses to a minimum. The Germans do not want to let the enemy enter the coming winter season in too strong a posture.

Behind the Scenes

Army Group South

During the night of 11/12 July 1943, formations of the Fifth Guards Tank Army (Lieutenant General Rotmistrov) moved into their operational area in the Kursk Salient. Early in the morning at 0315 the tanks of the 1st SS-Panzer Division "Leibstandarte Adolf Hitler" drove through pouring rain and with miserable road conditions into the center of Vasilyevka despite hard, house-to-house fighting. They were engaged in dogged battles with Soviet tanks coming from Petrovka.

At 0400 General Rotmistrov, who was just about to drive to his command post, received an order from the commander of the Voronezh Front that his reserves were to be moved immediately into the operational sector

Prokhorovka area, July 12, 1943: a unit of the German XLVIII Panzer Corps waiting for orders

of the Sixty-ninth Army (Lieutenant General Kryuchenkin) because the situation had grown worse. In turn, Rotmistrov ordered Major General Trufanov to conduct an immediate forced march toward Mal. Psinka-Podgarugi and attack German troops at Zhelyakhovoye-Izumenka in cooperation with the Sixty-ninth Army, to prevent the Germans from breaking through to the north.

To secure the left flank of the Fifth Guards Tank Army, the 26th Tank Brigade of II Guards Tatzinsk Armored Corps simultaneously was pushed into the sector of the Sixty-ninth Army. This concluded Rotmistrov's preparations for action. The units of his first echelon had reached their assembly points and were consolidating their new positions.

Army Group Center

On the eve of Operation "Kutuzov," the Second Air Army (Lieutenant General Krasovsky) under the command of the Western Front (Colonel General Sokolovsky) and the Fifteenth Air Army (Lieutenant General Naumienko) attached to the Bryansk Front (Colonel General Popov) flew a series of massive bomb attacks against German artillery and mortar positions, tank concentrations, and other significant positions in the northern part of the Kursk Salient.

Soviet troops on the left flank of the Western and Bryansk Fronts which had not yet had any contact with the Germans were finishing their final preparations for Operation "Kutuzov." Their mission was to attack the rear of the Ninth Army in the Orel Salient, aiming to encircle and annihilate Colonel General Model's formations as well as the Second Panzer Army. Marshal Zhukov: "After lengthy deliberations, we decided not to begin the attack after the preparatory artillery fire, as was customary at that time. This would have given the enemy information on when the attack would begin. Instead, we attacked when the artillery preparation was at its peak. This proved to be very effective."

Army Group South

In the southern part of the Kursk Salient, at dawn on 12 July 1943, the bridgehead at the northern bank of the Donets built by Colonel von Oppeln-Bronikowski with his battle group was reinforced by the 1st Battalion of Panzer Grenadier Regiment 114.

In the early morning hours, Soviet batteries in the northern part of the

Kursk Salient began the heaviest fire that the Eastern Front had ever experienced. The artillery of the Eleventh Guards Army (Lieutenant General Bagramian) assigned to the Western Front possessed more than 200 guns and mortars per kilometer of front in the area of the main effort. In the zone of the VIII Guards Rifle Corps, the Russians had 260 tubes per kilometer of front. In addition to this, the Eleventh Guards Army was reinforced with two tank corps whose 250 tanks were assigned the exclusive mission of immediate support of the infantry. As soon as the artillery preparation was over, the formations of the Bryansk and the Western Fronts took the offensive.

The Soviets quickly achieved deep penetrations in the flanks of Second Panzer Army (Colonel General R. Schmidt), advanced toward Orel, and at the same time threatened the Ninth Army. Model's formations were in grave danger. If the breakthrough were successful of the Soviet troops pushing forward from the north in cooperation with the Seventh Guards Army (Lieutenant General Shumilov) in the south, Model's divisions with approximately 600,000 men would have been encircled. A second Stalingrad of even greater dimensions was possible.

At the same time, Operation "Kutuzov" provided the Central Front the opportunity to finish its preparations for its own counteroffensive. General Rokossovsky's formations had the task of throwing back the troops of Army Group Center that had penetrated deeply into the Soviet defenses. Then they were to attack Kromy and proceed to the northwest in order to envelop German formations in the Orel area from the south and southwest. In conjunction with the Western and Bryansk Fronts, Rokossovsky's mission was to annihilate the encircled Germans.

Army Group Center

As this situation developed, Army Group Center had to redeploy at once the two divisions reinforcing Ninth Army. These divisions were committed with the three reserve divisions available in the Orel Salient to resist the Soviet counteroffensive. In addition, Ninth Army also had to relinquish two tank divisions and a number of extra heavy tank units which it had wanted to employ for its own assault operations. This made impossible the continuance of Operation "Citadel" in the area of Army Group Center.

Army Group South

At 0500 on 12 July, the 1st SS-Panzer Division "Leibstandarte Adolf Hitler" reported: "Linked up with Division 'Totenkopf.' Much rumbling of tanks before us. Intensive enemy air activity. Heavy artillery and infantry harassing fire in the area of Division 'Totenkopf.' Soviet strafing planes are beginning their attacks."

Toward 0600 the "Leibstandarte" repulsed a Soviet attack of regimental strength at the Prokhorovka-Petrovka line with very strong artillery fire. At 0745 Battle Group Horst attacked Sabyno in order to break through the last flank position of the Soviet defensive front.

At 0800 General Trufanov's troops reached the area allocated to him. Meanwhile the German III Panzer Corps (General of Pz. Tr. Breith) pushed elements of the Sixty-ninth Army to the north and threatened the left flank of the Fifth Guards Tank Army. Trufanov's troops, along with the 26th Tank Brigade, moved forward against the Germans and the II Guards Tat-

zinsk Armored Corps. The 53rd Guards Tank Regiment (Major Kurnozov) advanced to Novo-Alexeyevka–Vyzelok.

While the Fifth Guards Tank Army was preparing for action, Army Group South was finishing regrouping its forces at Prokhorovka. More than 700 tanks, predominantly Panzer IVs G and H with 75mm guns, and more than 100 Tiger and Panther tanks, plus heavy Ferdinand assault guns were waiting for the order to attack. The formations were to repeat their advance on Prokhorovka from the south and west in the morning in order to break through to Kursk. Lieutenant General Rotmistrov: "In order to forestall the enemy attack, the launching of the counteroffensive was moved up from 1000 to 0830. Because the weak artillery forces were not yet ready for action, I ordered artillery preparatory fire to last only fifteen minutes."

Thus at 0830 in the northern part of the Kursk Salient the formations of the Bryansk Front and the left flank of the Western Front opened the attack. At the same time the Fifth Guards Tank Army and Fifth Guards Army began their operations against Army Group South. As the relocation and final assembly of the Fifth Guards Tank Army occurred so rapidly and went unnoticed by the Germans, the appearance of General Rotmistrov's tank formations on the field of operations was a great surprise. Lieutenant General Rotmistrov: "At 0830 the Fifth Guards Tank Army received the order to attack in the sector three kilometers southwest of Yakovlevo, left of Beregovoye-Krasnaya Dubrava, right of Provorot-Belenikhino . . . The first echelon rolled at full speed toward the combat formations of the German tank forces."

Prokhorovka area, July 12, 1943, one dares to break through: A Soviet T-34/76B tank knocked out far behind the German lines by antitank fire

193

The Fifth Guards Tank Army and the elements of the Fifth Guards Army (Lieutenant General Zhadov) attacked with their main effort in the Prokhorovka area toward Yakovlevo. The Soviet First Tank Army and the bulk of the Sixth Guards Army attacked with the same objective north of Melovoye-Kruglik. East of Belgorod the three rifle divisions of the Seventh Guards Army (Lieutenant General Shumilov) attacked. The Soviet Command reinforced the troops with artillery, ordering the gunners to aim directly at the tanks.

General Rotmistrov decided to deploy his army, having a total of 850 tanks (mostly T-34s) and SU-86 self-propelled guns in two echelons. In the first there were three tank corps and in the second a mechanized corps supported by strong army reserves. The army reserve (Major General Trufanov) was composed of the 53rd Guards Armored Regiment, the 1st Independent Motorcycle Regiment, the 689th Tank Destroyer Regiment, and the 678th Howitzer Regiment. The II Armored Corps, which already had suffered heavy losses in previous actions, secured the boundary between II Guards Armored Corps and the main-effort troops of the Fifth Guards Tank Army with XVIII and XXIX Armored Corps and V Mechanized Guards Corps.

Every corps in the first echelon was reinforced with a guards launcher (Katyusha) regiment, one or two self-propelled gun regiments, and tank-destroyer regiments. The three tank corps in the first echelon were allocated a sector of approximately 3.5 kilometers for their offensive with forty-five tanks per kilometer of front. The XVIII Armored Corps (Major Gen-

194

eral Bakharev) was to annihilate the enemy in the Greznoye-Krasnaya Du-brava sector and deploy in a northwesterly direction, securing the attack of the bulk of the Fifth Guards Tank Army toward Tomarovka. The XXIX Armored Corps (Major General Kirichenko) was given the mission of de-stroying German forces in the sector of Zovkhoze "Komsomoletz"-Krasnaya Polyana and mopping up the Pokrovka area by evening. The II Guards Tatzinsk Armored Corps was to seize the Yakovlevo area by evening.

Immediately after the Fifth Guards Tank Army initiated its attack, II Tank Corps (Colonel General Popov) was ordered to reinforce the first echelon of the army to be able to attack the rear of the German XLVIII Panzer Corps (General of Pz. Tr. von Knobelsdorff) in the direction of Safanovo-Oboyan. The V Mechanized Guards Corps (General Skvortzov) was to continue the attack on Bykovka.

All around Prokhorovka, once a sleepy little town amidst green hills, bordered by golden, ripening cornfields, the greatest tank battle of the Sec-ond World War was escalating minute by minute. The protagonists for the Soviets were Lieutenant General Rotmistrov and his Fifth Guards Tank Army and for the Germans the formations of the Waffen-SS with Obergruppen-fuehrer Hausser and the II SS-Tank Corps assigned to him. The dust kicked up by the tanks; the smoke from the guns; and the detonations and greasy, black clouds from burning tanks covered the sky and turned the sun into an ugly orange-gray disc. Above the dust and smoke-enshrouded battle-field, incessant dogfights raged. Swarms of Soviet "Stormoviks" flying low roared over the German tank spearheads while howling Stukas attacked Soviet tanks.

In this greatest mobile battle in the history of war, two focal points became evident: one west of Prokhorovka (location of the Fifth Guards Tank Army) and the other south of the town. Two Soviet mechanized brigades, a tank brigade, and a tank regiment under Major General Trufanov, the deputy commander of the Fifth Guards Tank Army, were fighting here.

All told on both sides, 1,200 tanks and self-propelled guns supported by the same number of aircraft were participating in the battle. Their rel-ative combat strengths were fairly well balanced. One Soviet advantage was that their tanks were faster and more mobile, virtues the Russians were masters at exploiting. They kept attacking boldly and at full speed into Ger-man assembly areas, firing point-blank at the German tanks.

The 2nd Company of SS-Panzer Regiment 1 was the first to engage these attacking tanks. In a sector which was at most 500 meters wide and 1,000 meters deep the German and Soviet tanks clashed. Although Soviet troops resisted stubbornly at the southern edge of Sabyno, the 1st Company of Panzer Grenadier Regiment 73 captured the town at 0900.

Nevertheless, in the sector of II SS-Panzer Corps, elements of the So-viet armored forces were able to penetrate the flank of the 1st SS-Panzer Division "Leibstandarte Adolf Hitler" by swinging to the south out of the Psel valley. They managed to reach the German artillery positions where they were annihilated in close combat by direct artillery fire. The 2nd SS-Panzer Division "Das Reich" captured the town of Stokhorozhevoye after fierce fighting in a counterattack that followed the earlier-repulsed Soviet tank attack.

Lieutenant General Rotmistrov: "The enemy attacked the Fifth Guards Tank Army toward midday and started to envelop its flanks. This unfa-

Prokhorovka area, July 12, 1943, at the edge of the battle-field: the remains of the hull of a Soviet T-70 light tank, its track idling wheel, road wheels and top rollers

УНЫЛЫЙ ХОР

«Геринг намекнул, что предстоит основательная чистка высшего офицерского состава, в результате которой кое-какие генералы будут выброшены на свалку».
(Из показаний немецкого лейтенанта Гельчута М.).

Рис. Бор. Ефимова.

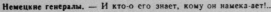

Немецкие генералы. — И кто-о его знает, кому он намека-ает!..

(*Left*) A caricature in PRAVDA, July 1943. Title: A Sad Choir. Caption: German generals: "And who knows whose head is going to roll!"

(*Right*) The Luftwaffe supporting the Panzer forces two Ju 87 just prior to a dive bombing attack

vorable situation was aggravated by an unexpected, serious crisis in the sector of the Sixty-ninth Army. In order to alleviate their situation, we had to commit not only the Army Reserve (Major General Trufanov), but also significant elements of the second echelon." The Soviet XXIX Armored Corps with the 32nd and 31st Armored Brigades in the first echelon held their ground against the attacks of the 1st and 3rd SS-Panzer Divisions ("Leibstandarte Adolf Hitler" and "Totenkopf").

At 1300 the Soviet XXIX Armored Corps was able to take hill 252.2. After being reinforced with a fresh tank brigade, it drove the German tanks back westward two kilometers and captured, in cooperation with the XVIII Armored Corps (Major General Bakharev), Sovkhoz Okatybrskiy. But at the same time, German armored forces succeeded in breaking through the front of the 95th and 52nd Guards Rifle Divisions of the XXXIII Guards Rifle Corps in the Krasniy Oktyabr-Kochetovka area. They advanced to the Vesely-Poleshayev line and drove the two Soviet Guards Rifle Divisions back to the north.

After the German tanks at Poleshayev had reached the sector of the Fifth Guards Army, they now threatened the right flank and the rear of the 5th Guards Tank Regiment. Lieutenant General Rotmistrov: "A very dangerous situation arose. My reserve, the attack formations of General Trufanov, advanced to the south, where elements of the second echelon also were marching. To secure the right flank, I could only fall back on the forces of the second echelon and commit the 24th Tank Brigade (Lieutenant Colonel Karpov) of the V Mechanized Guards Corps at Sovkhoz Vo-

198

roshilov. They were to use the XVIII Armored Corps to contain the enemy in the Poleshayev area. To alleviate the situation on the left flank of the Fifth Guards Army in the Ostrenkiy area, about nine kilometers northwest of Prokhorovka, the 10th Mechanized Guards Brigade (Colonel Mikhailov) of the V Mechanized Guards Corps was committed. Its task was to halt the enemy's advance with the support of the soldiers of the Fifth Guards Army. The situation was beginning to stabilize. The enemy's advance was stopped and he was forced to go on the defensive in this area." Gradually, the tide was turning.

At 1400 the first elements of the Fifth Guards Tank Army slowly and steadily pushed the II SS-Panzer Corps to the west, inflicting heavy losses in personnel and matériel. The XVIII Armored Corps, using the 181st and 170th Tank Brigades, took Koslovka and Vasilyevka after hard combat.

At 1430 the II Guards Tatzinsk Armored Corps broke through the German defensive line and reached the area east of Kalinin, where it encountered the 2nd SS-Panzer Division "Das Reich." Field Marshal von Manstein: "The battle had reached its climax. The decision on whether we would win or lose was imminent. On 12 July my headquarters knew that the Ninth Army had been forced to discontinue its assault and that the enemy had taken the offensive against the Second Panzer Army. But we resolved not to break off the battle prematurely. We still held one trump which we could throw into action, the XXIV Panzer Corps with the 17th Panzer Division and the SS-Division 'Viking'."

In the afternoon the situation was becoming unstable. The Fifth Guards Tank Army was forced to discontinue its attacks and go on the defensive along most of the line. But the II SS-Panzer Corps lost its momentum in the Prokhorovka sector for a few hours. It became crucial for mounted infantry to repulse the violent attacks of numerous Soviet tanks. The corps, however, was able to withstand the heavy Soviet onslaught both south and west of Prokhorovka and even to counterattack to the north at the Psel bridgehead. In the Pena Salient area, reinforced Soviet formations succeeded in making dangerous penetrations. There they forced the XLVIII Panzer Corps to go on the defensive.

At the same time the II SS-Panzer Corps was attacked in strength by the Soviet II Armored Corps which drove into the gap between II SS-Panzer Corps and III Panzer Corps. Here III Panzer Corps was engaged in heavy combat with the III Mechanized Guards Corps at Rzhavets and could not link up rapidly enough with the other German troops. Since strong Soviet attacks on the right flank and the front prevented further advances in the direction of Prokhorovka, the 3rd SS-Panzer Division "Totenkopf" attacked on the northern bank of the Psel. Having overcome two strong antitank defensive positions and defeated the attacking Soviet tank formation, it gained the Poleshayev hills.

In the afternoon, the bridgehead on the northern bank of the Donets, which Colonel von Oppeln-Bronikowski and his men were holding, received reinforcements from Battle Group Horst of the 19th Panzer Division (Lieutenant General G. Schmidt). Formations of III-Panzer Corps rolled quickly over the bridge toward Prokhorovka, seventeen kilometers away. This allowed them to overrun Soviet troops retreating to the north.

At the same time, superior Soviet forces attacked the right flank of the Raus Corps, assigned to the Kempf Army, penetrating it at one point. Ini-

tially, it was able to hold its position, but the situation in this sector remained extremely tense.

In cooperation with other units, the Fifth Guards Tank Army stopped the German Fourth Panzer Army (Colonel General Hoth) in its advance on Prokhorovka from the west, forcing it on the defensive. An attempt to break through to Prokhorovka from the south also was foiled. In the process, General Rotmistrov's tank brigades succeeded in penetrating deep into the right flank of the southern German spearhead. Colonel General Konev: "The enemy assault was stopped once and for all only by committing the Fifth Guards Tank Army commanded by Rotmistrov and the Fifth Guards Army under Zhadov."

On the same afternoon, the German III Panzer Corps was attacked simultaneously by the 96th Armored Brigade of the Sixty-ninth Army (Lieutenant General Kryuchenkin) and the 53rd Guards Armored Regiment of the Fifth Guards Tank Army. A dogged tank battle ensued with the 6th Panzer Division that lasted until after dark. The Soviet armored steamroller was brought to a halt late in the evening, but the II SS-Panzer Corps also had to break off its offensive and adopt a defensive posture. During the battle, all three Tiger companies that participated destroyed 120 Soviet tanks.

Neither Germans nor Russians could be judged the victors in the Battle of Prokhorovka, the greatest tank battle in the history of war. But its conclusion marked the end of Operation "Citadel." By the evening of 12 July 1943, the German tank reserves were exhausted, and the initiative went to the Red Army once and for all. Also, the heavy casualties among combat-experienced German tank crews took their toll. Freshly trained young crews often were killed in their first action before they had a chance to gain the slightest experience. One reason for the ultimate failure of the German advance toward the southern part of the Kursk Salient was the powerful counterthrust of the Voronezh Front reinforced with STAVKA's strategic reserves. The decisive role in this operation was played by General Rotmistrov and his Fifth Guards Tank Army.

Army Group Center

At the same time, furious battles were raging in the northern part of the Kursk Salient against the men of the Western and Bryansk Fronts supported by troop units of the Central Front. The objective of the Soviet offensive, Operation "Kutuzov," was to seize the greater Orel area. The left wing of the Western Front headed in the direction of Khotynets and Bolkhov, and the Bryansk Front was directed toward Bolkhov and Orel.

Colonel General Sokolovsky, a Soviet citizen descended from Polish nobility, was now commander of the Western Front. He energetically attacked on both fronts and was able to overrun German defenses by evening. Orel, Army Group Center's most important supply base, was in jeopardy, and the rear of the German Ninth Army was endangered. As of 12 July, Colonel General Model was assigned the command of both his Ninth Army and the Second Panzer Army (Colonel General R. Schmidt) on a group basis. Now for the first time, Model could demonstrate his skill at commanding operations of a defensive nature in a critical situation and on a large scale.

On that day, Field Marshals von Kluge and von Manstein received instructions to report to the Fuehrer's headquarters.

Also on 12 July, German prisoners of war held a meeting in a barrack in Krasnogorsk, a little town not far from Moscow. They had been brought here under Soviet guard from many camps scattered all over the USSR. A Communist writer, Erich Weinert, spoke to them about the primary goals of the National Committee "Freies Deutschland" (NKFD). The delegates at the founding conference elected thirty-eight members from those present, with Weinert as president of the National Committee. Unanimously they agreed upon the NKFD program which the exiled KPD (Kommunistische Partei Deutschlands, or Communist Party of Germany) had developed. The founding of the NKFD was achieved by the head of the Komintern, Man-

South of Orel, reviewing the situation in the middle of a cornfield: on the left, Col.Gen. Model, on the right, the commander of the Heavy Panzer Detachment 505, Maj. Sauvant

201

Prokhorovka area, July 12, 1943, a German tank company waiting for new orders: on the right, a Pzkpfw IV Model G with a 75 mm KwK 40 L/48 gun

uelsky, and NKVD General Melnikov, who had worked on this project for several months at the request of Stalin.

General of Artillery von Seydlitz, Lieutenant General von Daniels, Major Hetz, Flight Lieutenant Graf von Einsiedel, and Private Emendörfer were named vice presidents. In their black-, white-, and red-bordered leaflets intended for the troops at the front, the appeal to the German generals was no less than the ousting of Hitler as commander in chief, the immediate orderly withdrawal of German troops to the borders of the Reich before winter set in, and the resignation of Hitler's government, or no one would be willing to commence peace negotiations.

The Soviets, behaving with their usual secrecy, were careful that as little as possible be known about the NKFD even within the Soviet Union. In communicating with Soviet authorities or agencies, it was referred to simply as "USSR Institute No. 99." Practically none of the German prisoners whose names were connected with the NKFD realized that they were only chess figures in the Kremlin's game. Stalin referred to Hitler, but this really was aimed at his western allies.

By threatening to conclude a separate peace with Germany, Stalin wanted to persuade the Anglo-Americans to open soon a second front in Europe. The Soviets were not stingy with promises to the NKFD. They included, for example, unity of the German Reich as well as the 1938 borders that encompassed Austria. Significantly enough, they only gave this orally to the prominent members of the NKFD. Learning about the NKFD, the western allies saw this as evidence of a possible separate German-Soviet peace treaty. With the ghost of the 1939 Hitler-Stalin pact still spooking them, the west-

ern powers assured the Soviet Union that they would not conclude a separate peace with the Third Reich.

Later at the Teheran Conference (28 November–1 December 1943),
Stalin saw that his blackmail attempt had worked and that he was able to
prevail against the opposition of Roosevelt and Churchill in shaping Europe. It was obvious that the NKFD had fulfilled its main purpose for Moscow.

As the troops in combat became aware of the NKFD and its activities,
they considered it a Soviet propaganda operation. The severe hardships
and the violent fighting made it clear to them that in this war there was
only victory or doom.

Army Group South

On 13 July 1943, just before sunrise, in the southern part of the Kursk
Salient, the V Mechanized Guards Corps (Major General Kravchenko)
reached its assembly areas in the Rydinka-Avdeyevka sector. At this time
Major General Trufanov's tank formations and elements of the Sixty-ninth
Army were engaged in fierce fighting with the German III Panzer Corps
(General of Pz. Tr. Breith) in the Alexandrovka-Bol. Podyarugy area.

The 11th Mechanized Guards Brigade (Colonel Gritsenko) arrived in
the Prokhorovka area and attacked in the direction of Rydinka. The 26th
Guards Armored Brigade meanwhile was shelling Shchelokovo. The attack
was supported by heavy artillery and ground-attack aircraft.

The German 19th Panzer Division (Lieutenant General G. Schmidt) was

203

Rydinka area, July 13, 1943: A 15cm Nebelwerfer 41 (rocket launcher) being emplaced

decimated in this fight. It had to go on the defensive and subsequently was withdrawn. The 12th Mechanized Guards Brigade (Colonel Borisenko) reached Avdeyevka and attacked the high ground two kilometers south.

On the morning of 13 July 1943, the III Panzer Corps was crippled when an error by a Heinkel bomber He 111 practically wiped out the entire command group of the powerful German 6th Panzer Division, an irreplaceable loss for the troops who trusted implicitly these officers and their perfect teamwork. This tragic incident occurred when all the staff members were watching the air attack on Rzhavets from the front yard of the house in which the command post was billeted. Suddenly, one of the attacking aircraft dropped its bombs short of the target area. Fifteen dead and forty-nine seriously injured were the result of this error.

At the same time the Soviets were counterattacking strongly in the sector of the II SS-Panzer Corps and the 11th Panzer Division (Lieutenant General Balck). During the day the 6th Panzer Division, despite the heavy losses it suffered in the morning, broke through the Soviet defensive line between the Donets and Korotcha, stormed the dominating high ground of Alexandrovka, and opened the way to the north for an advance of the III Panzer Corps. Two other formations, the 7th and 19th Panzer Divisions of the III Panzer Corps, now moved from the bridgehead Rzhavets in the direction of Prokhorovka. Despite all their efforts, the last three kilometers to the town of Prokhorovka were unattainable.

On the same day in support of the Soviet army, fighter squadron "Normandie" of the Free French flew several sorties. It attacked German ground formations opposite the sector of the Eleventh Guards Army (Lieutenant General Bagramian) in the Ilyinskoye area and the Soviet Fourth Tank Army (Lieutenant General Badanov). The French had been assigned the newest Soviet type of Jak-9 fighters and often served as escorts for other Soviet ground-attack aircraft such as the "Stormovik" (IL-2).

On 13 July 1943, Hitler conceded that Operation "Citadel" had failed. Therefore, the OKW began to plan the removal of various large formations from Army Groups Center and South. Among them was the II SS-Panzer Corps (SS-Obergruppenf. Hausser) which was to be sent as rapidly as possible to Italy. Hitler: "The loss of Sicily practically is certain because of miserable Italian leadership. Perhaps Eisenhower will land tomorrow on the Italian mainland or in the Balkans. . . . I have to prevent that. This is why I need the divisions for Italy and the Balkans. As I have nothing more to withdraw anywhere after relocating the 1st Panzer Division from France to

South of Belgorod: the 6th Pz.Div. field repair shop. A maintenance team overhauling a tank out in the open

Orel area, mid-July 1943, first aid: an improvised medical station in the lee of a tank

the Peloponnesos, these reinforcements must be removed from the Kursk Front. Therefore, I am forced to discontinue 'Citadel.'"

Field Marshal von Manstein: ". . . Well, the situation developed as I had warned on 4 May in Munich, if 'Citadel' were postponed." Manstein, who had not yet utilized all the formations of his Army Group, insisted Operation "Citadel" be continued to exhaust the Soviets. To accomplish this, however, the Ninth Army (Colonel General Model) was ordered to hold its position.

Manstein continued to hope that he could prevent a major Soviet offensive at the other sectors of the Eastern Front by smashing their tank reserves in the Kursk Salient. Field Marshal von Kluge, commander of Army Group Center, considered it impossible for the Ninth Army to resume the offensive. Hitler, on the one hand, refused to hear anything about pulling Ninth Army back to its starting point, as Kluge demanded. On the other hand, he approved Manstein's plan to attack again with his weakened Army Group South in the sector of Fourth Panzer Army (Colonel General Hoth). Fourth Panzer Army was informed that II SS-Panzer Corps was to be transferred immediately to Italy and that the XLVIII Panzer Corps (General of Pz. Tr. von Knobelsdorff) was to transfer his most powerful troop unit, Panzer Grenadier Division "GD," to the command of Army Group Center.

It became a matter of concern to cover up the removal of numerous divisions of Army Group South that were needed to block Soviet penetrations in the Orel Salient. In order to conceal from the Soviets the withdrawal of these formations and the considerable depletion of Army Group South, these unit rotations were declared to be large-scale preparations for a massive attack on Kursk. The troops, however, were not to learn that these preparations were meant only to deceive the Russians. While discussions about the new Army Group South operations were in progress at Hitler's headquarters, the Red Army resumed its heavy offensive against Manstein's troops.

In the evening the Soviet 26th Guards Armored Brigade and the 11th and 12th Mechanized Brigades with elements of the 92nd Guards Rifle Division began an offensive at Shchelokovo, Rydinka, and Wypolsovka. This threw Manstein's troops back six kilometers to the south, enabling the Fifth Guards Tank Army to stop the advance of the III Panzer Corps, thus preventing it from interfering with the Soviet advance on Yakovlevo. By sundown, the Soviet Third and Sixty-third Armies had penetrated approximately fifteen kilometers into the German defensive lines.

205

In the northern part of the Kursk Salient the Eleventh Guards Army (Lieutenant General Bagramian) of the Western Front advanced on Bolkhov and Khotynets. They broke through the German defensive system, penetrating it to a depth of twenty-five kilometers. The attack of the Sixty-first Army of the Bryansk Front toward Bolkhov was developing. It achieved an eight-kilometer-long penetration in the German lines. Thus after two days of violent fighting, the defenses of the German Second Panzer Army were breached in three crucial sectors.

On Wednesday, 14 July 1943, by 0600, in the southern part of the Kursk Salient, Panzer Grenadier Division "Grossdeutschland" (GD) already was receiving heavy Soviet artillery fire while getting prepared for its own operations. During the morning, it was able to counter several Soviet thrusts from the north and west. Because of repeated attacks by strong tank units against the flank of its right battle group, which was moving toward hill 247.0, it could make only slow progress. The division was, however, able to destroy several tanks and inflict heavy losses on the mounted infantry which subsequently had to stream back to the west and southwest. Here the Russian troops ran into artillery fire of the XLVIII Panzer Corps and were smashed.

A Soviet thrust that began at 0700 from the direction of Zhakhovo against the 7th Panzer Division was repelled. An hour later the commander of the 6th Panzer Division, Major General von Huenersdorff, was shot fatally in

A Soviet poster, mid-July 1943: "We are sweeping the vile invader out of the way!"

208

On the morning of July 14, 1943, Melekhovo area: on the right the commanding general of the 6th PZ.Div., Maj.Gen. von Hünersdorff reviewing the situation. Shortly afterwards he was fatally wounded driving to the front line

the head by a Soviet sharpshooter while driving to his forward division command post.

The XLVIII Panzer Corps was engaged in heavy fighting all day, its infantry moving forward in several waves supported by continuous artillery fire. The Soviets attempted an attack with most of the units of its XXXI Armored Corps to break through the German positions despite high losses. General von Knobelsdorff: "I committed my last reserve battalion to support the front."

The armies of Army Group South still had not heard anything about Hitler's intention to break off Operation "Citadel." Now, Manstein informed his subordinate commanders of the OKW plan and simultaneously ordered Fourth Panzer Army to attack the Soviet troops between the Psel bridgehead and the road to Oboyan across the Psel and throw them back. But this order could no longer be carried out.

Meanwhile, II SS-Panzer Corps attacked once again. It pushed forward close to Prokhorovka and broke through the stubbornly defended Soviet position south of the town on the Lipovy Donets. The XLVIII Panzer Corps was able to push forward so far to the north that it could observe the Psel valley west of Oboyan.

Late in the afternoon in the Berezovka sector, elements of Panzer Grenadier Division "GD" contacted the 3rd Panzer Division (Lieutenant General Westhoven) which was attacking from the south. Repeated fierce Soviet counterattacks against them failed.

At 1930, the 19th Panzer Division (Lieutenant General G. Schmidt) in cooperation with the 7th Panzer Division (Lieutenant General Freiherr von Funck) which was encircling from the south seized the woods and the town of Zhakhovo.

After having repulsed new, strong assaults by the Soviets, the III Panzer Corps had cleared so much space east of Syeverny Donets to the east and to the north that General Breith planned to advance into the river triangle from his bridgehead at the Syeverny Donets the next morning.

Shortly after sunset, the 7th and 19th Panzer Divisions terminated their operations on the western bank of the Donets with a successful assault on the Soviet troops at Plota and Yablonova, enveloping a strong group of Russians near Zhakhovo. The Kempf Army was able to link up with Fourth Panzer Army about ten kilometers south of Prokhorovka.

14 July 1943 can be considered a successful day all along the front lines of Army Group South. Field Marshal von Manstein: "On 14 July, the SS-

Corps was able to seize Prokhorovka. . . . In this action, more well-disciplined and capable elements of the enemy's operational reserves were crushed, some severely exhausted." Yet all of this was too late to make Operation "Citadel" a success. From midnight on, it rained very heavily. The soldiers, wet to the skin, were forced to consolidate their positions and go on the defensive.

Arm Group Center

In the northern part of the Kursk Salient the Soviets again tore deep gaps in the front lines of the Second Panzer Army to the northwest, the north, and the east. Therefore, the Second Panzer Army, instead of covering the rear of Ninth Army, had to receive support from it in order to prevent annihilation. This situation forced Army Group Center to give up all further offensive operations. Lieutenant General Katukov, commander of the First Panzer Army: "Toward evening on 14 July, the Fascists brought their actions in our sector to a close. When I reported this to the commander of the front, he replied, to my joy: 'At the other sectors, too'."

On the morning of 15 July 1943, it was still raining. As early as 0300, the northern part of the Kursk Salient already was resounding with Soviet artillery fire that lasted until 0530 with undiminished strength. On that same day, following three days of intensive preparation, the armies of the Central Front's right wing (General of the Army Rokossovsky) launched a counteroffensive with the Forty-eighth Army (Lieutenant General Romanenko), Thirteenth Army (Lieutenant General Pukhov), Seventieth Army

(*Left*) Shakhovo area, July 14, 1943: a 19th Pz.Div. grenadier in a Soviet position just captured

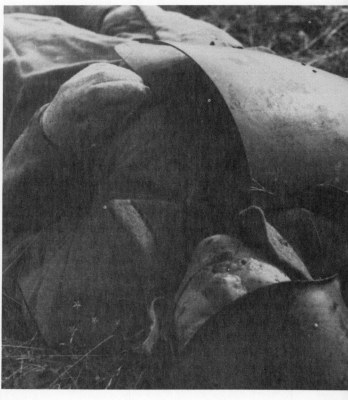

(Lieutenant General Galinin), and Second Tank Army (Lieutenant General Rodin). According to official Soviet information, the Central Front had massed up to 70 tanks and 230 guns per kilometer of front. The rifle divisions attacked on sectors about three kilometers wide. The main effort ran in a northwesterly direction toward Kromy-Orel and Gremyachevo, where Colonel General Model's troops were situated.

In the meantime, the Western and Bryansk Fronts kept pushing farther and farther into the German lines. Forward elements of Sixty-third Army (Lieutenant General Kolpakchi) and Third Guards Tank Army (Lieutenant General Rybalko) encountered the German XXXV Army Corps (General of Infantry Rendulic) east of Orel. The vital German supply route, Bryansk-Orel, was disrupted for two days by the advance of Soviet tanks and individual demolition parties. The initial result of this Soviet counterattack was that four German major units were forced to go from the offensive at Kursk to the defensive at Orel.

Army Group South

In the southern part of the Kursk Salient, Manstein's divisions reached their objective at the Donets, Seym, and Vorskla, but their advance came to a standstill at the main road from Belgorod to Oboyan. On 15 July 1943, Hitler ordered Army Group South to terminate offensive operations along the entire front. Lieutenant General Moskalenko: "On this day the fate of Operation 'Citadel' finally was sealed. The enemy had to go on the defensive. Our High Command now had the initiative in its hands."

The OKH decided to withdraw the Fourth Panzer and the Kempf Armies to new assembly areas where impregnable defenses were to be built as rapidly as possible. They wanted to transfer certain units from the Belgorod area in the northern part of the Kursk Salient to Orel in order to anticipate a Soviet attack in this sector. Starting in the evening, the divisions moved in three steps to their point of departure on 5 July 1943. It was very disappointing for the German troops to have to give up the terrain for which they had fought so hard.

(*Right*) Before Tagino, July 14, 1943, following action between the 2nd Pz.Div. and sections of the Soviet 60th Guards Div.: the dead captain of a Guards Div. regiment, wearing a breast armor

211

16 July–5 August 1943

Third

*Soviet Summer
in the Northern and
of the Kursk
Evacuation of Orel*

Phase

*Offensive
Southern Sections
Salient
and Belgorod*

530 Tanks Destroyed

Friday, 16 July 1943. The German High Command reports:

Heavy fighting at the center of the Eastern Front continued yesterday, despite the bad weather. Our troops' attack north of Belgorod gained more ground and resulted in encircling a strong enemy group. The strength of the enemy's counterattack faded in this sector due to its heavy losses in previous actions. On the other hand, the Soviets led diversion attacks with strong infantry and tank forces along the entire front from Kursk to Sukhinichi. These attacks were repulsed everywhere and more than 250 enemy tanks were knocked out in only a single army sector. All told, the Soviets lost 530 tanks yesterday in this great battle. In southern Sicily, German and Italian troops again repelled many British-North American assaults yesterday in the Agrigento-Catania axis of attack, inflicting heavy tank losses on the enemy.

Civilian Population Clears Mines

16 July 1943: The German 281st Division's order on the forced use of the civilian population to clear mines:

To mitigate the danger of mines on supply routes, I hereby order the following on the basis of past experience: The mine-infested supply routes are to be cleared daily by the use of several panje vehicles made available by the localities situated along the roads. The vehicles are to be loaded with

Psychological warfare in the Kursk salient: a Soviet pamphlet dropped after July 16, 1943

Two Summer Offensives

Zwei Sommeroffensiven

Am 5. Juli begann Hitler die Generaloffensive auf Kursk. **In 10 Tagen verloren die Deutschen:**

1392 Flugzeuge, 2818 Panzer

(davon mehr als 700 „Tiger"),

an die 100 000 Soldaten und Offiziere

allein an Gefallenen.

Ohne den geringsten Erfolg erzielt zu haben, wurde Hitler in die Verteidigung gedrängt.

Am 12. Juli begann die russische Offensive im Ra von Orel. Die Russen durchbrachen die deutsche V teidigung in einer Front von 70 km und

rückten in 3 Tagen 45 km vor,

besetzten über 110 Ortschaften, machten über 2000 Gefangene,

erbeuteten 40 Panzer, 210 Geschütze u. a. m. Auf Schlachtfeld blieben die Leichen von mehr als 12 deutschen Soldaten und Offizieren zurück. **Die Offensive der russischen Truppen dauert erfo reich an.**

DAS SIND DIE TATSACHEN.

stones and, driving one behind the other, are to draw plows behind them weighed down with tree trunks in order to expose the mines or make them explode.

We suspect that some of the civilian population is working hand in hand with the guerrillas, helping them lay the mines. The measures that have been ordered will at the same time deter the inhabitants from aiding the partisans.

Abt. Ia draft signed: von Stockhausen

New Offensive
16 July 1943, Moscow. STAVKA informs:

The new offensive of the Soviet army commenced with heavy artillery fire lasting half an hour. This gunfire, also supported by numerous bomber formations, destroyed the extensive German fortifications that had been built during the past eighteen months. Subsequently, our armor and infantry assault began and met practically no resistance in its early phase. Our offensive against Orel is continuing to make progress both in the north and east. We were able to widen substantially the breaches in the two sectors. Our tank spearheads are pushing forward at a rapid pace. Despite unfavorable weather, there have been strong air battles near Orel for the past three days.

Strong Defensive Fighting
Saturday, 17 July 1943. The German High Command announces:

While operations north of Belgorod lessened, strong defensive fighting continued in the Orel area. The Russian attacks were repulsed in hard fighting, the advantage going first from one side to the other. In the entire sector another 251 tanks were destroyed yesterday.

The Suburbs of Orel under Fire
17 July 1943, Moscow. STAVKA informs:

Since yesterday our artillery has been firing with increasing intensity on the German defensive positions at the edge of Orel. The counterattacks in this front sector that were thrown back by our forces cost the Germans 3,500 soldiers killed and approximately 70 tanks destroyed. Our Red Army soldiers advanced in their frontal attack from the north along the Orel-Bryansk railroad line. At several points our troops are less than twenty kilometers from the railroad and have interdicted it at some places with artillery fire.

Unsuccessful Breakthrough of the Front
Sunday, 18 July 1943. The German High Command announces:

The battle on the Eastern Front also has extended to the Southern Front and has, on the whole, become more intense. Soviet attempts to break through our lines with strong infantry and armored forces were defeated by the stubborn resistance of our troops. Counterattacks are in progress to clear up small local breaches. In the Orel area, strong defensive fighting is con-

A caricature in the *Daily Express*, London, July 1943: THE TWO GENTLEMEN OF VERONA, an allusion to Hitler's and Mussolini's last meeting before the latter's fall in Feltre, near Verona

"THE TWO GENTLEMEN OF VERONA"

tinuing, undiminished in intensity. Yesterday, 415 Soviet tanks were destroyed.

The fighting in Sicily also has become more intense. The city of Agrigento was evacuated under the pressure of strong enemy armored forces.

Strong Enemy Resistance Before Orel
18 July 1943, Moscow. The Sovinformburo announces:

The Soviet offensive against Orel has gained another ten to fifteen kilometers during the last twenty-four hours. Despite massive commitment of Fascist reserves which are being thrown into battle directly from the marching line, heavy Soviet pressure is still being felt.

Enemy resistance is strongest east of Orel. Since Saturday noon, German armor and infantry divisions have conducted no less than twelve determined counterattacks which were repulsed in bloody hand-to-hand combat. Numerous German strong points were wiped out and up to eight kilometers of terrain seized. The vanguard of a Soviet armored brigade whose objective is Orel was still standing eighteen kilometers east of the city at noon on Sunday.

German air defense has diminished considerably, to the extent that the Soviets now have air supremacy.

216

From the OKW War Diary
Monday, 19 July 1943:

Front situation: The enemy continued his offensive with strong artillery and armored forces supported by his air force. In the Kharkov-Orel area our front lines were held everywhere, whereas northwest of Orel very heavy enemy attacks resulted in new breaches. In view of the violent enemy offensive, it no longer seems possible to complete Operation "Citadel." In order to shorten the front our offensive operations will be discontinued.

News Blackout
19 July 1943, Moscow. The Sovinformbüro announces:

The Soviet army is continuing to advance along the entire front at Orel. At the Southern Front, strong Soviet attacks are still in progress, according to unofficial reports. Our High Command has forbidden all detailed reports for the time being.

Three Focal Points of the Battle
19 July 1943, Berlin. The Office Français d'Information reports:

The Soviets continued their offensive from Orel to the Sea of Azov with undiminished pressure, but were apparently unable to achieve any decisive results. Presently, three distinct focal points of the battle have developed.

Orel area, July 19, 1943, "calling off their own attack": an armored infantryman laboriously bringing MG ammunition forward

The first lies at the Mius, where the Red Army attempted to break through the German front; according to official German reports they, however, failed. The second is at Kursk, where Russian pressure let up yesterday. In Berlin this is attributed to the fact that the enemy is beginning to feel the heavy losses he sustained in the German offensive. Orel marks the third focal point. The fighting there is the fiercest, and the situation is apparently extremely tense.

From the OKW War Diary
Tuesday, 20 July 1943:

Front situation: The enemy continued his violent attacks that on the whole could be repulsed by the Sixth Army and the First Panzer Army. In the Belgorod area, reserves were released when our front-line troops were pulled back. In the sector of Second Panzer Army, the enemy achieved a breakthrough with strong armored forces and pushed forward to the Bryansk-Orel railroad line. The Luftwaffe combatted hostile troops and tank concentrations, directing their main attention to the breakthrough area at Bolkhov.

Partisans are Supporting the Fighting at Orel
20 July 1943, Moscow. STAVKA informs:

During the past twenty-four hours, our heroic troops have been able to deepen and widen the wedge driven from the north against the Bryansk-

There's some soup left! Belgorod area, July 20, 1943: The troops have to be fed even while the battle is in progress. The crew of a medium armored personnel carrier (SdKfz 251) receiving its hot rations

Tomarovka, west of Belgorod, July 20, 1943: a collecting point for captured weapons. Here a stack of the tried and true Soviet-Type PTRD antitank rifles (cal. 14.5mm) that were often also employed as antiaircraft guns against the slow Ju 87 in the Battle of Kursk

219

Orel railroad line. At various places, our troops, in overcoming dogged German resistance, are only fifteen kilometers north of the enemy's defensive line. Karachev is being threatened by our pincer movement whose two prongs are directed northeast and northwest of the city. Strong Fascist formations are defending the railroad line. Meanwhile, large partisan detachments also have become engaged in the fighting at Orel. They are destroying the German communication lines and strong points behind the front.

From the OKW War Diary
Wednesday, 21 July 1943:

Front situation: The main effort of the enemy attack was along the Kursk-Orel road, where the enemy was able to penetrate to a depth of ten kilometers in the direction of Orel with three armored corps. At the other fronts, the enemy is conducting holding attacks with strong artillery support. The Luftwaffe attacked troop objectives and tank concentrations at the Donets and Orel.

Sudden Soviet Advance at the Southern Front
21 July 1943, Moscow. The Sovinformbüro reports:

Concerning Red Army attacks on the Southern Front, we now may report that they were accompanied by exceptionally strong artillery support. They were conducted along a wide front from Izyum to Taganrog and had the goal of attaining jump-off positions for our offensive in the Donets Basin. Our troops encountered a very strongly built enemy defensive system in which the Germans fought doggedly in order to prevent a penetration in the Donets Basin that would threaten the Fascist army at the Mius with encirclement. Following a few hours of heavy fighting, the Soviet army crossed the Donets at many points between Izyum and Lisichansk and the Mius at Krasny Lukh and built extensive bridgeheads.

The Battle for Orel
21 July 1943, Moscow. Reuters reports:

The offensive against Orel is continuing to favor the Russians. Their two pincer arms northwest and southwest of the city are beginning to close.

While the German troops in Kursk are withdrawing, the people at home have to continue to believe in victory:

Berlin, Thursday, July 22, 1943

Incredible Bolshevik Losses, OVER 5000 TANKS IN 14 DAYS!

"Forward, comrades—we have to withdraw!" Belgorod area, July 22, 1943, armored infantrymen changing position

The German army numbering approximately 200,000 men in the Orel area is threatened by envelopment, although the encircling ring is still open about fifty-five kilometers in the southwest.

Increasingly Difficult Situation for the German Defense
21 July 1943, Berlin. *Svenska Dagbladet* reports:

On Tuesday in Berlin one gained the impression from the news coming from the Eastern Front that German troops were, on the whole, able to hold their positions against the attacking Russians. The Russian offensive has, according to German reports, made considerable, even decisive progress. Military circles, however, warn against hasty predictions about the final success of the defense. They emphasize rather that the battle has not yet reached its climax.

In fact, this seems to be the case according to present reports. The situation apparently has become more serious during the past twenty-four hours. German news coverage, which up to now endeavored to be moderately optimistic, has taken on a subdued tone. It is saying that military circles report that one cannot ever foresee the outcome of a battle. They seem to be anticipating that certain sectors of the front will have to be moved back for they now are talking of "an elastic defense," an expression that one has encountered in connection with earlier German reverses. The German High Command is applying tactics designed to exhaust the Russians and inflict great losses on them, while sparing German troops as much as possible.

Close-Quarters Combat at the Main Fighting Line
Thursday, 22 July 1943. The German High Command announces:

Yesterday, the Russians continued their unsuccessful attempts to break through German positions along the entire front from the Sea of Azov to the Orel sector. Some of their attacks were conducted with fresh forces. Their focal points were at Kuybyshevo, Izyum, north of Belgorod, and in the Orel Salient. They collapsed because of our defensive ground fire and bombing in front of our lines or were brought to a halt in combat at close quarters in the primary defensive line. All local breaches have been cleared immediately with counterattacks.

221

German Defensive Line at Orel Penetrated
22 July 1943, Moscow. STAVKA reports:

East and north of Orel the fighting within the German defensive zone continues. In view of the numerous concrete machine-gun and artillery positions, tank traps, mine fields, and wire obstacles, our assault operations can make only slow progress. Every kilometer gained is consolidated immediately and followed up by artillery. That we were able to push in the enemy fortification zone to a depth of from five to seven kilometers within thirty-six hours despite these difficulties shows how tremendously the strength of the Soviet army has grown.

The battle has turned into dogged fighting at close quarters practically along the entire length of the front. Fascist resistance continues to be most stubborn south of Orel. The action in the Belgorod sector is gaining constantly in intensity. Hitler's generals are conducting strong counterattacks, without, however, being able to stop our troops. Several towns have been stormed. The Soviet air force again led heavy attacks on Orel and Karachev last night. Both at the Donets and the Mius Fronts, tenacious fighting continues for control of river crossings and the domination of high ground.

From the OKW War Diary
Friday, 23 July 1943:

Front situation: On 22 July, the focal point of the enemy attack was at Orel, where our front had to be moved back. The withdrawal movement at Belgorod went as planned. Five hundred sixty-six enemy tanks were knocked out. The Luftwaffe supported the difficult defensive fighting despite unfavorable weather.

The Guards Tank Army in the Suburbs of Orel
23 July 1943, Moscow. STAVKA states:

North of Orel, our troops captured a strip of terrain about ten kilometers wide on the western bank of the Oka. A guards tank army broke through the enemy's fortified belt directly east of Orel yesterday afternoon against fierce and tenacious enemy resistance and is heading toward the city which, however, is still protected by German defenses.

Karachev area, July 23, 1943, a German supply column after being hit by Soviet ground attack planes

Radio Beromuenster (Switzerland)
23 July 1943:

Eight days ago today, on 16 July, Churchill and Roosevelt announced the political objective that they were pursuing with the Italian campaign by directing a proclamation to the Italian people. The Soviet government may be pursuing a similar goal by supporting the creation in Moscow of a committee called "Freies Deutschland" (Free Germany) composed of German prisoners of war and emigrated politicians. . . . At the Eastern Front the German offensive against the Russian salient in the front at Kursk no longer dominates the situation. Instead, the Russian counteroffensive against the German salient in the front at Orel now is the most important event.

The Russian High Command went on the offensive with the greatest commitment of tanks, mobile artillery, and aircraft and won back the terrain seized by the Germans during the first phase of the summer battle. Moreover, these actions were accompanied by renewed combat activities at the Donets and Mius Fronts in those areas between Kharkov and Rostov made famous by last year's battles.

Whether these are major Russian offensive thrusts, or simply actions of local significance to obtain improved jump-off positions for later offensive action, cannot be ascertained from here at this time.

From the OKW War Diary
Saturday, 24 July 1943:

Front situation: The enemy continued his attacks in existing sectors with strong artillery, tank, and tactical aircraft support everywhere. Army Group South warded off incessant attacks along the entire front all day.

At the Ninth Army sector, strong enemy attacks were repelled along the road Kursk-Orel. The Second Pz. Army was able to repulse the strong, enemy, armored assaults.

Soviet Counterattacks Repulsed
Sunday, 25 July 1943. The German High Command announces:

. . . Strong Soviet infantry and armored forces unsuccessfully attempted another breakthrough in the Belgorod area. In the Orel area in-

In PRAVDA, July 25, 1943: Directive from the High Command to Gen. of the Army Rokossovsky, Gen. of the Army Vatutin, Col.Gen. Popov. Yesterday, on July 23rd, the German July offensive in the area south of Orel and north of Belgorod in the direction of Kursk finally collapsed following successful combat on the part of our troops

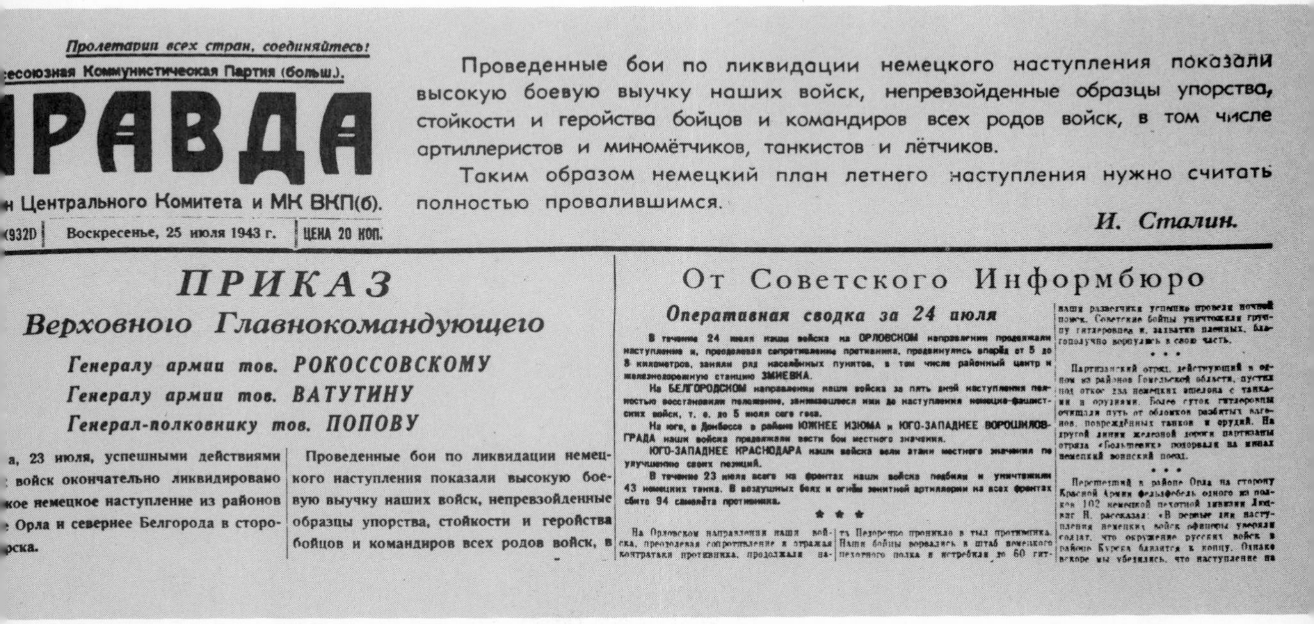
Пролетарии всех стран, соединяйтесь!
...есоюзная Коммунистическая Партия (больш.).
...РАВДА
...н Центрального Комитета и МК ВКП(б).
...(932D) | Воскресенье, 25 июля 1943 г. | ЦЕНА 20 КОП.

Проведенные бои по ликвидации немецкого наступления показали высокую боевую выучку наших войск, непревзойденные образцы упорства, стойкости и геройства бойцов и командиров всех родов войск, в том числе артиллеристов и миномётчиков, танкистов и лётчиков.

Таким образом немецкий план летнего наступления нужно считать полностью провалившимся.

И. Сталин.

ПРИКАЗ
Верховного Главнокомандующего

Генералу армии тов. **РОКОССОВСКОМУ**
Генералу армии тов. **ВАТУТИНУ**
Генерал-полковнику тов. **ПОПОВУ**

...а, 23 июля, успешными действиями ... войск окончательно ликвидировано ...кое немецкое наступление из районов ... Орла и севернее Белгорода в сторо...рска.

Проведенные бои по ликвидации немецкого наступления показали высокую боевую выучку наших войск, непревзойденные образцы упорства, стойкости и геройства бойцов и командиров всех родов войск, в ...

От Советского Информбюро

Оперативная сводка за 24 июля

В течение 24 июля наши войска на ОРЛОВСКОМ направлении продолжали наступление и, преодолевая сопротивление противника, продвинулись вперёд от 5 до 8 километров, заняли ряд населённых пунктов, в том числе районный центр и железнодорожную станцию ЗМИЕВКА.

На БЕЛГОРОДСКОМ направлении наши войска за пять дней наступления полностью восстановили положение, занимавшееся ими до наступления немецко-фашистских войск, т. е. до 5 июля сего года.

На юге, в Донбассе в районе ЮЖНЕЕ ИЗЮМА и ЮГО-ЗАПАДНЕЕ ВОРОШИЛОВГРАДА наши войска продолжали вести бои местного значения.

ЮГО-ЗАПАДНЕЕ КРАСНОДАРА наши войска вели атаки местного значения по улучшению своих позиций.

В течение 23 июля всего на фронтах наши войска подбили и уничтожили 43 немецких танка. В воздушных боях и огнём зенитной артиллерии на всех фронтах сбито 94 самолёта противника.

* * *

На Орловском направлении наши войска, преодолевая сопротивление и отражая контратаки противника, продолжали на-... ...ть Пезоречко проникло в тыл противника. Наши бойцы ворвались в штаб немецкого пехотного полка и истребили до 60 гит-...

...наши разведчики успешно провели ночной поиск. Советские бойцы уничтожили группу гитлеровцев и, захватив пленных, благополучно вернулись в свою часть.

• • •

Партизанский отряд, действующий в одном из районов Гомельской области, пустил под откос два немецких эшелона с танками и орудиями. Более суток гитлеровцы очищали путь от обломков разбитых вагонов, повреждённых танков и орудий. На другой линии железной дороги партизаны отряда «Большевик» подорвали на минах немецкий воинский поезд.

• • •

Перешедший в районе Орла на сторону Красной Армии фельдфебель одного из полков 102 немецкой пехотной дивизии Андреас Н. рассказал: «В первые дни наступления немецких войск офицеры уверяли солдат, что окружение русских войск в районе Курска близится к концу. Однако вскоре мы убедились, что наступление на ...

conclusive actions continued. The Soviets were repulsed in several places by our successful counterattacks. Local breaches were sealed off.

From the OKW War Diary
25 July 1943:

Front situation: At Army Group South, enemy breaches were cleared partially by counterattacks. The gap between the Ninth and Second Panzer Armies was closed. On the left wing of the Second Panzer Army, the enemy achieved deep penetration. The Luftwaffe supported all ground actions. The number of guerrilla attacks on railroad lines in the east reached a maximum of sixty attacks in one day's time.

The Battle of Orel
25 July 1943, Moscow. The Sovinformbüro states:

In continuing rainy weather, the heroic troops of General Vatutin carried on their encirclement of the Orel fortress. Progress was made at all the important sectors despite fierce Fascist resistance. Heavy Soviet siege guns were emplaced and put German strong points under concentric fire.

North of Orel the German units enveloped southeast of Bolkhov have been driven together into a restricted area under the concentric attacks of our troops. Soviet troops heading south along the western bank of the Oka are twelve kilometers from Orel. Northwest of the city, violent operations

are in progress between the Red Army and enemy armored formations south of Ilyinskoye. The railroad line from Bryansk to Orel has been disrupted at three points and all German attacks to secure the railroad embankment have failed.

To the south of Orel the Soviet army increased its pressure yesterday, advancing more rapidly than the previous day. The resistance of the elite Fascist troop units, however, continues to be extremely tenacious. On the Belgorod Front our troops occupied a series of additional towns yesterday. The fighting is now approximately twenty kilometers north of Belgorod.

The German Defense Strategy
25 July 1943, Berlin. *Svenska Dagbladet* reports:

Although the Russian High Command extended its offensive from the southern and central sectors to Leningrad a few days ago, according to German reports the focal point of operations in the east remains at Orel. Soviet efforts are depicted by the Germans as truly gigantic. How is the German eastern army resisting the Red Army offensive?

Military authorities in Berlin explain that the Russians have achieved only local successes up to now. The German plan is not so much to hold positions, as to exhaust the enemy. Thus, the public is being prepared for the eventuality that the front will be moved, which, in fact, has begun to happen to some extent. Nevertheless, there are no more doubts that German forces eventually will succeed.

Orel area, July 25, 1943, rescuing the wounded during the fighting: The troop doctor, who himself rode in a tank during the attack giving first aid. The waiting medium armored ambulance, Model C (SdKfz 251/8) gets the wounded out of the fighting zone to the main field hospital

Sacrificing terrain is part of the changed German strategy since Stalingrad. Until last winter German troops rigidly held the entire area that they had captured to the degree their strength allowed.

The German defense of the Ukraine this spring was already elastic and the exposed Demyansk and Rzhev salients have been evacuated. Military authorities hint that they are prepared to sacrifice some terrain that would cost too much to hold. Instead, the emphasis is on inflicting the greatest losses on the Soviets while sparing their own troops as much as possible.

From the OKW War Diary
Monday, 26 July 1943:

Front situation: The enemy is conducting very strong armored assaults against the center of the Ninth Army. The breach northeast of Orel could not yet be cleared. At Second Panzer Army, the enemy broke through the German main line of resistance with 100 tanks reaching a breadth of eight kilometers. At Fourth Army, active enemy movements and assembly areas were identified. In the air very strong hostile activity predominated while our own missions were reduced due to the weather.

Red Army Successes at Orel
26 July 1943, Moscow. STAVKA informs:

East of Orel, the enemy counterattacks lost much of their impetus yesterday and our troops moved forward several kilometers. They occupied

Belgorod area, July 26, 1943: The crew, dead tired, of an 88mm Flak antitank gun sleeping in the lee of their tractor

seventeen towns, some of which lie in the outer defensive zone of Orel. Several German units that had not withdrawn in time were cut off and crushed, with many prisoners captured. Enemy resistance also subsided north of Orel and General of the Army Rokossovsky's divisions made important terrain gains. The Hitler group that is enveloped south of Bolkhov was decimated in hard fighting following their repeated attempts to break out. The Red Air Fleet is supporting the advancing armored and infantry units with unprecedented commitment throughout the entire battle area.

Imminent Fall of Orel?
26 July 1943, Moscow. Associated Press reports:

The reports that the Germans are beginning to evacuate Orel are being confirmed. According to the latest dispatches from the front, General Rokossovsky committed strong reserves in all sectors and intensified the pressure on the fortress of Orel. Large Soviet formations are pushing toward Orel in the east, north, and south.

Soviet Breakthrough Attempt Repulsed
Tuesday, 27 July 1943. The German High Command announces:

The focal point of the fighting was in the Orel area yesterday. Our troops supported by many Luftwaffe sorties repulsed several enemy attempts to break through south, east, and north of Orel in bloody inconclusive actions and destroyed numerous tanks.

Actions Against the Last German Defensive Line
27 July 1943, Moscow. STAVKA informs:

The Soviet army is advancing systematically in the Orel area. While our troops at the center of the front (east of Orel) are engaged in heavy fighting against the last German defensive line, they have gained another five to ten kilometers in terrain to the north and south of the city. All told, seventy villages were recaptured yesterday.

Stubborn Enemy Resistance
27 July 1943, Moscow. The Sovinformbüro reports:

North of Orel the Soviet army built a new bridgehead on the western bank of the Oka. Our shock troops, that were committed in this operation, overran the German fortifications on the western bank and took more than a dozen villages in their attack. Toward evening, significant Fascist reinforcements intervened, slowing down the progress of the guards divisions. Northwest of Orel, the advance is continuing.

Scorched Earth at Orel
27 July 1943, Moscow. The Associated Press reports:

General of the Army Rokossovsky has again reinforced the flanks of his army at Orel while the attack directly east of the city against the well-constructed German inner defense system is proceeding inch by inch. By

(*Top*) This photograph taken at the sidelines of the Battle of Kursk is a rare coincidence: A Ju 87-G1 with a 37mm Flak 18 antiaircraft gun returning to its base from an antitank mission with its landing gear shot off and attempting a crash landing with its propeller upright

building a new bridgehead on the western bank of the Oka north of Orel, another section of flank cover for Orel was broken up. German troops, in as much time as the closely pursuing Russians give them, are destroying all communication routes and villages in their retreat.

Heavy Defensive Action Before Orel
Wednesday, 28 July 1943. The German High Command announces:

Heavy defensive operations in the Orel sector are continuing. On the remainder of the Eastern Front, the Soviet attacks have diminished in strength and size. Reports from the individual sectors of the fighting are that at the Kuban bridgehead and at the Mius and the Donets the enemy attacks are being defeated. In the Orel area, the enemy attacked again yesterday with undiminished strength. All attacks were repelled with heavy Soviet losses. The Rhenish-Westphalian 86th Infantry Division particularly distinguished itself at this front during the past weeks.

The Red Army Before Karachev
28 July 1943, Moscow. The Sovinformbüro reports:

Far to the west of Orel, General of the Army Rokossovsky has begun offensive operations against Bryansk. To the northeast of this city, Zhisdra already has been bypassed and nearly encircled. A strong, Soviet, armored formation is continuing to advance toward the west along the Orel-Bryansk

(*Bottom*) An example of the excellent air-tank cooperation between the Luftwaffe and the Panzer forces: A Stuka controller coordinating a bomb attack on Soviet positions via radio from his command armored car SdKfz 251/6. After the Soviet positions have been destroyed, the tanks are to advance

228

railroad line. At this time, it is approaching Karachev, which simultaneously is being encircled from the north.

German Withdrawal at Orel
28 July 1943, Moscow. The United Press reports:

Because the Soviets control a long stretch of the Orel-Bryansk railroad line and the roads leading from Orel to the southwest, the German High Command now is trying to withdraw strong German forces in the south of Orel to prevent their envelopment. The retreat is in full progress in several sectors of the front while rear guards are providing desperate delaying actions. According to the latest reports, the Germans are burning down the villages that they have evacuated and are taking their inhabitants with them; all bridges and roads are being destroyed. Eight Russian armies are pushing forward toward Orel. Some of them are already in the immediate vicinity of the city. Soviet air reconnaissance reports confirm that the Germans now are attempting to build a collecting area forty kilometers southwest of Orel.

From the OKW War Diary
Thursday, 29 July 1943:

Front situation: At Army Group South there are no engagements of any significance. On the other hand, at Ninth Army, enemy pressure continues to increase. The enemy is pursuing closely the Second Panzer Army's withdrawal. The commander of Army Group Center, FM von Kluge, turned to Hitler because of a teletype from the General Staff of the Army of 21 July and explained to him that the Army Group would be pulling strong forces out from the Orel Salient as soon as possible in the course of the current evacuation movement. Kluge protests about the criticism by the General Staff that he should have done this earlier because this course of action was not feasible any earlier.

Strategy of Mobile Defense
29 July 1943, Berlin. The DNB reports:

At the Eastern Front it is certain that the Russians will resume their massive attacks on the Kuban bridgehead, at the Mius, and south of Lake

Even the German press can no longer keep silent about the seriousness of the situation: (middle) Undiminishingly Fierce Defensive Fighting

Focal Point Near Orel

Ladoga after new troop units are reconstituted. To gain operational advantage, the German strategy of mobile defense in the Orel sector continues to deprive the Russians of realizing local terrain gains for which they must pay with the heaviest losses. Movements back and forth in various sectors are sapping Russian combat effectiveness as much as attacking multiple positions. The battle in the Orel area still shows all the signs of one of attrition in which the attacking Russians bear much greater losses than the defending Germans.

Dogged Fighting in the Orel Area
29 July 1943, Moscow. The Sovinformbüro reports:

In the course of their offensive, the troops of General of the Army Rokossovsky have recaptured 12,000 square kilometers to date, almost half of the 25,000 square kilometers making up the Orel Salient. All the roads and trails leading to the west are lined with destroyed or abandoned, as well as undamaged, Fascist war materiel. In the woods many German soldiers whose units have been wiped out are hiding. To the east of Orel, the battle is now raging within the inner German defensive ring just a few kilometers in front of the city. The Nazi troops are continuing to launch violent counterattacks at the Soviet wedge. The fighting is unusually dogged and has not led to any clear decision. Many villages have seen occupation troops change several times.

Human feelings of the sidelines of the Battle of Kursk: a prisoner, Col. Goryunov from the 29th Tank Corps of the 5th Guards Tank Army after having received first aid

230

Mobile action in the Orel area, July 29, 1943: a 20mm Flak 38 antiaircraft gun employed in ground combat

West of Orel, July 30, 1943: the sleeping crew of a horse-drawn field howitzer

South of Orel the enemy is withdrawing from attacks of elite Siberian troops. All Fascist attempts to hold in improvised positions have proved to be in vain. Since morning, forward Soviet units have been situated at the Kursk-Orel railroad line still sixteen kilometers away from the fortress.

German Withdrawal at Orel
29 July 1943, Moscow. Reuters reports:

The German army has begun to withdraw troops and materiel on a large scale from the Orel Salient through at most a thirty-kilometer-wide corridor.

Soviet Attacks Repulsed
Friday, 30 July 1943. The German High Command announces:

In the Orel sector, violent enemy infantry and armored attacks were repulsed.

Impending Decision at Orel
30 July 1943, Moscow. The Sovinformbüro announces:

After nineteen days of fighting for the Orel Salient, the battle is approaching its climax. To the north, east, and south our troops are situated approximately fifteen kilometers from Orel. Our guards formations are pushing forward along the Kursk-Orel railroad line and approaching the last railroad station near Orel which is being defended by a German artillery regiment. There are many indications that the Fascist High Command is preparing to withdraw, using major delaying actions, from the sector south of Orel. It is raining very hard at the front, so the earth is sodden to knee depth. In view of these ground conditions, Rokossovsky has been committing Cossack formations for several days now. These cavalry raids have disrupted German supply services as much as fifty kilometers behind the front line.

Radio Beromuenster (Switzerland)
30 July 1943:

Dramatic events of far-reaching significance have taken place during the past eight days. Practically no news has had such an impact on the world

231

since the war broke out as the downfall of the Fascist dictator, Mussolini, and the political system that he has led for twenty-one years. . . . According to an agency report from Moscow, the Russian High Command has an Army Group ready for an attack on Poltava, by which Kharkov is to be sealed off through an enveloping maneuver. The thrust is to be carried past Poltava to the bend of the Dnieper at Dniepropetrovsk. This is, by the way, the first time since the campaign in Russia began that the Red Army is the winning side in a summer offensive.

From the OKW War Diary
Saturday, 31 July 1943:

Front situation: The enemy resumed his assaults on the Kuban bridgehead. In the Orel area the Second Panzer Army repulsed numerous heavy attacks.

Bloody Soviet Losses
Sunday, 1 August 1943. The German High Command announces:

The actions that resumed at the Eastern Front on 31 July let up yesterday with the exception of the fighting in the Orel Salient.

At the Mius Front, our troops mounted a counterattack supported by strong Luftwaffe combat sorties north of Kuybyshevo. They encircled a strong Soviet battle group and annihilated them.

In the Belgorod area, the local Soviet attacks failed. Our counterthrusts in this sector were successful. In the Orel Salient, the Bolshevists continued attacking with strong infantry and armored forces all day. Their offensive collapsed with many bloody casualties and great materiel losses because of defensive fires from all weapons. A local penetration was sealed off.

Static War Before Orel
1 August 1943, Moscow. STAVKA informs:

In the combat sector north of Orel, our infantry was able to gain more terrain after having repelled a series of fierce counterattacks. Soviet armored formations have been attacking since yesterday evening. East of Orel, a guards division seized about two kilometers of terrain following hours of inconclusive fighting. South of Orel, Fascist resistance continues to be extremely strong. The battle for Orel has now assumed the characteristics of static warfare.

Return to Moscow
1 August 1943, Moscow. TASS reports:

After two years of working in Kuybyshevo, Foreign Minister Molotov now has authorized the Diplomatic Corps to return to Moscow. All embassies and legations have received notification from Vice Commissar Milochkov that he will, on behalf of the Kremlin, coordinate the move of the more than a hundred diplomats and nearly a thousand employees, for which special trains have been made available. The Diplomatic Corps had left the capital during the night of 15 November 1941, after Hitler's troops had

Belgorod area, August 1, 1943: soldiers of an SS-Panzer Division rescue a badly wounded Red Army soldier

broken through at Mozhaysk and seriously threatened Moscow. The return to Moscow is a sign of the deep confidence of the Kremlin and the General Staff that the war will be won and that our Air Fleet is now strong enough to be able to protect the capital.

From the OKW War Diary
Monday, 2 August 1943:

Front situation: The Sixth Army's attack on the breach at the Mius bridgehead was successful. The withdrawal of the Ninth Army and the Second Panzer Army occurred as planned. At the rest of the front, hostile thrusts by weak forces were repulsed.

Great Successes Before Orel
2 August 1943, Moscow. The Sovinformbüro announces:

The past twenty-four hours brought successes to our armies in the northeastern and southern sectors of the Orel Front exceeding by far those gained during previous days. The Soviet High Command reports that more than 100 villages in the vicinity of ten to fifteen kilometers of Orel have been liberated. The success is more remarkable because the ground is completely sodden due to constant rain and every movement makes enormous demands on the supply service. Nevertheless, Soviet troops were able to draw closer to the Orel-Bryansk railroad line on a wide front and have been situated at the railroad embankment since yesterday evening. Simultaneously, the highway running to the south of and parallel to the railroad line is under gunfire from our troops pushing forward from the south. Only the country road from the southwest to Orel is still open for the Germans to use.

Committee "Freies Deutschland" (Free Germany)

Orel area, a burning Soviet KW-1 heavy tank: This relatively slow tank suffered many losses

2 August 1943, Moscow. United Press reports:

In its editorial, *Pravda* deals extensively with the Committee "Freies Deutschland," which has been quite active politically since its founding. The

paper states that the new committee will play an active role in uniting the opposition against Hitler in Germany itself, significantly helping to overthrow the present German government and then assist Germany in its transition from war to peace.

In summarizing, *Pravda* lists the main points of its program: First, the overthrow of Hitler's regime by the people themselves; second, the formation of a national government possessing the confidence of the German people and the United Nations, and viewing a conclusion of peace as its first task; third, the reorganization of Germany according to democratic guidelines, guaranteeing that the future government of Germany shall suppress mercilessly any plot against the democratic state and the peace of Europe.

All Attacks Repulsed
Tuesday, 3 August 1943. The German High Command announces:

Several Russian attacks were repulsed fiercely at the Kuban bridgehead. The German attack north of Kuybyshevo is being continued with success. At the Donets Front, several weak enemy attacks collapsed.

In the Central Front, particularly southwest of Orel, the enemy continued his attempts to break through by committing new strong infantry, armored, and air forces. Our heroic fighting troops repelled all hostile assaults and retook, with air support, temporarily lost terrain. Again a great number of Russian tanks were destroyed.

Fighting for the Orel-Bryansk railroad line: the self-propelled gun "Wespe" with a light 105mm FH 18/2 field howitzer. This artillery vehicle on the chassis of a Pz-Kpfw II was quite unpopular. The high superstructure made it very top heavy, the hull was much too small for the five man crew, and the 32 round ammunition hardly permitted effective fire

237

Front situation: The enemy unexpectedly mounted an assault against the First Panzer Army with strong artillery and air support from the bridgehead at Izyum. It was possible with a counterattack to clear the breach.

At the Fourth Panzer Army the enemy broke through the right wing with 200 tanks but was repulsed finally following heavy fighting. At the Ninth Army he launched strong attacks with approximately 300 tanks and continued those west of the Orel-Kursk road. . . . One hundred thirty-one hostile aircraft were shot down and ten of ours were lost.

Rail traffic in the east was jeopardized greatly when the rails were blown up at numerous sites simultaneously (seventy-five large-scale attacks with approximately 1,800 detonations in the area of Army Group Center on 3 August). Incoming rail traffic was interrupted in the area of Army Group Center for forty-eight hours as of 4 August.

German Withdrawal at Orel in Full Progress
4 August 1943, Moscow. The Sovinformburo reports:

Our tank armies have been able to push closer to the railroad embankment between Orel and Bryansk during the last twelve hours despite fierce enemy resistance and to storm two more important barrier positions. The Fascist Germans now seem to have begun to withdraw from Orel. During the night, long columns were seen heading in the direction of Bryansk along the railroad embankment (normal rail traffic has not been possible for a long time) and on the highway running parallel to the railroad line. To cover these columns, the Fascist High Command has organized a strong concentration of rapid-firing guns and tanks.

From the OKW War Diary
Thursday, 5 August 1943:

Front situation: It was possible to regain the former main line in the operational area of Izyum. Fourth Panzer Army continued to push farther into the breach. The enemy attacked the east flank of the army with strong infantry and tank forces. The Second Panzer Army evacuated Orel ac-

On the Orel-Bryansk supply line, August 4, 1943, the last attempt to stop the overwhelming enemy: an 88mm Flak gun in rear guard action

(*Top*) Orel, August 4, 1943, the final moments in a completely evacuated town: The Obergefreite (corporal) at the steering wheel is wearing a "Kraftfahrer-Bewährungsabzeichen" (first class driver badge) on his lower sleeve

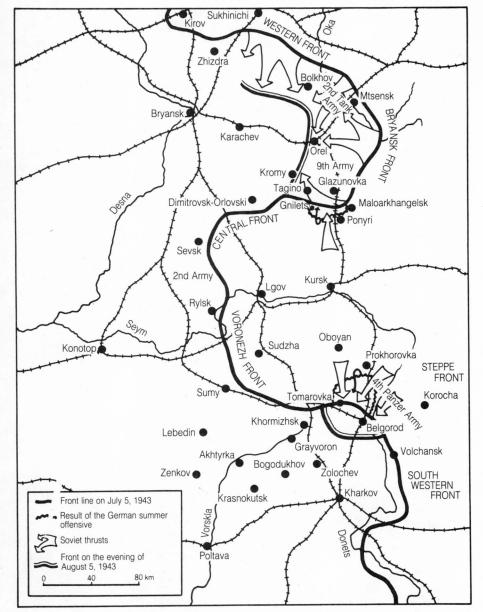

(*Bottom*) The Soviet summer offensive: In no time this operation nullified the gains won in Operation "Citadel"

239

cording to the withdrawal plan. . . . Both air forces were committed heavily. The enemy lost 126 aircraft, with 20 of our planes being downed. The railroad track was blown up at 1,763 sites in the rear area of Army Group Center, posing a serious threat to the movement of supplies to the troops.

Berlin Reports the Evacuation of Orel
5 August 1943, Berlin. The DNB announces:

Reports indicate that the Germans have moved their lines behind the ruins of the city of Orel after having smashed strong Russian attacks at the shortened flanks of the Orel Salient. The planned evacuation of all important military facilities and those vital to the war economy has been successful. The German forces were able to withdraw to more favorable positions that had been prepared in advance. The Russians did not detect this maneuver and therefore did not move against the new German positions until several hours after the evacuation. As a supplement to the Wehrmacht report, we are informed that a fundamental reason for the incessant Russian attacks in the area before Orel was that the Russian Command hoped to ameliorate their situation, even minutely, by seizing the city.

Orel has fulfilled its purpose for German tactics. . . . The German evacuation of the city was executed smoothly after all facilities important to the war had been destroyed. The Russians tried to retake the city before the systematic destruction of all important facilities and the withdrawal of German rear guards; this attempt failed.

Street Fighting in Orel
5 August 1943. STAVKA informs:

Yesterday our troops at the Orel Front continued their successful offensive. They advanced six to ten kilometers and pushed into Orel, where they are now engaged in street fighting with enemy forces. Our troops captured more than eighty villages in the area near Orel, as well as two railroad stations north and south of the city.

At the Belgorod Front, our troops again resumed operations against the Fascists, pushed forward ten kilometers, and improved their positions considerably. In the Donets Basin, in the area south of Voroshilovgrad, our

"Orel has served its purpose for the German direction of operations:" Under cover of a PzKpfw III German grenadiers (armored infantrymen) evacuating their positions in the suburbs

troops are engaged in local fighting and have improved their positions. At the Leningrad Front, in the area north and east of Mga, artillery and mortar fire was reported on both sides.

On 3 August, our troops destroyed or disabled 236 Fascist tanks at all fronts and have shot down 138 enemy aircraft in aerial combat or by antiaircraft gunfire.

Withdrawal in the Direction of Bryansk
5 August 1943, Moscow. Reuters reports:

West of Orel the German army is in the midst of withdrawing in the direction of Bryansk. The corridor is less than twenty kilometers wide. Through this, German main forces are streaming back to the west from Orel and are being attacked on both sides by strong Russian troops, trying to encircle as many of the enemy as they can. The long German motor vehicle columns that are being attacked by Russian ground-attack planes, fighters, and bombers are thronging the few, still-available roads. Some of these are also under Russian artillery fire.

In the south particularly, the advanced Russian detachments were able to drive far westward past Kromy. These units are for the most part raiding parties equipped with machine and submachine guns. They are riding in automobiles, light tanks, American jeeps, and other motor vehicles on side roads and paths through woods in the German rear area. They are attacking the flanks of the retreating columns in cooperation with the Red Air Fleet that has committed all available forces in pursuing the enemy.

Sudden Advance Near Belgorod
5 August 1943, Moscow. The Sovinformburo reports:

Having reduced the Orel Salient, our troops are now able to exploit the Kursk area as a jump-off position for an offensive toward the south and west. After about a two-weeks' pause in the fighting, Soviet pressure at this front intensified substantially yesterday and Red Army soldiers drove ten kilometers forward in a daring attack near Belgorod. As a result, the German front at Belgorod and Kharkov is in great danger.

Military action east of Bryansk, August 5, 1943: A Panzer detachment with PzKpfw V "Panther" during a break in the action. Foreground: captured Red Army soldiers waiting for transportation

241

From the OKW War Diary
Friday, 6 August 1943:

Front situation: With the Kempf Army, Orel was lost following dogged fighting. The right wing of the Fourth Panzer Army also had to be pulled back after several strong penetrations and breakthroughs. At the Ninth Army, the enemy continued to try to break through with strong forces at the flank. The Luftwaffe supported our own actions effectively. One hundred sixty-eight hostile aircraft were shot down compared to only twelve losses on our side. . . . Meanwhile, the rail situation has changed completely because of the simultaneous detonation of a mass of planted bombs that paralyzed all traffic in the rear area of Army Group Center. Fuehrer Directive No. 9 for Army Group Center prescribed measures to be taken in the operational area in the east. All army personnel not assigned vital tasks, those in available training units, dispensable air force personnel, and emergency units are to be used to guard the tracks. . . .

Orel and Belgorod Liberated
6 August 1943, Moscow. STAVKA's special communique:

On Thursday following fierce fighting, our armed forces at the Bryansk Front have occupied the city of Orel in cooperation with the troops situated at their flanks. On the same day, our troops broke enemy resistance at the Voronezh Front and occupied the city of Belgorod.

Enemy Successes Foiled
Saturday, 7 August 1943, Berlin. The DNB reports:

The Russians have been forced to give up the major objective of their summer offensive to tear open the German front to the west from the Kursk area. This resulted from a timely German counterstroke. Now they are trying

A cartoon in PRAVDA, August 1943: the Germans withdraw "according to plan"

to gain an operational success at least by committing mercilessly all of the considerable forces still left to them. The first attempt of this kind was aimed at the Orel area.

The German High Command, that had already intended to give up the Orel Salient to make more reserves available, was able to prevent the Russians from shortening the front. Instead of the planned envelopment, Russian efforts ended with such high casualties that the enemy's fighting strength is noticeably diminishing in this sector. The Russians may now want to achieve an operational success at any price in the Belgorod area like they did at Orel. If so, this attempt can no more be considered a large-scale operation with a major objective than at most taking advantage of opportunities.

(*Top*) Mobile warfare in the Orel area, early August 1943: a burning Soviet tank

(*Bottom*) The withdrawal in the Belgorod area, early August 1943: A German infantry regiment disengaging

W. Churchill to J. V. Stalin
Thursday, August 12, 1943:

Your telegram of 9 August gives me the opportunity to express my most cordial congratulations on the latest extremely important victories achieved by the Russian armies at Orel and Belgorod which free the way to further advances in the direction of Briansk and Kharkov. Defeat of the German Army at this part of the front will be a milestone on the road to our final victory. . . .

I am sending you a slide projector with a great number of slides which show the damage inflicted on German cities by our bombing attacks. . . . I hope you will have half an hour in which to inspect them. We know with certainty that in Hamburg 80 percent of the houses were destroyed. Shortly the nights are becoming longer and we will cause yet greater destruction in Berlin. This depends solely on the weather. These attacks will last a number of days and nights and will be the heaviest to date. . . .

Behind the Scenes

Army Group Center
On Friday, 16 July 1943, Soviet troops broke through the defensive lines of the Second Panzer Army (now Colonel General Model) and reached the Oleshnya River. Within five days the Third and Sixty-third Armies of the Bryansk Front (Colonel General Popov) had ripped a 36-kilometer-wide and 17- to 22-kilometer-deep gap in the German defenses. Meanwhile, Hitler ordered the II SS-Panzer Corps pulled out and transferred to the Belgorod area. This was contrary to the desires of FM von Manstein of Army Group South. On 16 July 1943, Model received permission from OKH to withdraw his army to a new assembly area. This movement, which was executed at night, came as quite a surprise to the Russians.

A Soviet flier from August 6, 1943, dropped in the area of Army Groups Center and south: Read and pass on! *OREL* the strongest focal point of the German defense system and *BELGOROD* were taken by the Russians on August 5th, 1943. The Russians also attack in the *SUMMER*?

Lesen und weitergeben!

OREL
der stärkste Knotenpunkt des deutschen Verteidigungssystems
UND
BJELGOROD
sind am 5. August 1943

VON DEN RUSSEN GENOMMEN WORDEN

DIE RUSSEN GREIFEN AUCH IM **SOMMER** AN!

244

A village near Opolkova, southeast of Orel, August 7, 1943: this village, too, will fall victim to the "scorched earth" strategy

Army Group South

On Saturday, 17 July 1943, the offensive of the Southwestern Front (General of the Army Malinovsky) and the Southern Front (Colonel General Tolbukhin) opened in the Donets Basin at Izyum and at the Mius at the same time that Army Group South had decided to withdraw its fatigued formations from Belgorod to new positions. The entire Eastern Front was now in motion. At the Southwestern Front, the First Guards Army (Lieutenant General Kuznetsov) and the Eighth Guards Army (Lieutenant General Chiukov) attacked. They were able to build a 30-kilometer-wide and a 10- to 12-kilometer-deep bridgehead in hard fighting at the western bank of the northern Donets. Meanwhile, the troops of the Southwestern Front began to gain a foothold on the right bank of the Mius.

Because of these operations of the two fronts, OKH lost the opportunity to transfer forces from the Donets Basin to the Belgorod and Orel areas. Worse yet, this forced the German Command to throw five Panzer divisions from Kharkov and one Panzer Grenadier division from Orel into the Donets Basin. Field Marshal von Manstein: "On 17 July the OKH ordered the immediate removal of the entire II SS-Panzer Corps for other missions. On 18 July two other Panzer divisions were ordered to be attached to Army Group Center. In view of this loss of troops, my headquarters saw ourselves forced to give up our own planned offensive, to break off the fighting, and withdraw our armies to new defensive positions."

On the same day, 17 July 1943, Army Group South's forty-two divisions (thirteen of which were Panzer and Panzer Grenadier) faced Soviet divisions enjoying a seven-to-one advantage. Manstein was helped temporarily, however. In addition to the XXIV Panzer Corps (General of Pz. Tr. Nehring) heading toward the Donets area, he was able to keep the II SS-Panzer Corps that Hitler still wanted to move to Italy in the Donets area for the time being. But there were increasing signs of an impending crisis. A new buildup of strong Soviet forces became evident opposite the weakened north wing of Army Group South. It was assumed that the main effort of the Soviet summer offensive here was to cut off and annihilate Army Groups A (FM von Kleist) and South (FM von Manstein). The troops of Army Group South were now back at their positions of 5 July 1943.

245

Norddeutsche Ausgabe
198. Ausg. / 56. Jahrg. / Einzelpreis 20 Pf.

„Freiheit und Brot"

Norddeutsche Ausgabe
Berlin, Sonnabend, 17. Juli 1943

VÖLKISCHER BEOBACHTER

Kampfblatt der nationalsozialistischen Bewegung
Großdeutschlands

Im Kampf gegen „General-Sherman"-Panzer auf Sizilien

PK. . . . 18. Juli

„Da, Karl, schau mal hin, was sich dort bewegt", der Zeigefinger des Unteroffiziers weist in die Richtung der Kaktushecken, die hier in Sizilien noch üppiger gedeihen als auf afrikanischem Boden.

Im ersten Augenblick kann der Angesprochene nichts erkennen, doch mit einem Male verrät drüben eine verdächtige Bewegung, daß ein feindlicher Panzer auf eigene Faust versucht, in die Flanke der deutschen Anwahr zu stoßen.

Zögernd tastet sich das Panzerungetüm vorwärts. Man muß schon die erhöhten Augen des Unteroffiziers W. besitzen, um überhaupt zu erkennen, daß es sich hier der...

Die Belastungsprobe unserer Front östlich und nördlich Orel

An einem Tage 530 Panzer vernichtet!

Vom 10. bis 14. Juli 300 000 BRT. aus der Landungsflotte versenkt

Berlin, 16. Juli.

Seit den frühen Morgenstunden des 11. Juli ist der so oft schon heiß-

Einkesselung einer Kräftegruppe

Privileg ohne Verpflichtung?

Von Eugen Mündler

Die Morgennebel wogten im ungeheuren Absturz der Nordwand des Eiger, und der Gipfel der Jungfrau, der am Vorabend in zartem Rosa hoch im blassen Himmel leuchtete, war nun in dicke Wolken gehüllt. Der Gletscher war grau und der Fels düster in dieser kühlen Morgenstunde auf der Scheidegg, da auch die Berge noch zu schlafen schienen im Schleier der Nebel und im dichten Gespinst der Wolken, die der Westwind in der Nacht um ihre Flanken gelegt hatte.

De trat aus dem Haus eine Gruppe von Männern, die unbeschwert von den Sorgen

---

The reports on enemy losses are supposed to gloss over the seriousness of the situation

Army Group Center

In the Orel Salient for the time being, Colonel General Model was able to stop the advancing Soviet formations in hard defensive fighting at individual sectors. General Shtemenko: "After five days the attack of the Bryansk Front developed relatively slowly and came to a complete standstill at the enemy's rear line along the Oleshnya on 17 July."

On 17 July 1943, in the afternoon, the Fighter Squadron "Normandie" of the "Free French," in coordination with Soviet ground-attack aircraft, conducted strafing attacks against supply columns of the German Second Panzer Army moving along the Bolot-Orel road. In this mission the squadron commander, Major de Tulasne, was shot down and killed.

On Sunday, 18 July 1943, in the sector of the German Ninth Army, the Soviets committed 600 tanks in the Orel area. The main effort was against the 36th Infantry Division (Lieutenant General Gollnick) and the 18th Panzer Division (Major General von Schlieben). This was the greatest number of tanks to date in a relatively narrow strip of front.

The impact of the Soviet assault against the Second Panzer Army forced OKH to bring up forces immediately from other sectors. Thus by 18 July, within one week, four Panzer divisions and one motorized division of the Ninth Army were transferred into the area of the Second Panzer Army.

Despite its heavy casualties in the Battle of Kursk, STAVKA again conducted its summer offensive on a wide front. The concentric attacks of the Western and Bryansk Fronts in the rear of the Orel Salient was, however, halted initially by the Ninth Army at Karachev. In order to accelerate the pace of the attack and crush the newly arrived German reinforcements in the Orel area, STAVKA ordered several formations of its strategic reserve into this operational sector. Therefore, at that time, the Western Front received reinforcement from the Fourth Tank Army (Lieutenant General Badanov) and the II Guards Cavalry Corps (Major General Kruykov). The Bryansk Front received the Third Guards Tank Army (Lieutenant General Rybalko).

At the Central Front the biggest problem these days was that supplies were not arriving on a steady basis, because the capacity of the Kastornoye-Kursk supply route proved to be insufficient. Help came from the Air Transport Force (Lieutenant General Skripko). Urgently needed ammu-

nition, blood, and medical supplies were flown in. On return flights, the aircraft evacuated some 21,000 of the wounded. This was the greatest Soviet air evacuation for wounded during the Second World War.

Also on 18 July 1943, Luftflotte 6 (Colonel General Ritter von Greim) began to pull out its squadrons. Complying with orders for scorched-earth tactics, airfield facilities and billets were destroyed and the terrain was mined with bombs that still were available.

During the night of 18/19 July 1943, STAVKA ordered the Steppe Front (Colonel General Konev) to join the battle.

During the morning of 19 July 1943, the Eleventh Guards Army (Lieutenant General Bagramian) broke through the entire width of the German defense, penetrating more than seventy kilometers. Its spearheads pushed south in the direction of Khotynets and now were situated just twenty-five kilometers from Karachev and twenty kilometers from Khotynets. Ninth Army's most vital communication lines were seriously endangered. A Soviet tank brigade crossed the Bryansk-Orel railroad line and was heading toward the highway further to the south.

The situation reminded the Germans of the disaster at Kalach. At that time, November 1942, similar developments led to the encirclement and annihilation of the Sixth Army in Stalingrad. Luckily for General Model, the Eleventh Guards Army had spread its formations along a sector of 150 kilometers in order to attack Bolkhov and Khotynets simultaneously. This diluted the effect of the attack. Therefore, it no longer was able to thrust forward from the Orel area into the rear of the German Ninth Army. To secure his communication lines, Model rapidly brought up new formations and again overcame a difficult situation.

To STAVKA's surprise, the imminent German catastrophe was warded off chiefly by the Luftwaffe. These also were the Stukas' last days of glory. Without rest, the VII Flieger Corps (Major General Seidemann) and other squadrons of Luftflotte 4 (General of the Air Force Dessloch) and all of Luftflotte 6 (Colonel General Ritter von Greim) attacked the Soviet formations in the breaches. Schlachtgeschwader 9 (Lieutenant Colonel Kupfer) and Panzerschlachtflieger (Captain Meyer) in particular distinguished themselves in this action. Dive-bombing Junkers Ju 87 G-1's, Henschel Hs 129 B-2s, and fighter-bomber Focke-Wulf FW 190 G-1's from nearby Karachev Air Base were covered by the fighters of Fighter Squadrons 3 and 52. They attacked the units of the Eleventh Guards Army with armor-piercing weapons while bomber squadrons with He 111's and Ju 88s were conducting heavy horizontal attacks against concentrations of Soviet tanks.

Colonel General Model: ". . . we succeeded for the first time in stopping a tank advance in the rear of two armies solely with Luftwaffe action." Meanwhile the Soviet Sixty-first Army (Lieutenant General Bielov) advanced twenty kilometers accompanied by violent fighting, encircling Bolkhov from the north and east and coming within five kilometers of the town.

248

At the same time, the Soviets attacked the entire front of the XLVIII Panzer Corps (General of Pz. Tr. von Knobelsdorff) with the main effort against the 36th Infantry Division and were able to make strong penetrations. The corps still counted eight divisions, but they really possessed only a fraction of their normal strength. Particularly, insufficient infantry proved a problem. There were no more reserves. General von Knobelsdorff: "A radical measure was dictated to prevent a breakthrough to Orel. I decided to withdraw the corps for a few kilometers as I already had contemplated doing."

General Model racked his brain on how to transport the indispensable military stockpiles out of overflowing dumps about to fall into the hands of the Soviets. There were 900 tons of rations just in the area of the XLVI Panzer Corps (General of Infantry Zorn). At Kromy, which was being contested fiercely, there were 4,000 tons of high-quality ammunition stacked in the Ivanovsk camp.

The left wing of the Bryansk Front reinforced with a tank division was not able immediately to break through German defenses at the Oleshnya. It took until evening to push forward ten kilometers west of the river. Major General Yakubovsky: "Despite the enemy's tenacious resistance and his incessant air raids, our tank formations were able to throw him out of his position on the Oleshnya and push forward ten to twelve kilometers by nightfall. Thus the adversary's rear area had been penetrated and the situation in the Bryansk Front's line of attack had changed suddenly."

A Henschel Hs129B-1 being prepared for take-off: this heavily armored, one-seater ground attack plane—also called "can-opener"—was employed in particular in action against motorized columns and clusters of tanks

On Tuesday, 20 July 1943, at 1345, a Fuehrer order arrived at Second Panzer Army headquarters forbidding any withdrawal of the Ninth and Second Panzer Armies. At the same time the Soviets were intensifying their attacks in the sector of the XLVIII Panzer Corps, but without success. Twenty Soviet tanks were knocked out. Toward 1800, immediately upon his return from the front, General Model aired his opposition to the Fuehrer's order in a telephone conversation with von Kluge in Smolensk. Kluge promised to intervene at the Fuehrer's headquarters.

During the following night, a partisan bomb attack on the Osipovichy railroad station took on unexpected dimensions. A new kind of magnetic mine, attached to a fuel-transport train, exploded, immediately setting the station on fire. Two ammunition trains on the adjacent tracks blew up, destroying a freight train transporting new Tiger tanks.

At 2100, von Kluge informed Army High Command 9 that Hitler had agreed to Model's withdrawal. On the night of 21 July, the moment of truth came for Lieutenant General Scheller, the commander of the reliable Austrian 9th Panzer Division fighting in the Orel area. Scheller, who had been decorated with the Knight's Cross for superb leadership, demonstrated rare courage, this time not in the face of the enemy, but his superiors. The general, who had been a soldier since he was nineteen years old, knew when he must not obey.

During the night of 20/21 July 1943, Scheller was ordered by General Harpe, the commanding general of the XLI Panzer Corps, to throw the Soviets off the high ground west of Krasnikovo with Panzer Grenadier Regiment 11 and Panzer Regiment 33. Panzer Grenadier Regiment 10 was to advance with weak infantry cover toward Koptevo and hill 213.0.

Scheller and his Ia (Lieutenant Colonel von Ruecker) agreed that the action, if carried out as prescribed, inevitably would lead to enormous casualties. For Scheller the fate of Panzer Grenadier Regiment 11 and its new regimental commander were at stake. Until 0230 Scheller struggled with himself. Meanwhile, all preliminary preparations were in progress. He then reported to General Harpe that the mission was not feasible. He was convinced that "his duties to the troops entrusted to him took precedence over all orders."

Orel area, following a Stuka attack: the end of a Soviet horse-drawn battery. In the background note a passing 37mm Flak 36 gun on a chassis with a 5-t tractor (SdKfz 6/2)

A short rest between uninterrupted action: two armored infantrymen fast asleep with a light MG 34 (cal. 79.2mm) and some handgrenades

251

Lt. Gen. Scheller, Commander of the 9th Pz.Div. in his command post (photograph from fall 1942)

At 0345 his Ia transmitted a written message to the corps chief of staff repeating his views. At 0420 the 9th Panzer Division reported its alternate plan of attack and requested approval from Corps. According to this new plan, Panzer Regiment 33 and Panzer Grenadier Regiment 10 were supposed to attack first as a spearhead followed by Panzer Grenadier Regiment 11 to screen the flanks of the assault.

At 0435 a radio message from General Harpe to Colonel Jollasse arrived at the division asking whether the division would be able to attack as ordered. Jollasse explained that the division would be able to do only what General Scheller had already reported to Corps. Ten minutes later General Harpe relieved Scheller of his command.

North of Orel, during the morning of 21 July, the Soviets attacked in strength in the sector of the 10th Panzer Grenadier Division (Lieutenant General A. Schmidt) and 9th Panzer Division (Colonel Jollasse). Following a successful breakthrough, they reached a position close to the command post of Grenadier Regiment 20 with tanks and infantry. This penetration was contained with the help of a tank detachment from the 9th Panzer Division. A Soviet tank also was knocked out in front of the command post of the 10th Panzer Division. It was fate that just a few hours later General Harpe had to rely for tactical support on that element of the 9th Panzer Division that had been the stumbling block in his controversy with General

Scheller. In the morning, the Red Air Fleet bombed and strafed the 1st Battalion of Panzer Grenadier Regiment 10 in its assembly area. At 1030 elements of Panzer Grenadier Regiment 11 were overrun. The 2nd Battalion of Panzer Grenadier Regiment 10 had the mission of regaining hill 222.4 south of Krasnikovo in an immediate counterattack, but was itself attacked at the same time. The 1st Battalion of Panzer Grenadier Regiment 10 and 1st Battalion of Panzer Regiment 33, both of which were intended for the attack west of Krasnikovo, were ordered personally by General Harpe to attack at 1200. But by 1425, Harpe already had to break off the attack under great Soviet pressure and go on the defensive in the occupied Karantiayevo-Koptevo line.

By noon, troops of the Bryansk Front attacking north of Orel had made a breakthrough into German positions about fifty kilometers wide and deep. They were, at this time, immediately in front of Orel, approaching the Orel-Bryansk railroad line by which the entire Orel Salient was supplied. Thanks only to waves of strong German air force attack planes was it possible to hold up the Soviet assault spearhead until the divisions from the south arrived to block it.

STAVKA's plan to push forward to Orel and take the city thus was thwarted. This was the last great mission flown by German ground-attack aircraft. General von Knobelsdorff: "As of 21 July, the enemy undertook no further major assaults. He had suffered terrible losses in advancing in

Belgorod, July 22, 1943, A call for forced evacuation: "Acts to the contrary will be most severely punished." In plain words: the death sentence

The new main line of resistance in a suburb of Orel: armored infantrymen waiting among the graves of their comrades for the enemy to attack

253

Orel area. The German forces try to stop the enemy advance again and again: an armored infantry unit marching to new defensive positions

waves following closely behind one another, and lay exhausted at the front . . . During the next days there were only small thrusts, supported, however, by tanks."

The breaches were sealed off one by one. With this, conditions required for the evacuation of the Orel Salient were satisfied. This was called the "Hagan Movement." The German Ninth Army, seriously weakened, no longer was able to hold its positions in the Salient.

The following day, Thursday, 22 July 1943, Colonel Teske, chief of the Transport Center, ordered an immediate evacuation of his offices in the Orel Salient. At the same time at the Optukha River, the Task Force Traut was formed, composed of the 78th Storm Division, elements of the 36th Infantry Division (Lieutenant General Gollnick), and the 262nd Infantry Division (Lieutenant General Karsk), and was assigned to the XXXV Army Corps (General of Infantry Rendulic). Its mission was to prevent an enemy breakthrough to Orel and simultaneously to secure the withdrawal. The evacuation preparations of the transport offices signified primarily that all railroad repair shops, valuable technical equipment, and trained local personnel would be moved to the rear. Colonel Teske: "The evacuation of the Orel Salient was successful because the headquarters of Army Group Center constantly pressured Hitler. If that had not happened, there would have been a second Stalingrad."

From 22 July 1943 on, active partisan formations detonated up to 750 mass explosives during the day by using a new kind of mine on the stretches over which the reinforcements for the German formations in the Orel Salient were moving. The single-track railroad line from Khutor to Michailovsky, for example, over which urgently needed troop reinforcements from Army Group South were marching, was paralyzed for two days. These new mines, especially when attached to fuel trains, caused fires that often spread to other trains and resulted in considerable materiel damage.

On Friday, 23 July 1943, following their successes in the Orel area, troops of the Bryansk Front (Colonel General Popov) pushed the Germans back to the Mtsensk sector. But when they reached the western bank of the Oka, they encountered stubborn German resistance.

Meanwhile Stalin was urging his two deputy commanders of major units, Marshals Zhukov and Vasilevsky, to proceed westward at an increasingly rapid pace. The troops, however, were worn out from the hard fighting of the past weeks and supplies were scarce, particularly fuel and ammunition. Marshal Zhukov: "Due to the extreme exhaustion of our First Tank Army as well as the Sixth and Seventh Guards Armies, the enemy was able to withdraw his main forces to the Belgorod defensive line by 23 July. The troops of the Voronezh and the Steppe Fronts, at the enemy's main line of resistance, were not able to counterattack immediately as the commander in chief had demanded."

In the Orel salient: Whenever the Germans have to withdraw only "scorched earth" remains

257

Army Group South

On the evening of 23 July 1943, in the southern part of the Kursk Salient, the troops of the Voronezh and the Steppe Fronts once again reached the line that they had held prior to the beginning of Operation "Citadel." Now, at STAVKA's orders, they started preparing for the counteroffensive in the Belgorod Kharkov line. Colonel General Konev, commanding general of the Steppe Front: "Operation 'Citadel' had failed completely. The conditions for the planned counteroffensive were present. The representatives of Marshals Zhukov and Vasilevsky met in my command post to evaluate the experiences we had had in the defensive battle."

By morning, Saturday, 24 July 1943, the Soviets had concluded the buildup of their troop units north of Belgorod.

Army Group Center

On Sunday, 25 July 1943, soldiers of the Bryansk Front began their assault to liberate Orel at the Oka and Optukha rivers. Resisting desperately, the German divisions were able to counterattack at individual sectors. The Luftwaffe tried, albeit unsuccessfully, to check the Soviet armored spearhead.

On the same day, Hitler surprisingly agreed not only to an extensive withdrawal of the Ninth Army, but even demanded that it be speeded up. The reason was his concern about developments in Italy. He just had learned of the overthrow of Mussolini. He wanted to withdraw as many troops as

This Soviet flier confirms: That neither the Moscow nor the Stalingrad defeat decided the course of the war but the collapse of the German offensive in the Kursk salient. Its conclusion: "GERMAN SOLDIERS! leave Hitler's doomed army. Refuse to run into the annihilating Russian fire. Save your lives. SURRENDER! This flier is a valid pass for German soldiers and officers who surrender to the Red Army"

Im Sommer 1942 verloren die deutschen Truppen pro Tag:
37 Panzer, 44 Flugzeuge, 5000 Soldaten und Offiziere.

Im Sommer 1943 verlieren die deutschen Truppen pro Tag:
460 Panzer, 200 Flugzeuge, 10 000 Soldaten und Offiziere.

WOVON ZEUGT DAS?

Das zeugt davon, daß sich im Verlaufe des Krieges das Kräfteverhältnis von Grund aus zugunsten der Roten Armee geändert hat.

Das zeugt davon, daß von nun an alle Abenteuer Hitlers von vornherein zum Scheitern verurteilt sind.

Die Katastrophe, zu der Hitlers jetzige Offensive führt, wird viel furchtbarer als der Zusammenbruch vor Moskau und Stalingrad.

DEUTSCHE SOLDATEN! Verlaßt die todgeweihte Armee Hitlers. Weigert Euch, in das vernichtende Feuer der Russen zu rennen. Rettet Euer Leben.

GEBT EUCH GEFANGEN!

Dieses Flugblatt gilt als Passierschein für deutsche Soldaten und Offiziere, die sich der Roten Armee gefangengeben

Эта листовка служит пропуском для немецких солдат и офицеров при сдаче в плен Красной Армии.

2625

(*Top*) Belgorod area, July 24, 1943: In hard combat the German rear guard tries to slow down the Soviet advance

possible from the Eastern Front to stabilize the situation in Southern Europe.

On Monday, 26 July 1943, at sunrise the Soviet Fourth Tank Army (Lieutenant General Badanov) and the Eleventh Guards Army (Lieutenant General Bagramian) launched their new operation. The bulk of the units moved in the direction of the Orel-Bryansk railroad line. The remainder approached the Bolkhov area to support the Bryansk Front in crushing German resistance there. The advance of the Fourth Tank Army, however, progressed quite slowly, only about five kilometers a day.

At the same time, at a conference in the Wolfsschanze (Wolf's Lair) Hitler demanded that Field Marshal von Kluge immediately transfer several of his divisions to the Italian Front. Field Marshal von Kluge: "My Fuehrer! I must point out that at the moment there is nothing to withdraw. It is absolutely impossible at this time!"

The OKH already was planning the complete evacuation of the Orel Salient, a pullback of the troops to the so-called "Hagan line" west of Orel. Meanwhile, Soviet armored forces renewed their concentric thrusts in the sector of XLVI Panzer Corps (General of Infantry Zorn). At the 102nd Infantry Division (Major General Hitzfeld), the Russians pushed forward up to five kilometers between Muravtshik-Zolotoye Dno and Grankino.

(*Bottom*) A demolition squad blows up sections of a railroad line

259

On Wednesday, 28 July 1943, elements of the Bryansk Front drove forward in the morning from the north in the direction of Orel. Their left-wing troops approached within twenty kilometers of the city from the southeast. At the same time German forces in the Bolkhov area were being smashed, thereby menacing the flanks and rear of German formations which were preparing for the defense of Orel. Toward noon, the OKH issued the order for Operation "Herbstreise" (autumn journey), the final evacuation of the entire Orel Salient and the withdrawal of Ninth Army and Second Panzer Army to the Hagan line along the banks of the Desna.

In a western suburb of Orel: two old people with the last of their belongings on their way into the unknown

260

Preparations were beginning for the massive withdrawal of units as of 1 August 1943. Continuous rainfall turned the roads and trails into a muddy wasteland which considerably impeded troop movements. On the same day, the Wehrmacht report used the term "elastic defense" for the first time. Initially it was applied only in the Orel sector. They wanted to try systematically to avoid the enormous concentrations of Soviet artillery and thus combat Soviet armored formations out of the reach of their artillery batteries. These delaying tactics could be employed only until Soviet motorized batteries moved to new positions under cover of the armored brigades.

Simultaneously with the Red Army operations in the Orel area, STAVKA intensified the activities of the many partisan detachments in the rear of the German front, particularly against German supply lines. Between 22 July and 1 August there were almost 7,500 explosive attacks on railroad tracks just in the Orel area. According to STAVKA, a downright "rail war" broke out.

The partisan attacks were aimed not only at German railroad trains and military facilities. Even the Luftwaffe was not safe from them. A bomber squadron based near Roslavl to support the troops in combat in the Belev area lost several crews and planes. At night, partisans who had intermingled with the Russian volunteer helpers from the local population (Hiwis), performing rough repairs on the airfield, attached barometrically activated explosive charges at the rear of bomb-loaded and fully fueled Ju 88s. When the planes lost altitude during subsequent missions, for example in attack dives, the charges detonated automatically and destroyed the aircraft in midair. At first, these incidents were puzzling; then an explosive charge with magnetic plates was found in the egg basket of a seemingly harmless Russian peasant woman.

On Sunday, 1 August 1943, Operation "Herbstreise" commenced in the Orel Salient. This systematic withdrawal was supposed to occur in four large movements from line to line, a distance of about 100 kilometers. At the same time, the OKH informed Colonel General Model that, following the movement, twenty divisions would have to be released for other fronts, mainly Italy. The planned orderly withdrawal was impeded by Soviet actions. Although the Red Army made several breakthrough and outflanking attempts, the German troops streaming rearward did not lose the initiative. Many rivers, often running from north to south through the whole Army Group area, facilitated the retrograde movement in some sectors.

General Model was now faced with the threat that not only might the Soviet Fourth Tank Army (Lieutenant General Badanov) cut off the Orel-Bryansk railroad line, but also that the troops of the Bryansk and Central Fronts might envelope completely the city of Orel. Orel was one of the Wehrmacht's main supply centers on the Eastern Front. The evacuation of the many storehouses, containing about 20,000 tons of valuable supplies, plus several field hospitals became an almost insolvable problem. Headquarters of Army Group Center in Smolensk demanded that it and not Model's headquarters release the units on each movement from line to line out of the Orel Salient. This was completely beyond supervision from Smolensk, which lay 250 kilometers farther to the west. The enemy, however, was following up so strongly that some close-in fighting already had occurred. Meanwhile, the front lines were drawing closer and closer to the city of Orel.

On Monday, 2 August 1943, the Staff Officers for Propaganda at Army Groups Center and South evaluated the results of Operation "Silverstreif." This large-scale propaganda action had started promisingly during the night of 6/7 May 1943, but now had to be viewed as rather a disappointment. In the entire area of Army Group Center there had been only 899 defectors in May, 1,087 in June, 2,345 in July; all told, 4,331 men. At Army Group South there were somewhat more: in May 831, in June 665, in July 3,543; all told, 9,370. During this period nearly one billion leaflets had been

dropped, or 106,724 per defector, making a weight of 150 kilograms per head. This propaganda operation in which the German High Command had placed such hopes in weakening the Soviet army was coming to an end.

The evacuation of the Orel salient, the "elastic defense"—a new concept that is supposed to make the Kursk defeat look harmless

Army Group South

On Tuesday, 3 August 1943, in the southern part of the Kursk Salient, the Voronezh Front (General of the Army Vatutin) and the Steppe Front (Colonel General Konev) attacked the northern wing of Army Group South (FM von Manstein) from the areas north and south of Belgorod in the direction of Belgorod-Kharkov-Poltava.

Major General Popiel, member of the War Council of the First Tank Army: "It was a peaceful, quiet morning. The dense fog in the gorges was rising and disappearing slowly. Suddenly fire came from the Katyushas. Everything from heavy artillery to regimental artillery joined the infernal concert with their volleys."

This large-scale attack (STAVKA had 70 tanks and up to 230 mortars and guns concentrated per kilometer of front in some sectors) began the second phase of the Soviet summer offensive. It hit full blast the unprepared German troops who were relieving other units on the main fighting line that very night. According to Soviet information, the Red Army had more than six times as many tanks and artillery as the Germans. Within the next three hours, the Fifth Guards Army (Lieutenant General Zhadov) and the Sixth Guards Army (Lieutenant General Chistyakov) pushing forward from the area south of Yakovlevo made deep inroads in the German

Sections of the Panzer Grenadier Division (armored infantry division) "Grossedeutschland" changing position. Foreground: two Kpfw III, in the background two Kpfw IV

lines, followed up almost unimpeded by hundreds of tanks. They overran supply columns on their way to the front lines, command posts, and billets. The Germans did not have even enough time to remove the warning signs from their mine fields. More than 300 partisans also participated in these operations. During the night, they shut down nearly all rail traffic in the rear area of Army Groups South and Center for two days by blowing up substructures in a series of simultaneous explosions forcing the German Command to take stronger security measures.

By noon at Tomarovka-Borisovka, the formations of the Voronezh and Steppe Fronts had driven forward six kilometers into the second German defensive line. At 1300, the First Tank Army (Lieutenant General Katukov) and the Fifth Guards Armored Army (Lieutenant General Rotmistrov) were ordered into the sector of the penetration to increase the operational depth of the breakthrough. Field Marshal von Manstein: "On 3 August, the enemy first attacked the Fourth Panzer Army and the front of the Kempf Army west of Belgorod . . . The Fourth Panzer Army was pushed back to the west and the Kempf Army to the south toward Kharkov."

By the evening of 3 August 1943, the Soviet armored formations already had advanced twenty-six kilometers. They were also able to break through at the boundary between the Fourth Panzer Army (Colonel General Hoth) and the Kempf Army and within hours enlarge the gap in depth and width. The German troops in the Kharkov area now were threatened.

Army Group Center

In the northern part of the Kursk Salient the spearheads of the Third Army (Lieutenant General Gorbatov) and the Sixty-third Army (Lieutenant General Kolpakchi) pushed into the city of Orel during the night of 3/4 August 1943. During the same night, the troops of the VIII Mechanized Guards Corps broke through the second German defensive belt in the Demnino area and rapidly pushed forward to the south.

Army Group South

On Wednesday, 4 August 1943, German resistance in the southern part of the Kursk Salient stiffened and stopped the advance of the Steppe Front. Colonel General Konev: "All attempts to strike the enemy in the flank were unsuccessful. . . . Although our tank armies already were fighting against their reserves, the Fascist armored formations offered dogged resistance." The assault formations of the Voronezh Front were making steady progress and meanwhile were threatening the flanks of the Kempf Army. Late in the afternoon, General Kempf decided to withdraw his troops because there was an acute danger that they might be encircled.

Army Group Center

In the meantime, fierce street fighting and house-to-house combat were raging all day in Orel. As the Soviet formations were making only slow progress despite their tremendous superiority, the chief political instructor of the Third Army, Colonel Amosov, and the chief of the War Council of the Sixty-third Army, Major General Abramov, tried to improve the spirit of the fatigued soldiers in a special way. In critical moments during combat, selected Red Army soldiers who were faithful to the party appeared where everyone could see them; with raised troop banners they ran toward the German positions shouting "For the Fatherland, for Stalin!". Even the assault units received piles of red flags that they were supposed to display on the most important buildings in the liberated villages.

This evening, the evacuation of the central district of Orel began, and during the night of 5 August 1943, after blowing up all the important buildings and supply facilities, the German troops withdrew from the city with heavy losses. They took up new positions east of Bryansk behind the Desna. The soldiers of the 5th Rifle Division (Colonel Mikhalitsyn) and the Third Army were the first to occupy the rubble that remained of the city. The Soviets continued their violent attacks without letup and pushed Army Group Center back to the area around Smolensk.

On Thursday, 5 August 1943, at 0600, following bloody street fighting, the 89th Guards Rifle Division (Colonel Seryugin) of the Steppe Front pushed into Belgorod. With the Soviet capture of Orel and Belgorod, the Battle of Kursk was over. The major German formations that had launched Operation "Citadel" in the northern and southern parts of the Kursk Salient exactly a month earlier, on 5 July 1943, now were pulling out.

Dolbino, a village approx. 20 km southwest from Belgorod: withdrawing German troops passing a burning church

265

In the evening, Stalin ordered fireworks in Moscow and, as an honorary salute for the troops that liberated Orel and Belgorod, twelve volleys for each from fieldpieces. From then until the end of the war the Moscovites proclaimed the victories of the Red Army with artillery fire.

Orel, August 5, 1943: the 105mm tank howitzer "Wespe" in the last street fighting. Shortly after this photograph was taken, German troops finally evacuated this beleaguered city

Moscow at 9 P.M. on August 5, 1943. A salute: 12 volleys from 125 guns proclaim the liberation of Orel and Belgorod

269

Epilogue

It was no coincidence that Stalin ordered the victory in the Kursk Salient to be celebrated with fireworks and a gun salute. The Russian dictator knew that the Soviet Union had won the Second World War with the Battle of Kursk and Orel. At Stalingrad, Hitler had lost only one army and, despite its size, only one battle, but he had not lost the war at that time. In the Kursk Salient, however, the turning point of the Second World War came. Hitler's last attempt to seize the initiative on the Eastern Front had been thwarted; the failure of Operation "Citadel" meant the beginning of the end. From now on the Germans in the east would always be on the defensive.

Deprived of all opportunities to conduct large-scale assault operations, the Germans went on the defensive along the entire Eastern Front. In the most crucial sector of the Second World War, the Germans forfeited the initiative to the Red Army, so the end of the fighting was only a question of time. The Red Army would continue to fight dozens of large and small battles on its way from Kursk to Berlin. The fate of the Third Reich, however, already had been sealed at Olkhovatka and Ponyri, Oboyan and Prokhorovka.

The German High Command made exactly the same mistake in the Kursk Salient that it had the year before at Stalingrad. At that time German formations had attacked the fortress Stalingrad, but this time it was the Kursk Salient itself that was turned into a fortress. Both times the Germans neglected the advantages of mobile tactics and met the Soviets on a battlefield that the Red Army had chosen. German losses, according to Marshal

270

A Soviet poster from
the fall of 1943:
The road to the
west is open

Zhukov, totalled 500,000 casualties, 1,500 tanks, 3,000 guns, and 1,500 aircraft. To this day, Moscow has kept silent on its own losses. We can be
certain, nevertheless, that they were no less significant. The Fourth Panzer
Army alone, for example, captured some 32,000 prisoners and destroyed
more than 2,000 tanks plus an almost equal number of guns.

Soviet armor was a determining factor in the victory at Kursk; for the
first time, they were employed not only in concentrated counteroffensives
and counterthrusts, but also in holding sectors on the defensive, either as
independent formations or in cooperation with mixed formations. The Soviet High Command then immediately employed in its next summer offensive what it had learned in the Kursk battle. At Kursk, for example, they

271

learned that the rifle units in mixed tank armies lagged far behind the armor. From then on, STAVKA drew up uniform tank armies and employed them as fast-moving motorized troops in the main spearheads in July/August 1943.

The German tanks simply were no match for the firepower of these concentrated tank destroyers. Colonel General Konev called it the "swan song of German armor." In fact, German tank losses in the two battles of war materiel at Orel and Belgorod were so high that the German strategy of operations with powerful motorized formations had come to a halt.

Following the discontinuance of Operation "Citadel" and the loss of German air supremacy, the feasibility dwindled for air-ground cooperation

On August 12, 1943 the theater of Operation "Citadel" is already deep in the rear area of the Red Army front

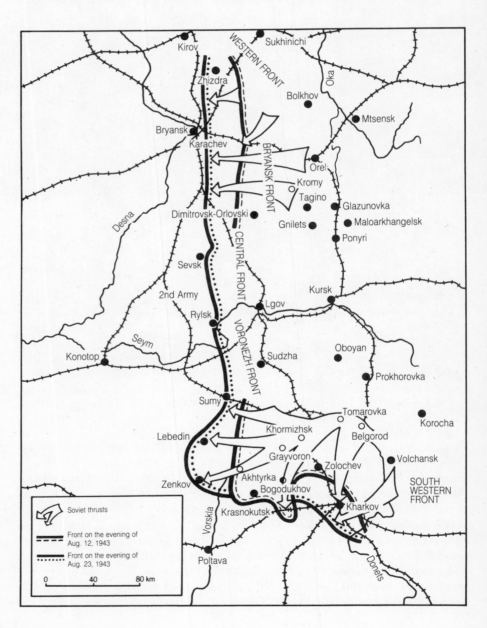

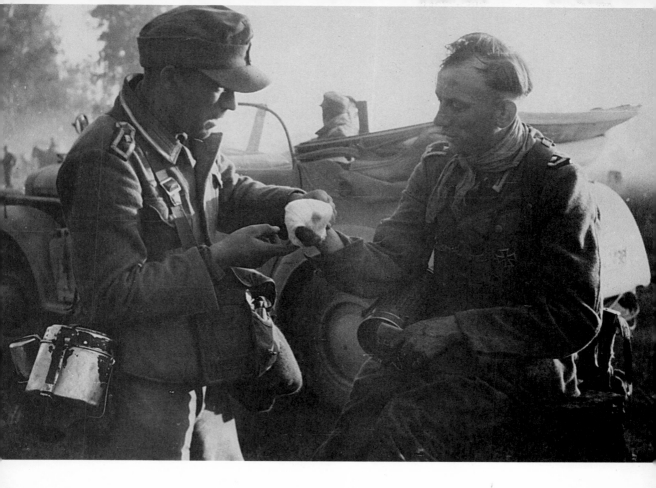

between the Luftwaffe and the Panzer forces, the basic principle for the former successes. The German Panzer formations now were faced with the difficult problem of protecting themselves from enemy air attack.

The Battle of Kursk was also a significant example of the right timing of a decisive counterattack. It did not start until the STAVKA strategic reserves had been concentrated and the German forces were worn out. The transition from strategic defense to a counterattack and then to an offensive testifies to the high standard of Soviet tactics. Typical was Soviet fronts entering the fighting at different times: the left flank of the Western Front and the Bryansk Front on 12 July, the Central Front on 15 July, the Voronezh and Steppe Fronts not until 3 August. This misled the German Command, and the consequent German attempt to ward off the Soviet assaults shattered any purposeful cooperation between Army Groups South and North. The battle itself and the repeated shifting from one sector of the front to another were disastrous for many German divisions.

The partisans contributed substantially to the success of the Red Army at Kursk-Orel. For instance, they blew up several railroad lines and bridges in the Orel area over which German reinforcements and reserves being moved from one sector of the front to another were just beginning to move.

Infantry divisions played no major role in Operation "Citadel." Organized as they were at that time, they already were a thing of the past. Although the operation was conducted in a confined area, the infantry di-

On one of the withdrawal roads: a Feldwebel (company sergeant) giving first aid to a comrade

273

vision's lack of vehicles made a real difference. A quick change in direction is a peculiar feature of a moving battle that involves concentrated use of tanks. The advance or assembly of infantry, the relief or new commitment of these troops marching on foot, tormented by heat and other hardships, required three times as much time as experience showed armor units needed for deployment.

The Soviet High Command used a simple domino effect for its successful offensive to make one sector of the front fall after the other. Following each breach in the German front, the Soviets shifted their main direction to the adjoining sector and in this way prepared the entire front for operational breakthroughs. Thus the entire Eastern Front was set into motion and it never stopped.

After the OKH began its "planned disengagement movements," "Panther," and "Buffalo" movements, the direction was nonstop back to the west. The Red Army employed its successful assault plan against German delaying tactics. It persistently attacked the same German front-line positions, no matter what the losses, until either the German defense yielded or the Soviets had exhausted their own strength. As long as the Wehrmacht was able to employ mobile tactics against the Soviet assaults, German losses were held within bounds. The Germans gave up terrain and let the Red Army follow up and wear themselves out. Then came a German counterattack, and the game started all over again. At this point the Germans still could afford this mobile defense; they were far inside Russia, so that withdrawing 150 or 200 kilometers meant nothing. But time was working against the Wehrmacht.

On Wednesday, 8 September 1943, the capitulation of Italy was announced. Now the "Case Axis" occurred. The German Wehrmacht had to occupy the entire Apennine peninsula and carry the burden of defense. By the end of September 1943, the Eastern Front ran west of Leningrad via Kiev along the Dnieper to the Black Sea. Despite the huge investment in materiel, personnel, and time, the OKH was not able to build up an effective defense following the collapse of the Orel-Kharkov-Belgorod sectors. It could only delay the defeat.

The Germans were in the process of creating a strategic defensive line running from north to south along the Narva, Lake Peipsi (Chudskoye), east of Vitebsk, along the Sozh, the Dnieper, and Molochnaya. The westward withdrawal was to stop at this line extending from the Baltic Sea to the Sea of Azov, the so-called "Ostwall" (eastern rampart). Meanwhile, with the outcome of Operation "Citadel" and the landing of the western allies in Sicily, Germany's allies knew that they no longer could count on an Axis victory. The secret peace efforts by Finland, Romania, Hungary, and Bulgaria beginning in summer 1943 show the increased discord between Hitler and his allies.

Soon, even the western allies began to feel the consequences of the Soviet victories at Orel and Kursk. Stalin, now convinced that his fast-growing military power could force the Third Reich to its knees even, if need be, without the aid of the Anglo-Americans, forced his will upon the others at the conferences of Yalta and Teheran. By this time, the political landscape of our world already was shaped.

A forward observation post. Like these two men, millions of German soldiers will see similar pictures after Operation "Citadel" until the bitter end; a gloomy cloud on the horizon prophesizing death and destruction

275

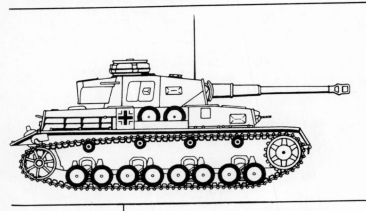

PzKpfw IV Medium Tank
Model H

Weight:	25 t
Crew:	5 men
Speed:	38 km/h
Range:	road 180 km
	cross-country 120 km
Armament:	one long 75mm L/48 gun
	2 machine guns

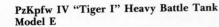

PzKpfw IV "Tiger I" Heavy Battle Tank
Model E

Weight:	55 t
Crew:	5 men
Speed:	38 km/h
Range:	road 90 km
	cross-country 60 km
Armament:	one 88mm KwK 36/L56 gun
	2 machine guns

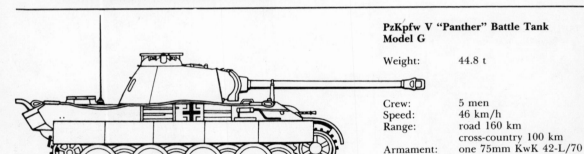

PzKpfw V "Panther" Battle Tank
Model G

Weight:	44.8 t
Crew:	5 men
Speed:	46 km/h
Range:	road 160 km
	cross-country 100 km
Armament:	one 75mm KwK 42-L/70 gun
	2 machine guns

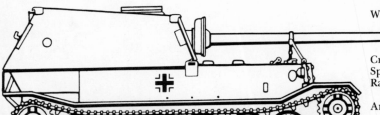

Jagdpanzer Tiger (P) "Elephant"
Destroyer Tank ("Ferdinand")

Weight:	68 t
Crew:	6 men
Speed:	20 km/h
Range:	road 130 km
	cross-country 90 km
Armament:	one 88mm 43/2-L/71 antitank gun

276

T-34/74A Medium Tank

Weight:	28.24 t
Crew:	5 men
Speed:	50 km/h
Range:	road 450 km
	cross-country 350 km
Armament:	one 76.2mm gun model
	1938 (L-11)
	1 machine gun

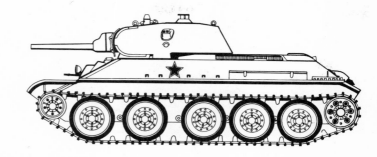

T-34/85-I Medium Tank

Weight:	32 t
Crew:	5 men
Speed:	50 km/h
Range:	road 336 km
	cross-country 208 km
Armament:	one 85mm gun Model 1943
	2 machine guns

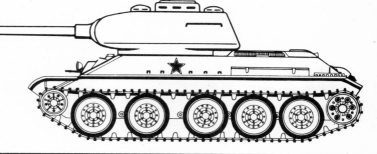

JSU-122 Destroyer Tank
Self-propelled Gun

Weight:	41.2 t

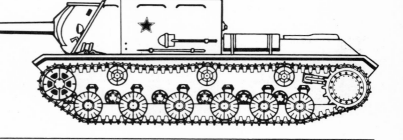

Crew:	5 men
Speed:	37 km/h
Range:	road 280 km
	cross-country 240 km
Armament:	one 122mm gun A-19
	1 machine gun

Rocket Launcher (officially Guards Launcher)

The Germans called this rocket launcher—several variants were built—"Stalinorgel" and the Red Army called it "Katyusha." The double T-shape of the tracks permitted launching two rockets simultaneously, one over the other. A bolt held the rockets on the tracks until launching. Elevation was variable. The launching direction was set by the position of the truck.

Max. shooting range: 8000–8500 m

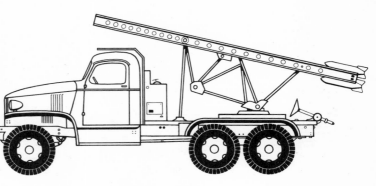

Junkers Ju 87 G-1 Ground-attack Dive Bomber (Stuka)

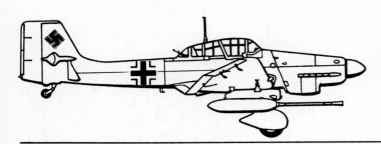

A variant of the Ju 87 D-5 with two 37mm cannons (Flak 18 or Flak 36) for antitank combat, which were mounted in containers underneath the wings. These containers were bomb-shaped. These two area cannons, which were fully automatic, were operated from the cockpit. The armor-piercing ammunition was fed via box magazines.

Messerschmitt Bf 109 G Fighter

Also employed as fighter-bomber (Jagdbomber—Jabo) along with the Focke-Wulf Fw 190 F fighter in the Battle of Kursk.

Max speed:	690 km/h
Operational ceiling	approx. 11,600 m
Combat radius (without extra tank)	approx. 700 km
Armament:	up to 5 machine guns

Henschel HS 129 B-2 Ground Attack Plane

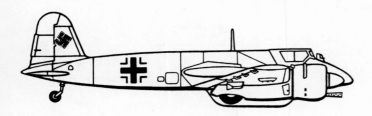

The only armored ground-fighting support plane with two French 690 HP Gnome-Rhone engines. The pilot sat in an armored cockpit behind an 8 cm thick bulletproof glass windshield. The 30mm MK 101 cannon was situated below the fuselage.

Max. speed:	408 km/h
Operational ceiling:	9000 m
Combat radius:	880 km

Junkers Ju 88 A-4 Dive Bomber

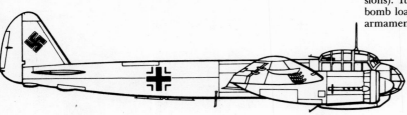

This was the most versatile plane in the German Luftwaffe (more than 50 versions). Its good flying qualities and high bomb load capacity were set off by its low armaments:

Crew:	4 men
Max. speed:	43 km/h
Combat radius:	1790 km
Armament:	3 machine guns
Bomb load	up to 1800 kg

Ilyushin IL-2m3 Ground Attack Light Bomber ("Sturmovik")

German soldiers called it "the black death." It was the best and most successful ground attack plane in the Second World War. The cowling and the cockpit are a single unit made of steel plates weighing approx. 700 kg. Most of the aircraft that took part in the Battle of Kursk had two 37mm 11-P-37 guns in the underwing pods and carried 200 small PTAB type armor-piercing bombs.

Crew: 2 men
Max. speed: 404 km/h
Combat radius: up to 765 km

Lavoshkin La-5FN Fighter

According to Soviet aces, this was the best fighter in the Red Air Force. The aircraft had several parts made of wood.
Max. speed: 626 km/h
Combat radius: 765 km
Armament: two 20 mm type ShVak
                guns

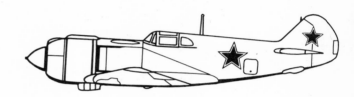

Petlyakov Pe-2 Fast Bomber

There were several versions of this aircraft and it formed the core of the fighting power of all Red Air Force bomber formations.
Crew: 3 men
Max. speed: 540 km/h
Combat radius: 1500 km
Armament: 4 machine guns
Bomb load: 1000 kg

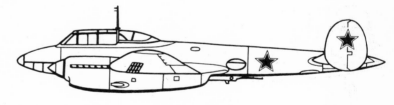

Tupolev SB-L Medium Bomber

Already employed as early as 1936, it was only used as a night bomber in the summer of 1943.
Crew: 3 men
Max. speed: 425 km/h
Combat radius: 1200 km
Armament: 4 machine guns
Bomb load: 600 kg

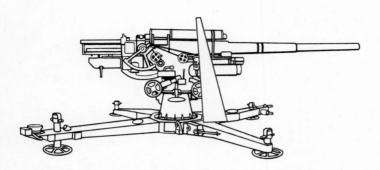

88mm-Flak 18 Gun

Max. range: 10.6 km, also employed to destroy bunkers and tanks.

Howitzer Model 1934

Cal. 152mm, max. range: 17.1 km

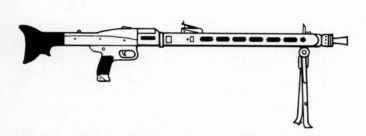

MG 42 Light Machine Gun

Cal. 7.92 mm, convertible into a medium machine gun or an antiaircraft machine gun. The first really practical multi-purpose machine gun in the world.

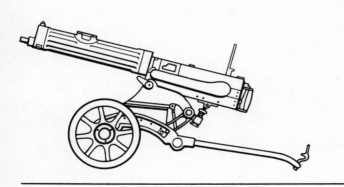

Maxim-MG Machine Gun

Cal. 7.62 mm, water-cooled, with a hand-carriage and a U-shaped trail

Composition of the German Forces (as of July 1, 1943)

ARMY GROUP CENTER	Field Marshal von Kluge
9th-Army	Col.Gen. Model
XX. Army Corps	Gen. of the Inf. Freiherr von Roman
45th Inf.Div.	Maj.Gen. Freiherr von Falkenstein
72nd Inf.Div.	Lt.Gen. Müller-Gebhard
137th Inf.Div.	Lt.Gen. Kamecke
251st Inf.Div.	Maj.Gen. Felzmann
XLVI Panzer Corps	Gen. of the Inf. Zorn
7th Inf.Div.	Lt.Gen. von Rappard
31st Inf.Div.	Lt.Gen. Hossbach
102nd Inf.Div.	Maj.Gen. Hitzfeld
258th Inf.Div.	Lt.Gen. Höcker
XLVII Panzer Corps	Gen. of the Pz.Tr. Lemelsen
2nd Pz.Div.	Lt.Gen. Lübbe
6th Inf.Div.	Lt.Gen. Grossmann
9th Pz.Div.	Lt.Gen. Scheller
20th Pz.Div.	Maj.Gen. von Kessel
XLI. Panzer Corps	Gen. of the Pz.Tr. Harpe
18th Pz.Div.	Maj.Gen. von Schlieben
86th Inf.Div.	Lt.Gen. Weidling
292nd Inf.Div.	Lt.Gen. von Kluge
XXIII. Army Corps	Gen. of the Inf. Friessner
78th Sturm Div.	Lt.Gen. Traut
216th Inf.Div.	Maj.Gen. Schack
383rd Inf.Div.	Maj.Gen. Hoffmeister
ARMY GROUP SOUTH	Field Marshal von Manstein
Army Kempf	Gen. of the Pz.Tr. Kempf
III. Panzer Corps	Gen. of the Pz.Tr. Breith
6th Pz.Div.	Maj.Gen. von Hünersdorff
7th Pz.Div.	Lt.Gen. Freiherr von Funck
19th Pz.Div.	Lt.Gen. G. Schmidt
168th Inf.Div.	Maj.Gen. Châles de Beaulieu
XI. Army Corps	Gen. of the Pz.Tr. Raus
106th Inf.Div.	Lt.Gen. Forst
320th Inf.Div.	Maj.Gen. Postel
XLII. Army Corps	Gen. of the Inf. Mattenklott
39th Inf.Div.	Lt.Gen. Loeweneck
161st Inf.Div.	Lt.Gen. Recke
282nd Inf.Div.	Maj.Gen. Kohler
4th Panzer Army	Col.Gen. Hoth
LII. Army Corps	Gen. of the Inf. Ott
57th Inf.Div.	Maj.Gen. Fretter-Pico
255th Inf.Div.	Lt.Gen. Poppe
332nd Inf.Div.	Lt.Gen. Schaefer
XLVIII. Panzer Corps	Gen. of the Pz.Tr. von Knobelsdorff
3rd Pz.Div.	Lt.Gen. Westhoven
11th Pz.Div.	Lt.Gen. Balck
167th Inf.Div.	Lt.Gen. Trierenberg
Pz.Gren.Div."Gross-deutschland"	Lt.Gen. Hoernlein
II. SS-Panzer Corps	SS-Obergruppenführer Hausser
1st SS-Pz.Div. "Leibstandarte Adolf Hitler"	SS-Brigadeführer Wisch
2nd SS-Pz.Div. "Das Reich"	SS-Gruppenführer Krüger
3rd SS-Pz.Div. "Totenkopf"	SS-Brigadeführer Priess

Notes

The secret documents pertaining to Operation "Ultra Secret" and how London passed on to Moscow the information it gained from deciphering radio communication between the German high staffs at the Eastern Front are in the archives of:
Public Record Office, Kew, Richmond, Surrey, Great Britain, and the Ministry of Defence, Cabinet Office, Whitehall, London SW1A2AS

1 CAB 66/20, WP(42)8 from January 5, 1942, pp. 15–17, SIC file D/Russia, JIC(43)25 from February 2, 1943
2 Dir/C Archive, 1645 from December 6, 1942
3 London/Moscow Signals file "unnumbered telegrams" from July 7 and 13, 1941
4 Dir/C Archive, MI telegrams to BMM 7666 from September 28, 1941
5 Dir/C Archive, MI telegrams to BMM 6908 from June 28 and 7098 from July 17, 1941
6 Dir/C Archive, MI telegrams to BMM 167 and 168/MI 14 from July 13, 1942
7 CAB 121/464, JIC(41)357 from September 13, 1941
8 Dir/C Archive, 1487 from November 23, 1942
9 London/Moscow Signals file, Y Board Chairman to BMM, SJ 86 from December 23, 1942
10 WO 208/3573 from March 22, 1943
11 H. Höhne, "Kennwort: Direktor". Frankfurt/M. 1970, p. 283
12 CX/MSS/2422/I 28
13 H. Höhne, "Kennwort: Direktor" Frankfurt/M. 1970, p. 283
14 CX/MSS/2499/I 4
15 H. Höhne, "Kennwort: Direktor". Frankfurt/M. 1970, pp. 283/284
16 London/Moscow Signals file "unnumbered telegrams" from July 7 and 13, 1941

Bibliography (Selected)

Andronikow, I. G./Mostowenko, W. D.: Die roten Panzer. München 1963.
Antipenko, N.: In den Hauptrichtungen. Berlin (Ost) 1973.
Arbeitskreis für Wehrforschung (Hrsg.): Der Feldzug gegen Sowjetrußland 1941–1945.
Batow, P. I.: Von der Wolga zur Oder. Berlin (Ost) 1965.
Bauer, E.: Der Panzerkrieg. Bonn 1964.
Bekker, C.: Angriffshöhe 4000. Oldenburg 1964.
Berndt, A. J./Oberst v. Wedel (Hrsg.): Deutschland im Kampf. Berlin 1943.
Boelcke, W. A.: Deutschlands Rüstung im Zweiten Weltkrieg. Frankfurt/M. 1969.
Breith, H.: Der Angriff des III. Panzerkorps bei "Zitadelle" im Juli 1943. In: Wehrkunde, Jg. 7, 1958, H. 10.
Buchbender, O.: Das tönende Erz. Stuttgart 1978.
Buchheit, G.: Hitler der Feldherr. Rastatt 1958.
Caidin, M.: The Tigers are burning. New York 1975.
Carell, P.: Verbrannte Erde. Berlin 1966.
Chant, C.: Kursk. London 1975.
Churchill, W. S.: Memoiren-Der Zweite Weltkrieg. Stuttgart, Hamburg 1952.
Clark, A.: Barbarossa. London 1974.
Conrady, A.: Wende 1943–Geschichte der 36. Panzer-Grenadier-Division. Neckargemünd 1978.
Constantini, A.: La bataille de chass de Prokhorovka (12 et 13 juillet 1943). In: Forces armées françaises, 1974, H. 25.
Deborin, G. A.: Der Zweite Weltkrieg. Berlin 1960.
Dierich, W.: Kampfgeschwader 51 "Edelweiß". Stuttgart 1973.
Dierich, W.: Kampfgeschwader 55 "Greif". Stuttgart 1975.
Dingleiter, J.: Die Vierziger. München 1963.
Dragunski, D. A.: Jahre im Panzer. Berlin (Ost) 1980.
Erickson, J.: The Soviet High Command. London 1972.
Förster, G./Paulus, N.: Abriß der Geschichte der Panzerwaffe. Berlin (Ost) 1977.
Fuchs, T.: Deutsche und sowjetische Führung. In: Wehrkunde, Jg. 9, 1960, H. 11.
Gareis, M.: Kampf und Ende der Fränkisch-Sudetendeutschen 98, I. D. Bad Nauheim, 1956.
Görlitz, W.: Der Zweite Weltkrieg 1939–1945, Bd. 2. Stuttgart 1953.
Görlitz, W.: Model. Strategie der Defensive. Wiesbaden 1975.
Gollikow, S.: Die Sowjetarmee im Großen Vaterländischen Krieg. Berlin (Ost) 1954.
Gosztony, P.: Die Rote Armee. Wien 1981.
Gottberg, H. L. v.: Das Wesen des sowjetischen Partisanenkampfes. In: Wehrkunde, Jg. 7, 1958, H. 12.
Graser, G.: Zwischen Kattegat und Kaukasus. München 1961.
Gretschko, A. A.: Geschichte des 2. Weltkrieges. 12 Bde. Berlin (Ost) 1972.
Groehler, O.: Geschichte des Luftkrieges 1910–1970. Berlin (Ost) 1977.
Großmann, H.: Gesch.d.rhein.-westfäl. 6. Inf. Div. 1939–1945. Dortmund 1958.
Großmann, H.: Rshew. Eckpfeiler der Ostfront. Bad Nauheim 1962.
Guderian, H.: Erinnerungen eines Soldaten. Heidelberg 1951.
Halder, GenOberst.: Kriegstagebuch, Bd. 2. Stuttgart 1963.
Haupt, W.: Heeresgruppe Mitte, 1941–1945. Dorheim 1968.
Haupt, W.: Bild-Chronik der Heeresgruppe Mitte. Dorheim 1969.
Heiber, H. (Hrsg.): Hitlers Lagebesprechungen. Stuttgart 1962.
Heinrici, G./Hauck, F. W.: Zitadelle. In: Wehrwissenschaftliche Rundschau, Jg. 15, 1965, H. 8–10.

Hermann, C. H.: 68 Kriegsmonate. Wien 1978.

Höhne, H.: Kennwort Direktor. Frankfurt/M. 1970.

Höhne, H.: Canaris. München 1976.

Holder, L. D.: Kursk: the breaking of the Panzer Corps. In: Armor 1975, Nr. 1.

Hoßbach, F.: Streiflichter aus den Operationen des Südflügels der Heeresgruppe Mitte vom Juli 1943 bis April 1944. In: Allgem. Schweizerische Militärzeitschrift.

Hubatsch, W. (Hrsg.): Hitlers Weisungen für die Kriegführung 1939–1945. Dokumente des OKW. Frankfurt/M. 1962.

Hubatsch, W.: Kriegswende 1943. Darmstadt 1966.

Jacobsen, H. A.: 1939–1945. Darmstadt 1961.

Jakubowski, I. I.: Erde im Feuer. Berlin (Ost) 1977.

Jukes, G.: Kursk—The Clash of Armour. New York 1972.

Kabonow, P. A.: Stählerne Strecken. Berlin (Ost) 1977.

Katukow, M. J.: An der Spitze des Hauptstoßes. Berlin (Ost) 1979.

Kleine, E./Kühn, V.: Tiger, Stuttgart 1976.

Klink, E.: Das Gesetz des Handelns. Die Operation "Zitadelle" 1943. Stuttgart 1966.

Knobelsdorff, O. v.: Gesch.d. niedersächs. 19. Pz.Div. Bad Nauheim 1958.

Kjoltunov, G. A./Solov'ev, B. G.: Kurskaja bitva. Moskwa 1970.

Konjew, I. S.: Aufzeichnungen eines Frontbefehlshaber 1943/44. Berlin (Ost) 1978.

Kozlov, L./Orlov, A.: La bataille de Koursk et son influence sur la seconde guerre mondiale. In: Revue Historique des Armées, 1974, No. 2.

Kurkotkin, S.: Tyl Sowietskich Wooruzonnych Sil w Wielikof Otieczestwiennoj Wojnie 1941–1945. Moskwa 1977.

Liddell Hart, B.: Geschichte des 2. Weltkrieges, Bd. 2. Düsseldorf 1972.

Mabire, J.: Légion des Volontaires Français (LVF). 3 Bde. Paris 1973–1975.

Mabire, J.: L'enfer blanc 1941–1943. Paris 1980.

Mackintosh, M.: Juggernaut. London 1975.

Manstein, E. v.: Verlorene Siege. München 1965.

Markin, I. I.: Die Kursker Schlacht. Berlin (Ost) 1960.

Mellenthin, F. W. v.: Panzerschlachten. Nekkargemünd 1963.

Merker, L.: Das Buch der 78. Sturmdivision. Dortmund 1955.

Meyer-Detring, W.: Die 137. I. D. im Mittelabschnitt der Ostfront. Petzenkirchen 1962.

Middeldorf, E.: Das Unternehmen "Zitadelle". In: Wehrwissenschaftliche Rundschau, Jg. 3, 1953, H. 10.

Militärakademie M. W. Frunse (Hrsg.): Die Entwicklung der Taktik der Sowjetarmee im Großen Vaterländischen Krieg. Berlin (Ost) 1961.

Morosow, W. P.: Westlich von Woronesch. Berlin (Ost) 1959.

Moskalenko, K. S.: Bitva na kusskoj duge. Moskwa 1975.

Moskalenko, K. S.: In der Südwestrichtung. Berlin (Ost) 1975.

Müller-Hillebrand, B.: Der Zweifrontenkrieg. Frankfurt/M. 1964.

Nazarov, V.: Kampf des 214. Schtz.Rgt. b. Bjelgorod am 5.7. 1943. In: Voenn.ist. Zurnal, 1963, H. 6.

Nitz, G.: Die 292. Infanterie-Division. Berlin 1957.

Nowarra, H. J.: Der Frontbogen von Kursk. Rastatt 1977.

Parotkin, I.V.: Kurskaja bitva. Moskwa 1970.

Parrish, M.: The battle of Kursk. In: The Army Quarterly and Defense Journal, 1969.

Paul, W.: Geschichte der 18. Panzer-Division, Kameraden-Kreis 18. Panzer-Division. Krefeld 1975.

Paul, W.: Brennpunkte—Geschichte der 6. Panzer-Division. Krefeld 1977.

Philippi, A./Heim, F.: Der Feldzug gegen Sowjetrußland 1941 bis 1945. Stuttgart 1962.

Piekalkiewicz, J. K.: Luftkrieg 1939–1945. München 1978.

Piekalkiewicz, J. K.: Krieg der Panzer 1939–1945. München 1981.

Platonow, S. P. (Hrsg.): Geschichte des Zweiten Weltkrieges 1939–1945, Bd. 1. Berlin (Ost) 1961.

Plotnikov, V.: Der Beitrag der Arbeiter des Kursker Gebietes zur Erreichung des Sieges bei Kursk. In: Voenn. ist. Zurnal, 1961 H. 10.

Popiel, N. K.: Panzer greifen an. Berlin (Ost) 1964.

Posnjak, W. G.: Die Schlacht bei Kursk. In: Die wichtigsten Operationen des Großen Vaterländischen Krieges 1941–1945. Berlin (Ost) 1958.

Redelis, V.: Partisanenkrieg. Heidelberg 1958.

Rendulic, L.: Die Schlacht von Orel Juli 1943. In: Österreichische Militärische Zeitschrift, 1963, H. 3.

Riedi, E.: Die Schlacht um Kursk, Juli/August 1943. In:Allgemeine Schweizerische Militärzeitschrift, 1974, Nr. 12.

Rokossovsky, K. K.: The Kursk battle. In: Soviet Military Review, 1968, Nr. 7, Nr. 8.

Rokossovski, K. K.: Soldatenpflicht. Berlin (Ost) 1971.

Rotmistrow, P. A.: Tankovoje srazenije pod Prochorovkoj. Moskwa 1960.

Rudakov, M./Lunin, V.: Die parteipolitische Arbeit in der Schlacht bei Kursk. In: Voenn. ist. Zurnal, 1963. H. 6.

Rudenko, S./Brajko, P.: Die 16. Luftarmee in der Schlacht bei Kursk. In: Voenn. ist. Zurnal, 1963, H. 7.

Schaub, O.: Panzer-Grenadier-Regiment 12. Bad Nauheim 1957.

Scheibert, H.: Panzer-Grenadier-Division Großdeutschland. Dorheim 1970.

Scheurig, B.: Verrat hinter Stacheldraht. Stuttgart 1969.

Schmidt, A.: Geschichte der 10. Inf.Div. (1933–45). Bad Nauheim 1963.

Schmiedel, K.: Die sowjetische Militärgeschichtsschreibung zur Schlacht bei Kursk. In: Zeitschrift der Militärgeschichte, 1964, H. 3.

Schtemenko, S. M.: Im Generalstab. Berlin (Ost) 1969.

Schukow, G. K.: Erinnerungen und Gedanken. Stuttgart 1969.

Schukow, G. K.: The battle of Kursk. In: Military Review, 1969, Nr. 8.

Sedlmeyer, E.: Landeskunde der Sowjetunion. München 1950.

Shilin, P. A.: Die wichtigsten Operationen des Großen Vaterländischen Krieges 1941–1945. Berlin (Ost) 1958.

Sokolowski, W. D. (Hrsg.): Militä-Strategie. Köln 1965.

Solovev, B. G.: Faktor strategiceskov vnezapnosti v bitve pod Kurskom. In: Vestnik Voennoj istorii. 1. Moskwa 1970.

Spaeter, H.: Die Gesch. d. Pz.Korps Großdeutschland, Bd. 2. 1958.

Stadler, S.: Die Offensive gegen Kursk 1943. II. SS-Panzerkorps als Stoßkeil im Großkampf. Osnabrück 1980.

Strelbizki, I. S.: Die Erde dröhnt. Berlin 1964.

Talenskij, N.: In der Schlacht um Orel. Berlin (Ost) 1962.

Tashjean, J.: Operation "Mincemeat"—5 deutsche Dokumente. In: Wehrwissenschaftliche Rundschau, Jg. 11, 1961, H. 5.

Telpuchowski, B. S.: Die sowjetische Geschichte des Großen Vaterländischen Krieges 1941–1945. Frankfurt/M. 1961.

Teske, H.: Die Silbernen Spiegel. Heidelberg 1952.

Teske, H.: Partisanen gegen die Eisenbahn. In: Wehrwissenschaftliche Rundschau, Jg. 3, 1953, H. 10.

Teske, H.: Die Bedeutung der Eisenbahn bei Aufmarsch, Verteidigung und Rückzug einer Heeresgruppe. In: Allgemeine Schweizerische Militäzeitschrift, 1955, Nr. 2.

Timokhovitch, I. V.: L'aviation Soviétique dans la bataille de Koursk. Bruxelles o. J.

Tippelskirch, K. V.: Geschichte des Zweiten Weltkrieges. Bonn 1959.

Tschetschnewa, M. P.: Der Himmel bleibt unser. Berlin (Ost) 1982.

Wagener, C.: Heeresgruppe Süd. Dorheim o. J.

Warlimont, W.: Im Hauptquartier der deutschen Wehrmacht 1939–1945. Frankfurt/M. 1962.

Wassilewski, A. M.: Sache des ganzen Lebens. Berlin (Ost) 1977.

Weck, H. de: Les pertes et al consommation en munitions des troupes blindées à la bataille de Koursk. In: Revue militaire suisse, 1969, Nr. 6, Nr. 7.

Werth, A.: Rußland im Krieg 1941–1945. München 1975.

Witzleben, J. v.: Vor Moskau und Stalingrad fiel die Entscheidung. Berlin (Ost) 1960.

Wolff, W.: An der Seite der Roten Armee. Berlin (Ost) 1979.

Woroschejkin, A. W.: Jagdflieger, Bd. 2. Berlin (Ost) 1976.

Wünsche, W.: Kursk 1943. Die Entschlußfassung der faschistischen deutschen Führung für "Zitadelle". In: Militärgeschichte, 1973, H. 3.

Zadov, A.: Battle of the Kursk Bulge. In: Soviet Military Review, 1966, Nr. 7.

Zeitzler, K.: Die ersten beiden planmäßigen großen Rückzüge des deutschen Heeres an der Ostfront im Zweiten Weltkrieg. In: Wehrkunde, Jg. 9, 1960, H. 3.

Zimmern, K.: Unternehmen Zitadelle, Juli 1943. Rastatt 1963.

Newspapers and Periodicals (1943)

Berliner Lokal-Anzeiger/Der Adler/Das Heer/Das Reich/Die Wehrmacht/Heeres-Verordnungsblatt / Izvestiya / Krasnaya Sviezda/Mitteilungen für die Truppe/Mitteilungsblatt der Arbeitsgemeinschaft ehem. Offiziere (Berlin-Ost) 1969/Prawda/Völkischer Beobachter

Archives

Britannic Majesty's Office, London
Bundesarchiv. Bern
Bundesarchiv. Koblenz
Cabinet Office, Whitehall, London
Institute for Marxism-Lennism at the Central Committee of the Communist Party of the Soviet Union, Dept. of History of the Great Fatherland War of the Soviet Union, Moscow.
Institut für Zeitungsforschung, Dortmund
Ministère de la Defense, Château de Vincennes
Ministry of Defense, Whitehall, London
National Archives, Washington D.C.
Politisches Archiv des Auswärtigen Amtes, Bonn
Public Record Office, Kew, Richmond Surrey
Staatsbibliothek Preußischer Kulturbesitz, Berlin
Weltkriegsbücherei, Stuttgart
Zentralbibliothek der Bw., Düsseldorf

Documents

Boberach, H.: Meldungen aus dem Reich. Neuwied, Berlin 1965.

Boelcke, W. A.: Wollt ihr den totalen Krieg? Stuttgart 1967.

Geheime Berichte des Sicherheitsdienstes der SS zur innenpolitischen Lage, SD-Berichte zu Inlandsfragen. Bundesarchiv, Koblenz: R 58 Reichssicherheitshauptamt (Nr. 160–178).

Hitlers Weisungen für die Kriegführung 1939–1945. Dokumente des Oberkommandos der Wehrmacht. Hrst. W. Hubatsch. Frankfurt/M. 1962.

Jacobsen, H. A.: 1939–1945. Der Zweite Weltkrieg in Chronik und Dokumenten. Darmstadt 1961.

Krümmer, K.: Aufzeichnungen über Teilnahme an den Ministerkonferenzen, Band 1 und 2. Politisches Archiv des Auswärtigen Amtes, Bonn, Auswärtiges Amt.

The Guides to Records Microfilmed at Alexandria, Va. (68 vols. Washington D.C.: National Archives, 1955 ff.).

Sources of the Illustrations

Bundesarchiv. Koblenz
E.C.E.P.D.A., Fort D'Ivry
Imperial War Museum, London
National Archives, Washington D.C.
US-Army, Washington D.C.
Archiv P. Carell, Hamburg
Archiv Dr. C. H. Hermann, Euskirchen
Archiv K. Kirchner, Verlag D+C, Erlangen
Archiv M. R. de Launay, Paris
Archives J. S. Middleton, London
Archiv Munin Verlag, Osnabrück
Archives A. Stilles, New York
Archiv J. K. Piekalkiewicz

Acknowlegements

I would like to thank for their kind help:

Dr. H. Trumpp and his staff, Bundesarchiv, Koblenz

Lt.Col. H. Rohde of the General Staff, Militärgeschichtliches Forschungsamt. Freiburg

Dr. M. Lindemann, Mrs. H. Rajkovic, Institut für Zeitungsforschung, Dortmund

Professor Dr. J. Rohwer, Mr. W. Haupt and their staff, Weltkriegsbücherei, Stuttgart

Dr. Sack and his staff, Zentralibibliothek der Bundeswehr, Düsseldorf

Mrs. I. Ritter, Staatsbibliothek Preußischer Kulturbesitz, Berlin

Col. C. H. Hermann, Dr. Phil. (retired Bundeswehr), Euskirchen

Mr. K. Kirchner, Verlag D+C, Erlangen

Mr. J. S. Lucas and his staff, Imperial War Museum, London

Mr. J. C. North, Ministry of Defense, London

Mr. V. J. A. Carr, Public Record Office, Kew Richmond, Surrey

Mr. Beaven, Cabinet Office, Whitehall, London

Lt.Col. W. G. V. Kenney of the General Staff, British Embassy, Bonn

Col. W. D. Kasprowicz, London

Col. M. Mlotek, London

Lt.Col. Dousset, Mr. P. Rolland, Mr. Basues, E.C.E.P.D.A., Fort D'Ivry

Mr. M. Spivak, Service Historique de l'Armée, Paris

Capt. C. L. Blische, Dept. of the Army, US-Army Audio-Visual Activity, Pentagon, Washington, D.C.

W. H. Leary, National Archives, Washington, D.C.

Col. B. J. Morden, Center of Military History, Dept. of the Army, Washington, D.C.

Mr. E. Klupsch-Linsbauer, Mr. A. Häring, Mr. R. Borner, Mr. R. Winkler, Gustav Lübbe Verlag

I am especially grateful to:

Mr. D. Bradley, Dr. Phil.; Münster

Major R. L. Walton, O.B.E., London

Capt. B. D. Samuelson, Washington, D.C.

for their generous support and letting me benefit from their extensive knowledge.

The photograph on the front side of the jacket was taken with the kind permission of the Munin Verlag (Osnabrück) from the book "Wenn alle Brüder schweigen." The illustration on the back side of the jacket was kindly made available to the Lübbe Verlag by Mr. Paul Carell (Paul Carell: Der Rußlandkrieg. Fotografiert von Soldaten. Frankfurt/Main, Berlin: Ullstein Verlag, p. 53).

"The spring and summer of 1943 at the Eastern Military Theater stood under the sign of Operation 'Citadel' . . .
Its discontinuance, which was equivalent to failure, gave the Soviet side the initiative once and for all . . ."

Field Marshal Erich von Manstein

Index